"Can We All Get Along?"

Dilemmas in American Politics

Series Editor **L. Sandy Maisel,** *Colby College*

Dilemmas in American Politics offers teachers and students a series of quality books on timely topics and key institutions in American government. Each text will examine a "real world" dilemma and will be structured to cover the historical, theoretical, policy relevant, and future dimensions of its subject.

BOOKS IN THIS SERIES

"Can We All Get Along?" Racial and Ethnic Minorities in American Politics, Paula D. McClain and Joseph Stewart Jr.

Remote and Controlled: Media Politics in a Cynical Age, Matthew Robert Kerbel

FORTHCOMING TITLES

The Dilemma of Congressional Reform, David T. Canon and Kenneth R. Mayer

Immigration and Immigrants in the Contemporary United States, Rodolfo O. de la Garza and Louis DeSipio

Economic Policymaking in the United States, G. Calvin Mackenzie and Saranna Thornton

Abortion in American Politics, Karen O'Connor

Payment Due: A Nation in Debt, a Generation in Trouble Timothy J. Penny and Steven E. Schier

Participation, Democracy, and the New Citizenship in Contemporary American Politics, Craig A. Rimmerman

Onward Christian Soldiers? The Religious Right in American Politics, Clyde Wilcox

"Can We All Get Along?"

Racial and Ethnic Minorities in American Politics

Paula D. McClain
University of Virginia

Joseph Stewart Jr.
University of Texas at Dallas

 WestviewPress
A Division of HarperCollinsPublishers

Dilemmas in American Politics

Copyright © 1995 by Westview Press, Inc., A Division of HarperCollins Publishers, Inc.

Published in 1995 in the United States of America by Westview Press, Inc., 5500 Central Avenue, Boulder, Colorado 80301-2877, and in the United Kingdom by Westview Press, 12 Hid's Copse Road, Cumnor Hill, Oxford OX2 9JJ

Library of Congress Cataloging-in-Publication Data
McClain, Paula Denice.
"Can we all get along?" : racial and ethnic minorities in American politics / Paula D. McClain, Joseph Stewart Jr.
    p. cm. — (Dilemmas in American politics)
Includes bibliographical references and index.
ISBN 0-8133-1968-4 (hardcover). —ISBN 0-8133-1969-2 (pbk.)
    1. Minorities—United States—Political activity. I. Stewart, Joseph, 1951–   . II. Title. III. Series.
E184.A1M127 1995
323. 1'1'0973—dc20   95-12634
                                                                                                        CIP

Printed and bound in the United States of America

The paper used in this publication meets the requirements
of the American National Standard for Permanence of Paper
for Printed Library Materials Z39.48-1984.

10   9   8   7   6   5   4   3   2

To

HAROLD M. ROSE,

friend, colleague, and mentor.
You taught me more about research
and the academy than you will ever know.
But more important, you taught me how to be a scholar.

—P.D.M.

To

JEWEL L. PRESTAGE,

for whom I was the "warm-up act" in
Black Politics courses a "few" years ago.
Without that experience, my part in this would
never have been possible.

—J.S.

Contents

List of Illustrations   xi
Preface   xiii

1 America's Dilemmas   1

Terms Used in This Book   5
Race and Ethnicity   7
American Government Foundation and Racial Minorities   9
The Constitution and Black and Indian Citizenship   11
Citizenship and Later Minorities: Latinos and Asians   16
The Constitution and Black and Indian Suffrage   19
Structure of This Book   23
Conclusion   24

2 Resources and Status of America's Racial Minorities   27

Population Size, Socioeconomic Status, and Concentration   29
Participation in a Civil Rights Movement   37
Voting Rights Law   49
Conclusion   53

3 America's Racial Minorities in the Contemporary Political System: Actors   55

Group Identity and Perceptions of Discrimination   59
Political Ideology   62
Partisan Identification   65
Voting Behavior   74

Interest Group Activities   79
Conclusion   83

4 **America's Racial Minorities and
the Policymaking Process**   85

Agenda Setting   88
Minority Representation   89
Federalism   105
State Elective Office   107
Equal Educational Opportunity   108
Conclusion   121

5 **Coalition or Competition? Patterns of
Interminority Group Relations**   123

Interminority Group Relations   126
Coalition or Competition Politics?   126
Los Angeles   130
Conclusion   143

6 **Will We "All Get Along?"**   145

The Dilemmas Revisited   148
Looking to the Future   151
Conclusion   152

Discussion Questions   155
Glossary   159
Timelines   165
Notes   189
References   191
About the Book and Authors   200
Index   201

Illustrations

Photographs

A group of bystanders view a lynched man in Slayden, Mississippi, 1935   22

Black youths are marched away from an Alabama courthouse
following their arrests for participation in civil rights demonstrations   41

Cuban Americans protest detainment of Cubans at Guantanamo   71

Voter registration during Chinese New Year, Monterey Park   72

Japanese American citizens placed on trains to Manzanar, California,
for internment   91

President Bill Clinton meets with representatives of the federally
recognized tribes   92

Senator Ben Nighthorse Campbell   101

Koreatown Crime Team checks out an attempted car theft   142

Maps

2.1   African American population by county   35
2.2   Hispanic American population by county   36
2.3   American Indian population by county   38
2.4   Asian American population by county   39

Tables

2.1   Selected characteristics of black, Asian American,
       American Indian, and non-Latino white populations   30
2.2   Selected characteristics of the Latino population
       and selected subgroups, 1993   31
2.3   Selected characteristics of selected Asian American
       population subgroups, 1990   32

3.1   Proportion of blacks perceiving that they share a common
       fate with other blacks   60
3.2   Perception of discrimination against African Americans
       and Asians by Latino national origin groups   61
3.3   Black ideological identification   63

3.4   Latino ideological identification   64
3.5   Black partisan identification   68
3.6   Latino partisan identification   69
3.7   Asian Pacific American registered voters   73
3.8   Registration and voting by race for twenty states   75
3.9   Registration and voting by race, national sample   77
3.10   Registration and voting by race and sex, national sample   79

4.1   Black members of the 104th Congress, 1995–1997   96
4.2   Latino members of the 104th Congress, 1995–1997   97
4.3   Asian–Pacific island members of the 104th Congress, 1995–1997   98
4.4   American Indians who have served in the U.S. Senate and
       House of Representatives   99
4.5   Representation of racial–national origin groups in federal civilian
       workforce and civilian labor force, September 1993   104
4.6   Distribution of racial–national origin groups in federal
       civilian workforce by pay grades, September 1993   105
4.7   American Indian–Alaska native state legislators, 1995   109

6.1   Groups with which blacks, Latinos, and Asians feel they
       have the most in common   150

Preface

THIS BOOK is the result of a collaboration that began over a bottle of cabernet sauvignon at the 1992 American Political Science Association (APSA) meeting in Chicago. What started as an evening to be devoted to reading papers for discussion at the next morning's panels quickly turned into a discussion of the difficulties of teaching a true Minority Group Politics course.

Some universities, depending on their location, have a course devoted to a particular group—for example, Black Politics or Latino Politics or Asian Politics or American Indian Politics—or even a more specialized course such as Mexican American Politics or Puerto Rican Politics. Indeed, we have both taught such courses. But more commonly the demand is for an umbrella course, offered under the rubric Minority Group Politics, that, ideally, compares the politics of the four principal U.S. racial and ethnic minority groups—blacks, Latinos, American Indians, and Asian Americans—and their relationships with the majority. This is the situation at our current institutions.

Such umbrella courses generally take one of two forms. The less-than-ideal alternative is a course that is offered under the broader title but that is focused on one ethnic group because that is where the interest and expertise of the instructor lie. In such situations, it is possible for a student to take the same course twice from different instructors, to never encounter overlapping materials, and to never explicitly consider interminority group relations.

The second, preferable, form involves undertaking a comparative examination of the politics of America's major racial and ethnic minorities. This is an idealized alternative because, as we can report from personal experience, it is difficult to implement. One must spend countless hours amassing data from various sources in an attempt to draw out the similarities and the differences among the groups and to develop the depth and nuance that characterize a good course.

We decided, toward the bottom of the bottle of wine, that between us we had sufficient expertise on black and Latino politics and enough familiarity with the American Indian and Asian American politics literature to write a book for a true junior-senior-level Minority Politics class. We mentioned our "prospectus from a bottle" to Cathy Rudder, executive director of APSA, who discussed it with Sandy Maisel of Colby College, the editor of Westview's new series "Dilemmas in American Politics." Sandy contacted us, indicated that this was the book the series' editorial advisory board had decided was a high priority (McClain, a member of the board, had missed the meeting!), and convinced us to write a shorter, less detailed volume for use as a supplement, primarily in American government courses. The larger, upper-division book is still in our plans.

The words for the title were appropriated from Rodney King's first news conference following the acquittals of his attackers and the subsequent Los Angeles riots. His words crystallize the dilemmas faced by the nation, by members of both minority and majority groups.

We could not have accomplished what turned out to be a larger undertaking than we had imagined without the help of numerous people. Steven C. Tauber, Ph.D. candidate and research assistant in the Woodrow Wilson Department of Government and Foreign Affairs at the University of Virginia, served as our principal factotum. (Hint: This word appears in the GRE verbal exam. Look it up. Fans of the old TV series, *The Fugitive*, will have already encountered it.) Steve spent countless hours on numerous tasks, with perhaps the worst being an attempt to get the National Black Election Study data file to run again after a transfer from one computer system to another. Steve has served as McClain's teaching assistant for her Minority Group Politics course since 1991. His intellectual contributions to the study of racial minority group politics are present throughout the book.

Thanks also to Don Nakanishi of the Asian Americian Studies Center at UCLA for helping us identify Asian American elected officials; to Larry Bobo of the Department of Sociology at UCLA for sharing his Los Angeles County Survey data with us; to Paul Waddell and his staff at the Bruton Center for Development Studies of the University of Texas at Dallas for generating the maps in Chapter 2; the research staffs of the Joint Center for Political and Economic Studies and the National Association of Latino Elected and Appointed Officials; and to Paula Sutherland, head of Government Documents, and Linda Snow, reference librarian, McDermott Library, University of Texas at Dallas, for tracking down or pointing us toward valuable information we knew existed somewhere but had no idea where. Our colleagues and students over the years, especially those in McClain's Fall 1994 Minority Group Politics class, helped by enduring our on-the-job efforts to fashion a coherent, comparative course, by asking questions that forced us to seek more answers, and by answering questions we posed.

We are also indebted to Sandy Maisel; to Jennifer Knerr, our acquisitions editor, Shena Redmond, our project editor, and Cheryl Carnahan, our copyeditor, at Westview Press; and to the reviewers of a very rough first draft—Stephanie Larson of Dickinson College, Roderick Kiewiet of California Institute of Technology, and F. Chris Garcia of the University of New Mexico. Each offered helpful comments, some of which we heeded. Ted Lowi also read the rough draft and gets a special nod for pushing us to put more politics in the book. This book is better for their efforts, and none of them is responsible for any errors that remain. We blame those errors, as has become the convention in our discipline, on Paul Sabatier.

Perhaps most important, we thank Don Lutz, University of Houston, for giving us the bottle of wine that began this process, and we also thank our families. Paul C. Jacobson, Kristina McClain-Jacobson, Jessica McClain-Jacobson, and Paula Sutherland have patiently, lovingly, and supportively endured this lengthy and, at points, contentious (between the authors) process.

Finally, the book is dedicated to two individuals who have had a great deal of influence on our personal lives and professional careers. Harold M. Rose, an urban geographer at the University of Wisconsin–Milwaukee, has shared almost two decades of research collaboration on black urban homicide with McClain. They are now intellectual partners, but in 1977 Rose befriended the new assistant professor, shared his ideas for a major collaborative project, mentored her in the ways of the academy, and taught her the importance of maintaining one's intellectual integrity, of paying attention to detail, and of being thoughtful and reflective in one's scholarship. McClain affectionately dedicates this book to him.

Stewart's efforts are another step in a process that began when, as an assistant professor at the University of New Orleans, he decided he wanted to teach the sophomore-level Black Politics course. Jewel L. Prestage, who had been teaching the class, may have seen this as an opportunity to avoid those long drives across the bridges from Baton Rouge and to free her to teach other, more interesting upper-division classes. Whatever the reason, she approved of Stewart being her "warm-up act" and was supportive and helpful, as she has been in the years since. Had she not been so, Stewart's career would have probably taken a different track, and he would have missed some interesting intellectual endeavors. Jewel Prestage made Stewart's efforts on this project both possible and necessary, and he is grateful.

Paula D. McClain
Charlottesville, Virginia

Joseph Stewart Jr.
Dallas, Texas

1

....

America's Dilemmas

A white train station employee orders a black customer to leave, saying blacks are not allowed in the train station.

Matawan, N.J., March 17, 1993[1]

O N APRIL 29, 1992, rioting erupted in Los Angeles after the announcement that a predominantly white jury in a suburban municipality had acquitted police officers who had been videotaped beating black motorist Rodney King. These riots were widely reported as black reactions to an obvious injustice perpetrated by whites against blacks. Indeed, Americans are used to interpreting political and social relations in white-versus-black terms. The facts are more complex. The brunt of property crimes was borne by Korean retailers; the majority of those arrested during the civil disorders were Hispanic (Morrison and Lowry 1994). As America approaches the twenty-first century, the variety and identity of the actors are changing, but racial and ethnic conflict is an old story.

In his *Democracy in America*, published in 1835, Alexis de Tocqueville, an early French visitor to the republic, notes that the treatment and situation of blacks in the United States contradicted the American passion for democracy. He saw slavery and the denial of constitutional rights and protection to blacks as the principal threats to the U.S. democratic system: "If there ever are great revolutions there [in America], they will be caused by the presence of the blacks upon American soil. . . . It will not be the equality of social conditions but rather their inequality which may give rise thereto" (Tocqueville 1835 [original], Mayer and Lerner, eds. 1966:614). This same disparate treatment was noted over a century later by sociologist Gunnar Myrdal who published the first comprehensive scholarly examination of the oppression of blacks in the United States, *An American Dilemma* (1944). Myrdal argues that the contradiction within American society between an allegedly strong commitment to democratic values on the one hand and the presence of racial oppression on the other creates a moral dilemma for white Americans and is the root of the U.S. race relations problems.

Although many doubt that Myrdal's argument is correct—that is, that most white Americans are terribly cross-pressured by the presence of both democratic ideals and racial discrimination—the use of the term *dilemma* is invaluable in an examination of racial minority group politics in the United States. This book focuses on two dilemmas. The first dilemma harkens back to the founding of America, is the subject of de Tocqueville's concern, and continues to resonate today: *How does a governmental system that professes in its Constitution and its rhetoric to be democratic and egalitarian handle the obvious reality of its systematic denial of basic rights and privileges to its own citizens based on color? When forced to confront and correct the inequalities, how does it provide for and protect the rights of identifiable racial and ethnic minority groups?* The questions this reality-versus-rhetoric dilemma engenders are amazingly similar over time: How shall blacks be counted when apportioning congressional seats (1787)? Is it impermissible to draw "funny-shaped" congressional districts in an attempt to enhance minority group representation (1994)?

The second dilemma is less often articulated, perhaps because it exists within the perspective of the minority groups: *What strategy—coalition or conflict—should be used by minority groups in dealing with other minority groups and with the majority group?* In essence, this dilemma poses the "what do we do about it" question, given the political realities of the first dilemma. In many, if not most considerations of this second dilemma, members of minority groups are treated as passive subjects in a majoritarian system and as natural allies against members of the majority. The present volume challenges this perspective and considers a broader range of strategic choices that are available to members of racial and ethnic minority groups as actors within the polity.

In focusing on these dilemmas, this book addresses the importance of race and ethnicity in American politics—the decisions about who gets what, when, where, and how—in general and in the politics (historical, legal, attitudinal, and behavioral) of the four principal racial minority groups in the United States: blacks (African Americans), Latinos, Asians, and Indian peoples in particular. These groups are the foci because unlike other ethnic minorities—for example, the Irish, Italians, and Jews—who have also suffered from social discrimination, blacks, Latinos, Asians, and American Indians have lived in the United States *under separate systems of law* for varying periods of time. Because each has a history of differential legal status and because this history has led to special attention in contemporary law in an attempt to remedy the effects of historical discrimination, these groups require special attention in political analysis.

There is a tendency in the political science literature to assume that all racial minority groups within the United States share similar experiences and political behaviors. Consequently, blacks, Latinos, Asian Americans, and American Indians are often merged under the rubric "minority group politics." But the increasing recognition of differences among and within these groups has generated debate over whether the concept of minority group politics is useful in thinking about and studying the political experiences of all nonwhite groups in the United States. Although these groups share racial minority group status within the United States, there are fundamental differences in their experiences, orientations, and political behaviors that affect the relationships among the four groups as well as between each of the groups and the dominant white majority. Similarities in racial minority group status may be the bases for building coalitions, but they may also generate conflict. Consequently, this book focuses on the groups separately at times and comparatively at other times.

Terms Used in This Book

Before proceeding, it is important to define the terms used throughout the book. The way individuals identify themselves and how they are identified by others in the polity is of more than semantic interest. Self-identification, often referred to as **group political consciousness,** and other-identification can promote or thwart nation building and affect, as we shall see later, people's ability and willingness to participate in the political system.

First, the terms *black* and *African American* are used interchangeably. Recent survey data indicate that seven of ten African Americans prefer the term *black* (Gomes and Williams 1992). We also prefer the term *black* for theoretical reasons. It concisely describes an identity and a status within American society that are based on color. The black experience in America differs markedly from that of the white ethnics, and the use of African American may convey the impression that blacks are just another ethnic group similar to Italian Americans, Irish Americans, or Polish Americans. Blacks have been subjugated and segregated, on the basis of color, from *all* whites regardless of their ethnic backgrounds. Further, after one generation white ethnics have been able to shed their ethnicity and blend into the mainstream of white America, but blacks, because of their skin color, remain identifiable generation after generation. We also use *black* because it is a convenient proxy term for an insular group that is more or less politically cohesive, that has historically been stigmatized, that is generally depressed economically, and that remains socially isolated.

Similarly, we use *Latino* and *Hispanic* interchangeably as umbrella terms when we cannot distinguish among subgroups of the nation's Spanish-origin population. The largest of the Latino groups are Mexican Americans, Puerto Ricans, and Cuban Americans. The term *Hispanic* is eschewed by many intellectuals because it is Eurocentric—the term literally means "lover of Spain"— which, given the national origins of the overwhelming majority of U.S.

Latinos, is inappropriate. Moreover, *Hispanic* is a term devised by the U.S. Census Bureau for classifying individuals and is devoid of any theoretical or political context.

The Latino National Political Survey, discussed more fully in Chapter 3, suggests that Latinos do not primarily identify themselves as members of a Hispanic or Latino community. Although Latino is the preferred identifier among the intelligentsia, few Mexican Americans, Puerto Ricans, or Cubans self-identify themselves with either pan-ethnic term. The preferred identification terms are *Mexican* or *Mexican American* among Mexican Americans, *Puerto Rican* among Puerto Ricans, and *Cuban* among Cuban respondents (de la Garza et al. 1992).

Third, we use the term *Indian peoples* or *American Indian* peoples rather than *Native Americans*. The reasons for this choice are simple yet profoundly important. The term *Native American* was used during the nativist (anti-immigration, antiforeigner) movement (1860–1925) and the antiblack, anti-Catholic, and anti-Jewish Ku Klux Klan resurgence during the early 1900s (Higham 1963). The rhetoric of these groups was couched in terms of "native-born" white Protestants vis-à-vis those of "foreign" origin, for example, Catholics. There was even a political party known as the Native American Party. Thus, whereas popular culture may refer to Indian peoples as Native Americans, we feel it is important to separate this group from the white supremacist terms used by the nativist movement. Moreover, we seek to defuse the specious argument made by some that if one is born in the United States, one is a native American, thereby dismissing the unique situation and status of American Indian peoples. Indian peoples encompass a variety of tribes, each with its own history and different structural relationships with the U.S. government. Finally, many native Hawaiians consider themselves Native Americans, although the U.S. Census Bureau puts them in the Asian–Pacific Islander category. Native Hawaiians are not included in our discussion here, so our terms separate American Indians from native Hawaiians.

The question of who is an Indian is central to any discussion of American Indian politics. The essence of the "Indianness" issue rests not with Indian peoples themselves but with the federal government. Self-identification traced through descent, lineage, and tribe is a matter of pride for Indian peoples. But the Anglo-American preoccupation with formal definition has generated a host of problems for American Indians, in part because federal, state, and tribal definitions of Indian identification have wide variations. Moreover, the question of who is subject to Indian law also depends on the relationship of the tribe to the federal government and on whether the federal government recognizes the tribe. Federal recognition takes a variety of forms: through treaty-based reservations, reservations created directly by Congress, and state-created reservations or state-recognized tribes. In addition to federally recognized Indians, there are hundreds of groups that are no longer recognized as Indian tribes but that are composed of Indian peoples nonetheless and are recognized as such by other Indian peoples (Chaudhuri 1982).

Finally, the term *Asian American* envelops a multiplicity of ethnic origin groups—Japanese, Koreans, Chinese, Filipinos, Southeast Asians, Pacific Islanders, and East Indians (Kitano 1981). Each of these groups has a different history of entrance into the United States, but "Asian Americans have been here for over one hundred and fifty years, before many European immigrant groups" (Takaki 1993:7). The Chinese arrived first in significant numbers, followed by the Japanese, Koreans, Filipinos, Asian Indians, and, later, Southeast Asian refugees. We find no local, contemporary survey data that address ethnic identity for Asian Americans, but the historical record suggests a situation even less unified than that of Hispanics. National rivalries often survived the immigration process, so that, for example, early Japanese immigrants were as anti-Chinese as any of their non-Asian counterparts (Ichioka 1988). Furthermore, unlike Latinos, first-generation immigrant Asians have not shared a common language, a situation that provides a formidable barrier to any pan-Asian identification (Espiritu 1992).

Race and Ethnicity

Although this is not a book about **racism**—the belief in and practice of using race as a justification for discrimination among individuals—per se, each of the groups considered has been affected by racism, albeit differently. Furthermore, social class and gender differences are variables that both compound the effects of racism and affect the way group members can and do respond to the situations in which they find themselves. When information is available to allow us to take these factors into account, we shall do so. But over and above class and gender, race has been and continues to be a central theme of the American polity and society.

Race—initially construed in terms of white, black, and Indian—has never been a benign concept in the United States. We should remember that the first Africans to arrive at Jamestown, Virginia, in 1619 were indentured servants, not slaves. Slavery was not instituted on a broad scale until 1661 in Virginia (twenty

years after slavery had first been incorporated into colonial law in Massachusetts) as the need for labor increased and whites found Indian servitude and
slavery inadequate and the supply of white indentured servants insufficient. The
permanent enslavement of Africans and African Americans was the answer to a
"vexing" labor problem. The supply of blacks appeared to be endless, and "if they
ran away they were easily detected because of their color. If they proved un-
governable they could be chastised with less qualms and with greater severity
than in the case of whites, because Negroes represented heathen people who
could not claim the immunities accorded by Christians" (Franklin 1969:72).

With the institution of slavery and the mass importation of black slaves,
whites—although solving their labor problems—began to fear the mixture of
races and to be concerned that growing numbers of blacks would rebel against
the institution of slavery. These fears and the whites' disdain and contempt for
blacks created a dynamic of white oppression that manifested itself in a multiplicity of ways. Many states, concerned about the purity of the white group, codified into law the degree of black ancestry that qualified one to be legally defined
as black and thus subject to legal restrictions. Louisiana and North Carolina used
the one-sixteenth criterion (one great-great-grandparent); one-eighth (one
great-grandparent) was the standard in Florida, Indiana, Maryland, Mississippi,
Missouri, Nebraska, North Dakota, South Carolina, and Tennessee; Oregon used
a one-quarter standard (one grandparent) (Spickard 1989:374–375).

This obsession with "black blood" was also codified into legal restrictions on
marriage partners, which were referred to as **antimiscegenation laws.**
Throughout most of their history, twenty-nine states maintained laws forbidding interracial marriage between blacks and whites. Over time, many of these
laws were amended to include a prohibition on marriages between other racial
combinations in addition to blacks and whites. The fourteen states with additional prohibitions included California, between white and "Mongolian";
Georgia, between white, American Indian, Asiatic Indian, or Mongolian;
Nebraska, between white and Chinese or Japanese; and Arizona, between white
and Mongolian or Indian. The penalties for interracial marriages ranged from
maximum imprisonment of more than two years in fourteen states to no
penalty in California. These antimiscegenation laws were not nullified until
the U.S. Supreme Court decision *Loving v. Virginia* in 1967 (Spickard
1989:374–375).

We are also concerned with issues of ethnicity—in a specific sense of the
term. We use the term **ethnicity**—generally meaning the grouping of people
on the basis of learned characteristics, often associated with national origin—
because we recognize that within the four groups addressed in this book there

are different ethnic origin groups that may have different political attitudes and behaviors. Issues of ethnicity are particularly pertinent within the Latino, Asian, and Indian groups. The U.S. Bureau of Census currently has only four official racial categories—white, black, Asian–Pacific Islander, and American Indian–Alaska native; anyone who does not fit into one of these categories is classified as "other." Thus, for example, Hispanic is used as an ethnic, rather than a racial, category. Although many Hispanics view themselves as a separate nonwhite race, they are forced to classify themselves as either white or black. This practice has caused consternation among several of the groups, particularly Mexicans, who are a mixture of Indian, African, and European—principally Spanish. Until Hispanic is deemed to be a racial category, we will continue to use ethnicity in conjunction with racial minorities in recognition of the idiosyncratic situation of Latinos vis-à-vis the U.S. Census Bureau.

Such formal identification may define who is included in and who is excluded from the political system. In official terms, the issues are citizenship and voting rights. We now consider the key values in the foundation of the U.S. Constitution, including citizenship and suffrage, and their application to the nation's original minorities—blacks and American Indians.

American Government Foundation and Racial Minorities

April 13, 1993, marked the 250th anniversary of the birth of Thomas Jefferson, the third president of the United States and author of the Declaration of Independence. Despite all of the celebrations around the world, the contradictions and inconsistencies between Thomas Jefferson the man and Thomas Jefferson the statesperson were not lost. The man who wrote in the Declaration of Independence that "all men are created equal and are endowed by their Creator with certain inalienable rights . . . and among these are life, liberty, and the pursuit of happiness" was also a slave owner. The tension that existed between the venerated values of the American political foundation—democracy, freedom, and equality—and the enslavement of a sizeable segment of its population was not limited to Thomas Jefferson. It is an ever-present tension and a continuing struggle for the citizens of the United States and the values contained in the organizing document, the Constitution, which is the nation's foundation.

The political values contained in the Declaration of Independence in 1776 and spelled out later in the U.S. Constitution, drafted in 1787 and ratified in

1789, have their origins in classical liberal theory. **Classical liberalism** refers to a particular body of Western European political thought that sought to justify the "liberation" of the individual from feudal positions and to deride those who benefited from feudalism. In classical liberal theory private interests are given priority over public or governmental authority, and the economy receives priority over the polity. Liberalism finds expression in the writings of John Locke and others, writings with which Thomas Jefferson was very familiar. The free individual in Locke's liberalism was free from the confines of the state—free to seek private ends. States and governments were coercive; despite declarations that they should be representative, their main purpose was to control and regulate the conduct of individuals. To paraphrase Locke, if individuals are to be free, mechanisms must be developed to limit government's powers and to ensure that those limits will be preserved. Classical liberal thought runs throughout the *Federalist Papers,* the essays written to justify the ratification of the Constitution. Government's responsibility to protect private property and to provide an environment in which the pursuit of private property can be facilitated is a fundamental principle of the papers.

Given the emphasis on property in classical liberal theory in general, and in the *Federalist Papers* in particular, it is not surprising that the 1787 Constitution was explicitly intended not to apply to blacks and Indians. Article I, Section 2, of the original Constitution states: "Representatives and direct Taxes shall be apportioned among the several States which may be included within this Union, according to their respective Numbers, *which shall be determined by adding to the whole Number of free Persons, including those bound to Service for a Term of Years, and excluding Indians not taxed, three-fifths of all other Persons*" (emphasis added). "Other Persons" refers to the 92 percent of the black population held in slavery in the United States in 1790, the year the government began the census; the remaining 59,557 blacks were free individuals (Pohlman 1991:34; Jarvis 1992:21). In fact, there was no ambiguity regarding the founders' views on slavery or their position regarding the legal status of blacks within the United States.

Jefferson's original draft of the Declaration of Independence included an indictment of King George for "violating the most sacred rights of life and liberty in the persons of a distant people who never offended him, captivating and carrying them into slavery in another hemisphere or to incur miserable death in their transportation hither" (quoted in Jarvis 1992:20). However, this indictment of slavery was unacceptable to both southern and northern delegates because the southerners argued that slavery was fundamental to the economy of the new nation and the northerners viewed slavery as a business that needed to be regulated.

The issue of slavery and the ensuing debate influenced the final compromise contained in Article I, Section 2, of the Constitution quoted earlier. The framers were cognizant of the fact that slavery would affect the "issues of representation, apportionment among the states, direct taxation, and commerce" (Jarvis 1992:20). Compromise was the watchword of the individuals who drafted the Constitution, and several important compromises were struck over the issue of slavery and suffrage requirements. Whereas Article I, Section 9, mandated a twenty-year time period before Congress could limit the importation of African slaves, Article IV, Section 2, maintained that escaped slaves would not be freed from slavery but should be returned to their owners (the fugitive slave clause). The **three-fifths compromise,** in which the delegates decided to count a slave as only three-fifths of a person, resolved the issue of how to count slaves for representational and direct taxation purposes.

Although blacks were counted for representational and taxation purposes, they were not considered citizens of the United States: "Slaves were persons, but they were also property, which meant that a Negro's right to liberty conflicted with his master's right to property. In the colonial ideology, the right of property was central" (Robinson 1971:86). The compromise was momentous because

> it gave Constitutional sanction to the fact that the United States was composed of some persons who were "free" and others who were not. And it established the principle, new in republican theory, that a man who lived among slaves had a greater share in the election of representatives than the man who did not. With one stroke, despite the disclaimers of its advocates, it acknowledged slavery and rewarded slave owners. It is a measure of their adjustment to slavery that Americans in the eighteenth century found this settlement natural and just. (Robinson 1971:201)

"This twisted logic satisfied the issue of apportionment but failed miserably in setting the right of blacks, particularly those who were not enslaved, to vote" (Jarvis 1992:21).

The Constitution
and Black and Indian Citizenship

After ratification of the Constitution, two important issues remained to be addressed—suffrage and citizenship. Issues of **suffrage**—voting eligibility—were left to the states because reconciling differences in state voting qualifications at the national level was thought to be too difficult. Moreover, and critically important, the criteria for **citizenship**—determining who was and was not a citizen of the United States or of a state—were also left to the states. The fact that these two important issues were left up to the states set the stage for the systematic exclusion from the political process of blacks, Indian peoples, women of all colors, and other racial minority groups.

Prior to the Declaration of Independence, the Continental Congress defined the colonies' citizens as "all persons abiding within any of the United Colonies and deriving protection from the laws of the same owe allegiance to the said laws, and are members of such colony" (Franklin 1906:2). Several events surrounding the institution of the Declaration of Independence and the Articles of Confederation indicate that initially "the right to citizenship was to be opened to all white people who were willing to identify with the struggle against the King" (Robinson 1971:135). As evidence, the committee—consisting of Benjamin Franklin, John Adams, and Thomas Jefferson—that had been appointed to devise a new national seal proposed that the seal be representative of the countries from which the peoples of the new nation had originated: England, Scotland, Ireland, France, Germany, and Holland. "Apparently neither the Africans nor the Indians were thought, even by this cosmopolitan committee, worthy of representation" (Robinson 1971:135).

Another event that lends credence to the contention that citizenship was reserved for whites was the manner in which a committee of Congress under the Articles of Confederation, of which Thomas Jefferson was also a member, wrestled with the issue of Indian inclusiveness in the new country. The initial committee report advised Congress to urge the states to make it easy for Indians to become citizens. After all, the colonists had enjoyed generally friendly relations with the American Indian nations with which they had come into contact. Most Indians traded with, protected, and supported European settlers until conflict erupted over control of land. The support of the Iroquois Confederacy, a government that at the time was over seven hundred years old, in the French and Indian War had been crucial to the English victory. Likewise, two of the six tribes—including the most powerful, the Oneidas—had sided with the colonists against Great Britain in the Revolutionary War.

This report, however, was tabled. A subsequent report by a different committee "referred to the Indians, not as potential citizens, but as possible allies" (Robinson 1971:136). These events, combined with others, led to the conclusion "that the 'one people,' to whom Jefferson referred in the opening paragraph of the Declaration of Independence, were the white people of the thirteen colonies" (Robinson 1971:136). In addition, the Articles of Confederation, when discussing privileges and immunities, continually referred to "free inhabitants" and "free citizens" (Franklin 1906:1–18).

Although the U.S. Constitution, which replaced the Articles of Confederation, used the word *citizen* in several places, it did not confront citizenship directly; it assumed it. The assumption was that if individuals met the conditions of citizenship developed by the states, they were entitled to the rights and privileges extended in the Constitution. For example, Article I, Section 2, when discussing voting qualifications for election of members to the House of Representatives, states that if an individual meets the voting requirements in the state in which he resides, he is eligible to vote for members of the House of Representatives. Article IV, Section 2, states that "the Citizens of each State shall be entitled to all Privileges and Immunities of Citizens in the several States." The result was that each state was free to determine citizenship as well as voting requirements.

Following the ratification of the Constitution, Congress passed the **Naturalization** Act of 1790 in response to the Constitution's granting congressional power to pass a uniform rule to deal with the process by which foreigners could be "admitted to the rights of citizens" (Franklin 1906:33). This act granted citizenship as a matter of right to free white aliens who had lived in the United States and shown good behavior for two years, who expressed the intention of remaining in the United States, and who took an oath of allegiance. Between 1790 and 1854, Congress passed fifteen laws concerning naturalization and retained the phrase "free white person" in all of these laws without discussion: "The reason for the adoption of the phrase 'free white person' was manifestly the conviction that Indians and slaves, since they did not understand our life and political system, were not freemen and, therefore, were not fitted to be members of the body politic, nor to exercise the duties and responsibilities of citizenship" (Gulick 1918:55–56). Only after the Civil War, in the Naturalization Act of 1870, were naturalization laws "extended to aliens of African nativity and to persons of African descent" (Gulick 1918:56).

Although it could be argued that the Constitution, as it was framed, only excluded enslaved blacks from being citizens, the citizenship status of free blacks was debatable. Whatever doubt existed about the citizenship status of blacks under the Constitution was clarified with the Supreme Court decision in *Dred Scott v. Sanford* (1857). Writing for the majority in its attempt to settle the most explosive political issue of the time, Chief Justice Taney said the question was whether the provisions of the Constitution, in relation to the personal rights and privileges to which the citizen of a State should be entitled, embraced the negro African race, at that time in this country, or who might afterwards be imported, who had then or should afterwards be made free in any State; and to put it in the power of a single State to make him a citizen of the United States and endue him with the full rights of citizenship in every other State without their consent? Does the Constitution of the United States act upon him whenever he shall be made free under the laws of a State, and raised there to the rank of a citizen, and immediately clothe him with all the privileges of a citizen in every other State, and in its own courts? . . . It becomes necessary, therefore, to determine who were citizens of the several States when the Constitution was adopted. (*Dred Scott v. Sanford,* 19 Howard 393, 406–407 [1857])

Taney argues that on the surface the words of the Declaration of Independence that state "that all men are created equal" and "are endowed by their Creator with certain unalienable rights" appear to apply to blacks. Yet, he concludes, "it is too clear for dispute, that the enslaved African race were not intended to be included, and formed no part of the people who framed and adopted this declaration" (*Dred Scott v. Sanford* 1857:393, 410) and that this exclusion extended to the Constitution when ratified. Taney argues that two clauses in the Constitution, the right of the states to ban the importation of slaves after twenty years and the return of fugitive slaves (property) to their owners, provide evidence that the framers of the Constitution excluded blacks as "people" or citizens of the states in which they reside and thus as citizens of the United States. The Supreme Court thus declared that Dred Scott was not a citizen of the state of Missouri "in the sense in which that word is used in the Constitution" and that blacks, whether free or enslaved, "had no rights that the white man was bound to respect" (*Dred Scott v. Sanford* 1857:454, 407).

The issue of defining national citizenship and citizenship for blacks was not confronted directly until the ratification of the Fourteenth Amendment to the Constitution in 1868. Section 1 of that amendment says, in part, that "all persons born or naturalized in the United States, and subject to the jurisdiction thereof, are citizens of the United States and of the State wherein they reside." Thus, the issue of the citizenship status of African Americans was resolved, and national citizenship was added to the Constitution. Yet the rights, privileges, and immunities granted to blacks by this amendment were illusionary, as is discussed later. (The ratification of the Fourteenth Amendment to the Constitution also modified the three-fifths provision in Article I, Section 2. The Fourteenth Amendment implied that blacks would be counted equally with whites for purposes of representation.)

Although the Fourteenth Amendment established the citizenship status of blacks, American Indian peoples were still not considered citizens. In *Cherokee Nation v. State of Georgia* (1831:16), the Supreme Court had ruled that Indian tribes "are in a state of pupilage [a minor child under the care of a guardian], and the relationship between the Indian tribes and the United States government [is] likened to that of 'a ward to his guardian.'" Based on this wardship status, Indian peoples were considered to be "domestic subjects" and were not entitled to be thought of as citizens. Thus, they could be denied civil, political, and economic rights because "the framers of our constitution had not the Indian tribes in view, when they opened the Courts of the union to controversies between a state or the citizens thereof" (*Cherokee Nation* 1831:16). In fact, the Supreme Court in *Elk v. Wilkins* (1884) refused to extend the right of citizenship conferred in the Fourteenth Amendment to Indian peoples. The decision said, in part:

> Indians born within the territorial limits of the United States, members of, and owing immediate allegiance to, one of the Indian tribes (an alien, though dependent, power), although in a geographical sense born in the United States, are no more "born in the United States and subject to the jurisdiction thereof," within the meaning of the first section of the Fourteenth Amendment, than the children of subjects of any foreign government born within the domain of that government or the children born within the United States, of ambassadors or other public ministers of foreign nations. (*Elk v. Wilkins* 1884:102)

The Court ended its decision by stating:

> The plaintiff, not being a citizen of the United States under the Fourteenth Amendment of the Constitution, has been deprived of no right secured by the Fifteenth Amendment and cannot maintain this action. (*Elk v. Wilkins* 1884:109)

Thus, Indian peoples were left in a status much like that of slaves prior to the Civil War—they were neither aliens nor citizens.

Citizenship came to Indians only in piecemeal fashion. In response to a Supreme Court ruling that Indian peoples who left their tribes voluntarily were not U.S. citizens, Congress passed the Dawes Act in 1887, which granted citizenship to those who received individual allotments of tribal land (a new procedure meant to destroy the tribes and make Indians private-property owners) and to those who voluntarily left their tribe. Tribal Indian peoples remained noncitizens.

In 1901, Congress formally granted U.S. citizenship to the "five civilized tribes," originally of the Southeast—Cherokee, Chickasaw, Choctaw, Creek, and

Seminole—which had been displaced to "Indian territory," centered in Oklahoma.[2] In 1919, citizenship was granted to American Indians who had served in the U.S. armed forces in World War I. Not until the Indian Citizenship Act of 1924 was citizenship conferred on all American Indian peoples.

Citizenship and Later Minorities: Latinos and Asians

Although citizenship denial was most egregious in the cases of blacks and Indian peoples, an exclusion purposely crafted in the Constitution and upheld by the Supreme Court, other racial groups faced similar situations as they entered the United States. Citizenship for the various Latino groups—Mexicans, Puerto Ricans, and Cubans—came at different times and in different ways. In 1836, Anglos and dissident Mexicans in Texas revolted and seceded from Mexico, creating the Republic of Texas. Hostilities between Texas and Mexico continued for nearly a decade until 1846 when the United States declared war on the Republic of Mexico. The Treaty of Guadalupe Hidalgo in 1848 officially ended the war, and Mexico ceded what are now the states of Arizona, New Mexico, California, Colorado, Texas, Nevada, Utah, Kansas, Oklahoma, and Wyoming to the United States. Mexican citizens living in the territories that were ceded who chose to stay on the land and live under U.S. rule were granted U.S. citizenship and all of its guarantees.

Spain granted autonomy to the island of Puerto Rico in 1897, but when the Spanish-American War began in 1898, U.S. troops landed on the island. With the ratification of the Treaty of Paris in 1899, which ended the Spanish-American War, the United States annexed Puerto Rico. The 1900 Foraker Act made Puerto Rico an "unincorporated" U.S. territory with a presidentially appointed governor. Puerto Rico remained an American colony until 1952 when it became a "commonwealth" of the United States. Immediately after the U.S. acquisition, Puerto Ricans were in a political netherworld; they were not citizens of the United States nor of Spain nor of an independent nation. However, with the passage of the Jones Act in 1917, Puerto Ricans became citizens of the United States, although citizenship was conferred over the objections of the island's legislature (Hero 1992). Puerto Ricans residing on the island are subject to the military draft, when there is one, but do not pay U.S. income taxes and do not participate fully in federal social service programs (Moore and Pachon 1985). But Puerto Ricans who live on the mainland are not distinguished from other U.S. citizens for taxation and government assistance purposes.

U.S. involvement with Cuba can be traced to the Monroe Doctrine of 1823. In 1895, with the help of the United States, Cuba launched a War of Independence against Spain. Intense U.S. involvement, as with its involvement with Puerto Rico, stems from the time of the Spanish-American War, after which Cuba achieved its independence from Spain although it was still under U.S. military rule. In 1901, Congress passed the Platt Amendment granting Cuba conditional independence, with the United States reserving the right to intervene—militarily and otherwise—on "Cuba's behalf."

Although many think Cuban Americans first came to the United States after 1959, the 1870 U.S. census indicates that just over 5,000 persons living in the United States had been born in Cuba (Boswell and Curtis 1983:39). In the 1860s and 1870s several Cuban cigar manufacturers relocated their operations to the United States, settling principally in Key West, Tampa, and New York City. However, the majority of Cubans arrived in the United States after 1959. Census data indicate that in 1960 there were approximately 124,500 Cubans, just over one-third of whom were second- or third-generation Americans. Just a decade later the Cuban population had increased to over 560,000 persons, slightly over 78 percent of whom had been born in Cuba.

Little is known about the naturalization of the early Cuban immigrants to Florida, but until the 1980s 96 percent of the Cuban immigrants were considered to be white (Boswell and Curtis 1983:102). Thus, it is possible that they were also considered white under the naturalization acts and thus were eligible for citizenship. Cubans entering the United States after Castro's rise to power in 1959 generally enjoyed handsome financial support from the U.S. government and were encouraged to seek U.S. citizenship.

The citizenship status of Asian Americans—primarily the early Chinese and Japanese immigrants—although similar to the Latino case, also has close parallels with the legal status of blacks and Indians under the various naturalization acts. Two events—the Treaty of Guadalupe Hidalgo (1848) and the California gold rush—precipitated the Chinese immigration to the United States, which began in 1848. With the annexation of California under the treaty, a plan was sent to Congress for expansion of the railroad to the Pacific coast. The plan proposed that Chinese laborers should be imported to build the transcontinental railroad as well as to cultivate the land in California. At the same time, gold was discovered in California, thus generating the need for both Mexican and Chinese miners who were seen as the best source of cheap labor. Consequently, the 1850s saw a substantial increase in the number of Chinese immigrants to the United States, principally, but not exclusively, to

California. By 1870 there were sixty-three thousand Chinese in the United States, 77 percent of whom lived in California (Takaki 1993:192–194).

At first the Chinese were welcomed because their labor was essential to the expansion into California and the development of the territory. But in 1850, the California legislature enacted, then quickly repealed, a foreign miners' tax designed to eliminate Mexican miners (Takaki 1993:194). In 1852, the legislature passed another foreign miners' tax, this one targeted at Chinese miners. This tax required that every foreign miner who did not wish to become a U.S. citizen pay a monthly fee of three dollars. "Even if they had wanted to, the Chinese could not have become citizens, for they had been rendered ineligible for citizenship by a 1790 federal law that reserved naturalized citizenship for 'white' persons" (Takaki 1993:195). This exclusion barred most Chinese, but the interpretation of who was "white" was left to administrative officials. Thus, a small number of Chinese were able to be naturalized. The first Chinese applied for citizenship in 1854, another was naturalized in New York in 1873, and thirteen applied for citizenship in California in 1876 (Gulick 1918:59).

But anti-Chinese and Chinese immigration antipathy and nativist sentiments were on the rise. President Rutherford B. Hayes warned Americans about the "Chinese problem," saying that "the present Chinese invasion . . . should be discouraged. Our experience in dealing with the weaker races—the Negroes and Indians . . . —is not encouraging. . . . I would consider with favor any suitable measures to discourage the Chinese from coming to our shores" (quoted in Takaki 1993:206). Acceding to anti-Chinese agitation and violence in the 1870s and 1880s, Congress passed the Chinese Exclusion Act in 1882, which reduced Chinese immigration to a trickle (Higham 1963:25; Takaki 1993:200). Additionally, part of the act mandated "that even those Chinese who might otherwise qualify should not be given citizenship privileges" (quoted in Gulick 1918:59). Section 14 of the Chinese Exclusion Act stated that "hereafter no State Court or Court of the United States shall admit Chinese to citizenship; and all laws in conflict with this act are hereby repealed" (quoted in Gulick 1918:59).

As a result of World War II and the participation of Chinese Americans in the war effort, in 1943 Congress repealed the Chinese exclusion laws and extended the right of naturalized citizenship to Chinese immigrants: "At last after almost one hundred years in America, Chinese immigrants could seek political membership in their adopted country" (Takaki 1993:387). Although Chinese immigrants were initially denied citizenship, their children who were born in the United States were considered U.S. citizens.

The first known Japanese immigrants arrived in the United States in 1843, yet the need for labor on Hawaiian plantations in the mid-1860s precipitated the search for labor in Japan. (The United States officially acquired the Hawaiian Islands in 1898 as a territory.) The first Japanese contract workers arrived in Hawaii in 1868, and in 1885 the Japanese government officially allowed Japanese workers to migrate to Hawaii and to the U.S. mainland. Between 1885 and 1924, "200,000 [Japanese] left for Hawaii and 180,000 for the United States mainland" (Takaki 1993:247). On the mainland, Japanese were initially employed as migrant workers in agriculture, railroad construction, and canneries (Takaki 1993:267).

Eventually, the Japanese—primarily those in California—became farmers with extensive landholdings, and their success and increasing presence engendered great animosity. In 1908 the U.S. government pressured Japan to prohibit the emigration of Japanese laborers to the United States, and in 1913 the California legislature passed the California Land Act, which prohibited aliens—principally the Japanese—from owning and leasing land. Other states passed similar legislation. Drawing on the 1790 act, which limited naturalization to "white" persons, these restrictive alien land laws were based on the Japanese ineligibility to become naturalized U.S. citizens: "In 1922, the United States Supreme Court affirmed that Takao Ozawa, a Japanese immigrant, was not entitled to naturalized citizenship because he 'clearly' was 'not Caucasian'" (Takaki 1993:273). Moreover, in 1924 Congress passed the Immigration Quota Act—which was aimed specifically at the Japanese but also covered other Asians—which excluded all aliens who were ineligible for citizenship (those who were not "white," as stated in the 1790 and subsequent naturalization laws, or "African," as the naturalization laws were amended after the Civil War). Once again, however, although Japanese immigrants were denied citizenship, their children born in the United States were citizens. Only with the passage of the McCarran-Walter Act in 1952 were the racial restrictions contained in the 1790 Naturalization Act rescinded and Japanese immigrants allowed naturalization rights.

The Constitution
and Black and Indian Suffrage

The Constitution left voting requirements to the individual states and did not specifically prohibit free blacks from exercising the franchise (Foner 1992:57). Moreover, the concepts of citizenship and voting were not linked in colonial and postrevolutionary America (Kleppner 1990). Because the thirteen original colonies were settled primarily by the British, it is not surprising that they adopted the British system of restricting the franchise to property owners. Voting qualifications varied from colony to colony and were based on criteria such as property ownership, status ("freeman"), race (white), gender (male), age, religion, and length of residence (Jarvis 1992:18). Although only Georgia and South Carolina adopted state constitutions that expressly limited voting to white males on the basis of race, voting restrictions based on race were soon instituted in other states as the number of black slaves increased following the introduction of slavery. At the time the Constitution was framed, "free black men could vote in some of the original states, including the southern one of North Carolina" (Davidson 1992:7).

As the black slave population increased in the South, white colonists became concerned about their ability to control slaves and prevent slave insurrections. Thus, numerous slave codes were introduced. As a result, free blacks in the South saw their political and social access restricted and eventually curtailed. Free blacks were forced to carry certificates of freedom or risk being captured and sold as slaves. In addition, "They could no longer vote (except in Tennessee until 1834 and North Carolina until 1835), hold public office, give testimony against whites, possess a firearm, buy liquor, assemble freely (except in a church supervised by whites), or immigrate to other states" (Jarvis 1992:19). Free blacks in the northern regions fared better and lived under less restrictive conditions, but they were regarded as inferior and undesirable, and their employment opportunities were limited. In some instances, northern jurisdictions prohibited their immigration to other regions through the threat of punishment or enslavement (Jarvis 1992:19). By the time of the Civil War, free blacks were denied suffrage everywhere in the United States except in New York and in all of the New England states except Connecticut.

Following the Civil War and in response to the southern states' refusal to extend suffrage to blacks, numerous actions were taken by the Radical Republican–dominated Congress. For example, the Civil Rights Act of 1866 "anticipated the Fourteenth Amendment by making United States citizens of all native-born people except untaxed Native Americans, and guaranteeing to all citizens regardless of race or previous servitude the right to enforce contracts, file lawsuits, testify in court, own property, and enjoy all benefits of law to which white citizens were entitled" (Jarvis 1992:25). However, neither these laws nor the Fourteenth Amendment explicitly prohibited racial discrimination in the area of voting. This prohibition was not achieved until the ratification of the Fifteenth Amendment in 1870, which states, "the right of citizens of the United States to vote shall not be denied or abridged by the United States or by any State on account of race, color, or previous condition of servitude."

Although in theory the Fifteenth Amendment provided a constitutionally protected guarantee of black male suffrage, resistance—often violent—by white southerners to black voting was evident. Although three Enforcement Acts (1870, 1871, and 1975) were passed in an attempt to put teeth into the amendment, white resistance was not overcome (Davidson 1992:10). Moreover, two Supreme Court decisions undercut the effectiveness of the Fourteenth and Fifteenth Amendments. In *U.S. v. Cruikshank* (1876), in a case involving white defendants who had killed approximately one hundred blacks in a mob attack, the Supreme Court ruled that because these individuals were private actors and were not acting on behalf of the state, the Fourteenth and Fifteenth Amendments did not apply to them. Although it did not find the Enforcement Act of 1870 unconstitutional, the Court severely limited the act's application.

In the other decision, *U.S. v. Reese* (1876), in a case involving Kentucky election officials' refusal to accept the votes of a black person in a municipal election, the Court ruled that Congress could protect against interference only in congressional elections and not in state elections. Thus, Sections 3 and 4 of the Enforcement Act of 1870 were ruled unconstitutional because they went beyond the Fifteenth Amendment's prohibition against the denial of suffrage. The end of a national commitment to protect the suffrage and other constitutional rights of blacks came with the compromise of 1877 in which Rutherford B. Hayes, to gain the support of the southern states in the contested presidential elections of 1876, agreed to remove federal troops and protection from the former states of the Old Confederacy and leave the South free to deal with "the Negro problem" as the states saw fit.

After the removal of federal protection, the southern states moved quickly to disenfranchise blacks. This disenfranchisement was achieved through a combination of structural discrimination (e.g., gerrymandering, annexations, at-large election systems, and appointive offices), violence, voting fraud, and eventually through disenfranchising conventions that rewrote state constitutions with clauses to prohibit blacks from voting or participating in politics. By the 1890s, blacks—primarily in the South but in some northern jurisdictions as well—had been legally and very effectively removed from the electoral process (Kousser 1992).

Additionally, in 1896 the Supreme Court, in *Plessy v. Ferguson,* upheld Louisiana's practice of racial discrimination, essentially declaring that separation of the races was allowable under the U.S. Constitution as long as the facil-

A group of bystanders view A. B. Young after he was lynched by a mob of fifty men in Slayden, Mississippi, March 12, 1935. Members of the mob placed a rope around his neck while Young stood in a truck, tied the rope to a tree limb, and drove the truck from under him. Scenes like this were not uncommon during the period in which blacks were deprived of political power. Photo courtesy UPI/Bettmann.

ities were "equal." This reasoning became known as the **separate but equal doctrine.** The end of the nineteenth century and the beginning of the twentieth century constituted the nadir of black political history (Logan 1954).

Although American Indians were the first "Americans," they were the last large group to be granted voting rights and citizenship (Sigler 1975:156). The ruling in *Elk v. Wilkins* (1884) that Indians were not citizens of the United States under the Fourteenth Amendment kept "all Indians unable to prove that they were born under United States jurisdiction from registering to vote" (McCool 1985:106). Moreover, because Indians were not made citizens until the Indian Citizenship Act of 1924, the Fifteenth Amendment, which extended the right to vote to all male citizens regardless of race, did not apply to Indians until that time.

Even after the conferring of citizenship, many states—including Arizona, New Mexico, and Utah—through their state constitutions, continued to deny

Indians the right to vote. These states argued that because Indians were in a "guardianship" relationship with the federal government and were subject to federal rather than state jurisdiction, Indian reservations, therefore, could not be considered part of the state in which they existed. Therefore, Indians were not state citizens and were not eligible to vote in state and local elections. Beginning in 1927, federal as well as state courts began to reject this argument, but many states continued to find mechanisms to deny Indians the right to vote. The twin issues of state residency and federal guardianship were used in a long series of court cases in various states in attempts to keep Indians from voting. Indians in Arizona, through a series of court challenges, won the right to vote in 1948, and Indians in New Mexico won their case shortly thereafter.

Challenges continued. For example, in 1956 the Utah state attorney general issued an opinion based on an 1897 state law "that withheld residency from anyone who lived on an 'Indian or military reservation' unless that person had previously established residency in an off-reservation Utah county" (McCool 1985:109). In effect, this ruling denied Utah Indians the right to vote. The Utah Supreme Court upheld the attorney general's interpretation of the law, so the state legislature had to amend state statutes to allow Indians to vote. In another case, in 1962 a defeated non-Indian candidate in New Mexico challenged the validity of Indian voting rights, claiming Indians were not residents of the state. In this instance, the state Supreme Court upheld the right of Indians to vote (McCool 1985:109).

Structure of This Book

This chapter has articulated the dilemmas we address in this book. Furthermore, it shows that the roots of the first dilemma, the clear presence of racial inequality in a nation that promises equality, precede the founding of the current constitutional system. The remainder of the book elaborates on this dilemma and sets the stage for a consideration of the second dilemma, the choice between coalition or conflict as a strategy.

Chapter 2 provides a brief survey of some of the political resources and the status of each of the groups treated in this book. Several key variables—relative size and geographic concentration, socioeconomic status, degree of participation in a civil rights movement, and coverage by contemporary voting rights legislation—are highlighted to provide both comparable data and a context within which to discuss the contemporary political situations of racial and ethnic minorities, both as individual groups and comparatively.

The chapter also discusses the importance of the Voting Rights Act of 1965 and its extensions for the ability of various racial and ethnic groups to gain elective office.

Chapter 3 explores the attitudes members of racial and ethnic minority groups bring to the public policymaking process and the ways they choose whether to participate. The aspects of political participation we address are (1) perceptions of discrimination, (2) political ideology, (3) partisan identification, (4) voting behavior, and (5) interest group activities. For each of these areas, when applicable, class and gender differences are noted.

When a government chooses whether to undertake a purposive course of action in an effort to address a problem, that decision can be affected by whether members of racial and ethnic minority groups are present in policymaking positions. Furthermore, the impact of that decision is unlikely to be uniform across all racial and ethnic groups. Chapter 4 employs a sequential model of the policymaking process to explore the ways members of racial and ethnic minority groups can affect what government does and does not do and what difference these policies make for these groups. The representation of these groups within policymaking institutions offers another perspective on the continuing manifestation of the first dilemma. Analysis of the efforts made to achieve policy goals should provide evidence to help articulate a response to the second dilemma.

Chapter 5 uses the question posed by Rodney King at his first postverdict news conference, which we have appropriated for the title of this book, in an attempt to address squarely the second dilemma. This chapter focuses on the increasing tensions among minority groups and between minority groups and the majority. What options are available to members of minority groups within the American political system, and what are the consequences of pursuing each of these options? The bulk of the discussion compares the viable alternatives of coalition and competition and the arguments, both theoretical and practical, for and against each position. The consequences for both the nation and minority groups of following either track are explored. The last chapter discusses the future of American minority groups' politics and the authors' perspective on the resolution of the dilemmas.

Conclusion

This chapter shows that certain groups have been treated differently in our legal system based on their race or ethnicity. Thus, who is identified as being a member of one of these groups has had important legal implications, at times extending so far as to classify individuals as property rather than as citizens and to impose restrictions upon whom one could marry. This unequal treatment began before the current Constitution was adopted, with the nation's original minorities—blacks and American Indians. The treatment was applied as other racial and ethnic minorities—Latinos and Asians—immigrated, and it continues despite a common rhetoric of equality.

2

....

Resources and Status
of America's
Racial Minorities

A plastic surgeon is shot to death because his
confessed killer believes the doctor to be making
non-whites look "Aryan."

Wilmette, Ill., August 6, 1993

· ·

THE FACT THAT ALL American racial and ethnic minority groups have not been treated according to the rhetoric of the nation's founding principles has resulted in differences in these groups' contemporary political status based on differential resources, histories of political activism, and levels of access to political participation. The size, economic well-being, and geographic concentration of the group's population; the extent to which the group has participated in a civil rights movement; and the amount of protection that is provided under contemporary voting rights law all affect the way members of each of the groups will be treated within the American polity, what kind of role members of the group will be expected to play in the political system, and what kind of strategy—cooperation or conflict—will be chosen. A consideration of these factors identifies the commonalities and the differences among the various groups that are often lumped together under the rubric "minority group politics."

Population Size, Socioeconomic Status, and Concentration

The number of people and where they are located are important pieces of data in the U.S. political system. The population of a certain location affects important factors such as the number of members each state will have in the U.S. House of Representatives, the way electoral districts will be drawn, the number of votes each state will have in the electoral college to choose the president, and the way some government resources will be distributed. The latest population surveys (which vary in date by group) provide a detailed picture of the populations with which we are concerned. Tables 2.1, 2.2, and 2.3 present these data and provide basic information about the populations of each group, the groups' age structures, and some indicators of socioeconomic status—the general social and economic conditions of these groups—a variable that is related to political participation. In addition, we are able to see the variations that exist within the Latino and Asian communities.

TABLE 2.1

Selected Characteristics of Black, Asian American, American Indian, and Non-Latino White Populations, Latest Estimates

	Black (1992)	Asian American (1991)	American Indian (1990)	Non-Latino White (1993)
Est. population (in thousands) (1995)	33,117	9,756	2,226	193,900
% of total U.S. population (1995)	12.6	3.7	0.8	73.6
Median age (in years)	28.2	30.4	27.0	35.5
% age eighteen and older	66.7	69.6	65.8	75.9
% H.S. graduates (of population ≥ age twenty-five)	67.7	81.8	65.6	84.1
% Unemployed (of population ≥ sixteen)	14.1	6.3	MD[a]	6.1
Males	15.2	6.3	MD	7.1
Females	13.0	6.3	MD	5.0
Median family income (in dollars)	21,548 (1991)	42,245 (1990)	21,619 (1989)	33,335 (1992)
% Living in poverty	32.7 (1991)	12.2 (1990)	31.2 (1989)	9.6 (1992)
% Households without phones	MD	MD	MD	2.7

[a]Missing data.

Sources: Claudette E. Bennett, 1992. *The Asian and Pacific Islander Population in the United States: March 1991 and 1990.* U.S. Bureau of the Census, Current Population Reports, P20-459 (Washington, D.C.: Government Printing Office); Claudette E. Bennett, 1993. *The Black Population in the United States: March 1992.* U.S. Bureau of the Census, Current Population Reports, P20-471 (Washington, D.C.: Government Printing Office); Patricia A. Montgomery, 1994. *The Hispanic Population in the United States: March 1993.* U.S. Bureau of the Census, Current Population Reports, P20-475 (Washington, D.C.: Government Printing Office); Jennifer Cheeseman Day, 1993. *Population Projections of the United States, by Age, Sex, Race, and Hispanic Origin: 1993 to 2050.* U.S. Bureau of the Census, Current Population Reports, P25-1104 (Washington, D.C.: Government Printing Office).

Despite the growth in the populations of the various minority groups, non-Latino whites constitute about three-fourths of the nation's population. Blacks are the next largest single group, composing approximately one-eighth of the nation's population. Thus, in any political issue in which raw population

· ·

TABLE 2.2

Selected Characteristics of the Latino Population and Selected Subgroups, 1993

	Puerto Rican	Mexican	Cuban	Total Latino[a]
Est. 1993 population (in thousands)	2,402	14,628	1,071	22,752
% of total U.S. population	0.9	5.6	0.4	8.9
Median age (in years)	26.9	24.6	43.6	26.7
% age eighteen and older	62.8	62.5	84.5	65.5
% H.S. graduates (of population ≥ age twenty-five)	59.8	46.2	62.1	53.1
% Unemployed (of population age sixteen)	14.4	11.7	7.3	11.9
Males	17.2	12.1	7.6	12.4
Females	11.0	11.1	7.3	11.1
Median family income (in dollars) (1992)	18,999	22,938	25,874	22,859
% Living in poverty (1992)	36.5	30.1	18.1	29.3
% Households without phones	17.2	12.0	4.1	11.9

[a]Total Latino includes data on Central and South Americans and "other Latinos."

Source: Patricia A. Montgomery, 1994. *The Hispanic Population in the United States: March 1993.* U.S. Bureau of the Census, Current Population Reports, P20-475 (Washington, D.C.: Government Printing Office).

counts matter, from a national perspective whites will clearly maintain an upper hand for the foreseeable future.

Electoral politics, however, depends not just on the number of bodies but also on the number of those who vote. The one consistent legal restriction on the right to vote is age. In no U.S. jurisdiction can one vote until one is eighteen years old. If each group's age distribution is approximately the same, the translation of the potential power of numbers into the actual power of votes becomes an issue of mobilization. But as the tables show, there are broad variations in age structures. In general, the non-Latino white population is older than the other groups, and a higher proportion of its population is over age

TABLE 2.3

Selected Characteristics of Selected Asian American Population Subgroups, 1990

	Chinese	Japanese	Korean	Filipino
1990 population (in thousands)	1,649	866	797	1,420
% of total U.S. population	0.7	0.3	0.3	0.6
Median age (in years)	32.3	36.5	29.1	31.3
% age eighteen and older	76.7	81.8	69.2	72.7
% H.S. graduates (of population ≥ age twenty-five)	73.6	87.5	80.2	82.6
% Unemployed (of population ≥ age sixteen)	3.1	1.6	3.3	3.7
Males	3.2	1.8	3.1	3.9
Females	2.9	1.5	3.4	3.4
Median family income (in dollars) (1989)	41,316	51,550	33,909	46,698
% Living in poverty (1989)	14.0	7.0	13.7	6.4

Source: U.S. Bureau of the Census, 1993. *Asians and Pacific Islanders in the United States,* Series 1990 CP-3-5 (August).

eighteen. The only exceptions to this pattern are the Cubans, Chinese, and Japanese—who cumulatively account for only about 1.5 percent of the nation's population. Thus, whites not only continue to constitute the overwhelming majority of the population nationwide but they also maintain an advantage over most other racial and ethnic groups in the proportion of their population that is old enough to vote. Minority groups' numerical disadvantage is therefore exacerbated by the relative age distributions.

Beyond the numbers and age structure, socioeconomic status has been found to be important in determining levels of participation. Simply put, people who fare better economically have a greater stake in the system and are more likely to be able to afford the time to participate in politics, to engage in activities that stimulate political participation, and to have peers who are politically active. If one is struggling to subsist, political participation—even the simple act of voting—may be perceived as a luxury, a not very profitable investment of one's time and energy.

Tables 2.1, 2.2, and 2.3 also present some selected indicators of socioeconomic status. These indicators reflect a number of different perspectives on such status, and the picture that emerges from these data is clear. Only Asian Americans approximate the educational attainment levels of whites, and as Table 2.3 shows, there is significant variation within the Asian American community. Blacks are the next closest group, but even they fail to come within 15 percentage points of whites' educational attainment levels.

Only Asian Americans approach whites' unemployment levels, and the rate for each of the major Asian American groups is, in fact, lower than that for whites. The rates for other groups, however, are almost or more than twice as high as that for whites, with the exception of Cubans, whose unemployment rate is "only" 20 percent higher than that for whites. Thus, it should not be surprising that the median white family enjoys a $7,400 income advantage over Cuban families and at least a $10,000 advantage over any other group, with the exception of Asian Americans. Asian Americans report a median family income almost $9,000 higher than that of whites, with Japanese, Filipinos, and Chinese reporting median family incomes 55 percent, 40 percent, and 24 percent higher than those of white families, respectively.

Despite the family income advantage enjoyed by Asian Americans, a smaller proportion of whites live below the poverty line than any other major group. Japanese and Filipino individuals hold down the Asian American poverty figures to only half again as high as those for whites; Cubans are almost twice as likely and each of the other groups is three or four times as likely as whites to live in poverty. Even access to a telephone where one lives shows broad gaps. Except for Cubans, there is a nine-percentage-point gap between the proportion of whites who lack access to a telephone and any other group for which we have data. Clearly, by whatever measure one wants to use, the numerical and age-distribution disadvantages of racial and ethnic minority groups in the United States are generally compounded by the lack of resources that might be used to compensate for these disadvantages. Only Asian Americans and Cubans have some apparent equity with or advantage over whites on some of the variables, but there are several areas of disadvantage. Further, Asian Americans and Cubans make up only 2.8 and 0.4 percent of the U.S. population, respectively.

Despite these apparently cumulative disadvantages, there are clearly examples of each of these communities mobilizing for political success. How is this possible? The answer lies in looking lower than the national level. Just as the population figures must be considered in light of age structure and socioeconomic resources, we must also look at the way these groups' populations are distributed geographically. Although the figures suggest that minority groups are certain to be overwhelmed in any type of national contest, if former U.S. House Speaker "Tip" O'Neill's dictum "all politics is local" is correct, we should be looking at the subnational level.

Maps 2.1 through 2.4 report the concentration by county within the United States of each of the groups considered here. These maps confirm that each of the minority groups has very different geographic distribution patterns and that areas exist in which each of the "minorities" is either a majority or has the potential to be an important political player.

For each of the groups, on a separate map, we have identified areas in which it is totally or virtually nonexistent (< 5 percent of the population), in which the group is small but represents more than a "token" presence (5 percent–20 percent), in which the proportion is sufficient to be perceived as a potential ally or threat in electoral politics (20 percent–50 percent), in which a "minority majority" exists in population if not in voting-age population (50 percent–80 percent), and in which overwhelming minority majorities are found (> 80 percent). Because our data are aggregated at the county level, it is possible and even likely that subcounty-level jurisdictions (e.g., cities, school districts) exist in which minorities may constitute majorities but not appear on our maps. Likewise, there are areas within what appear on our maps as heavily minority that maintain a majority white population. Still, these maps give us some sense of where minority group members are most likely to be found in our nation and where potential minority group political power exists.

Map 2.1 reveals that the African American population is concentrated in a crescent that runs from Maryland down the Atlantic seaboard across the Deep South to east Texas. The heaviest concentrations of black population are found in the traditional "Black Belt," where blacks were concentrated during the days of slavery. The overwhelmingly black counties in the nation are found in rural Alabama and Mississippi. There are, however, more than token populations of blacks scattered throughout most U.S. regions, with the exception of the upper Great Plains. Much of the non-South concentration of blacks consists of residents in predominantly black central cities ringed by "whiter" suburbs; therefore, the county populations depicted here do not adequately reveal the black concentration.

Map 2.2 shows a similar pattern for Hispanics but in a different area of the country. The Hispanic "crescent" runs along the U.S.-Mexico border from the Rio Grande Valley in south Texas through New Mexico and Arizona and into southern California. An appendage of this crescent juts up through New Mexico into southern Colorado, and separate pockets of significant concentra-

MAP 2.1

African American Population by County

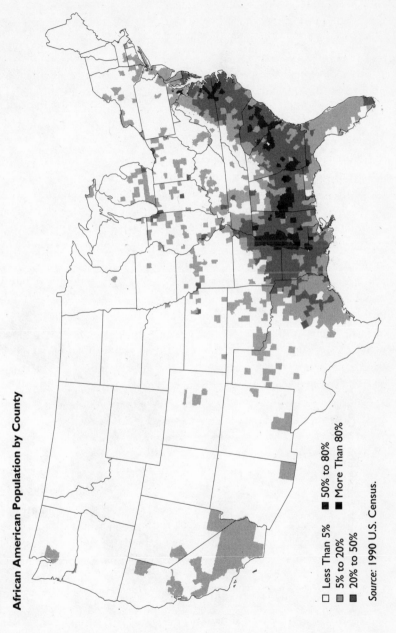

☐ Less Than 5%   ■ 50% to 80%

■ 5% to 20%   ■ More Than 80%

■ 20% to 50%

Source: 1990 U.S. Census.

MAP 2.2

Hispanic American Population by County

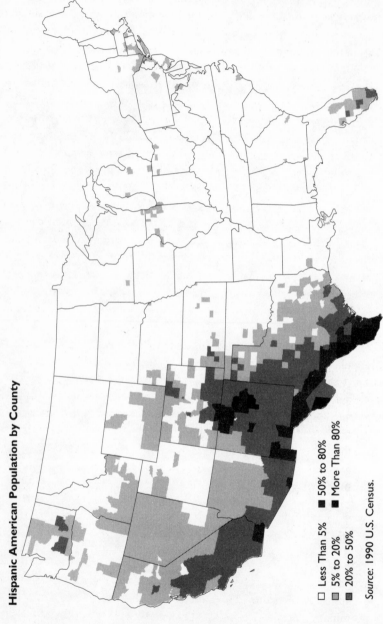

☐ Less Than 5%　■ 50% to 80%

■ 5% to 20%　■ More Than 80%

■ 20% to 50%

Source: 1990 U.S. Census.

tions appear in central Washington state. The overwhelmingly Hispanic counties in the nation are found along the Rio Grande in south Texas and in northern New Mexico. The only significant Hispanic concentrations east of Texas are found in urban areas, particularly around New York City, and in south Florida. This pattern reflects the different settlement patterns of the three major Latino groups. Although Hispanics of different origins are found in each of the three major areas of concentration, in general Mexican Americans are concentrated in the southwestern states that were added after the Mexican War, Puerto Ricans are concentrated in the New York metropolitan area, and Cubans are concentrated around Miami. Indeed, a majority of Cuban Americans in the United States live in Dade County, Florida.

The distribution of the American Indian population, shown in Map 2.3, reflects the effects of the group's push westward. Although there are pockets of Indian concentration in the eastern states, the areas of greatest concentration are found in the Great Plains and westward. One county in Wisconsin is overwhelmingly populated by American Indians, which is an exception to the previous statement. Generally, the American Indian population concentrations reflect the process of putting Indians on reservations in rural areas where whites showed little demand for the land. This map shows the continuing effects of this policy.

Finally, Map 2.4 illustrates the intense concentration of the Asian American population. Except for some pockets in eastern urban areas and areas just outside Chicago and Houston, Asian Americans are concentrated in the Pacific coast states, particularly in California. No majority Asian American counties are found in the United States, but the size of the counties in California probably dilutes the reporting of significant concentrations of Asian Americans living there in subcounty jurisdictions.

How well have these population and economic resources been mobilized? We now turn to this question.

Participation in a Civil Rights Movement

With the level of resources just described, even without a knowledge of the history depicted in this text in the timelines, one would guess that these minority groups are at a disadvantage in the political system. They fit under the rubric "dominated groups"—groups that have generally been excluded from participation in the decisionmaking process by which society's benefits are distributed. "Because of this exclusion, dominated groups at different times attempt

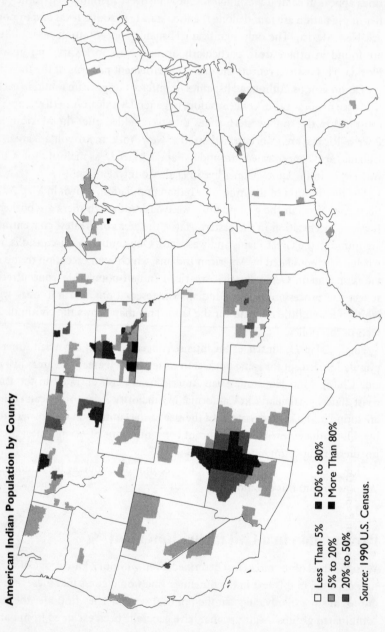

MAP 2.3

American Indian Population by County

☐ Less Than 5% ■ 50% to 80%

 5% to 20% ■ More Than 80%

■ 20% to 50%

Source: 1990 U.S. Census.

MAP 2.4

Asian American Population by County

☐ Less Than 5%

▨ 5% to 20%

▨ 20% to 50%

■ 50% to 80%

■ More Than 80%

Source: 1990 U.S. Census.

to change their situation of powerlessness by engaging in nontraditional and usually nonlegitimized struggles with power holders" (Morris 1984:282). These overt efforts by groups to empower themselves constitute **social movements.**

Certain prerequisites appear necessary for a social movement to have a chance to enhance the group's power. First, successful social movements generally tap a reservoir of social organizations for experienced leaders, potential followers, communication networks, money, and labor. The ability to draw from preexisting organizations minimizes start-up costs and provides stability in the early, tenuous days when the movement is vulnerable to a serious countereffort by the dominant group.

Second, successful social movements require catalytic leadership—social activists who create or recognize opportunities to protest the groups' subordinate status. Furthermore, they must be able to organize and motivate people to engage in the effort over what may be an extended period of time.

The movement will be stronger if these two prerequisites are combined— that is, if the leadership is taken from preexisting organizations. These organizations have already demonstrated their ability to raise money and to organize people sufficiently that, at the least, they still exist. If the leadership arises from such organizations, the task becomes one of redirecting energies toward a new goal rather than of having to create an entirely new organization.

Third, successful movements tap outside resources. They elicit money and personnel from the environment that is not immediately affected by their struggle. These resources, although they may be sporadic and may come with strings attached, can be valuable in sustaining the movement and in expanding the scope of conflict. As part of a dominated group, people active in social movements have little to lose by getting others involved. The existing social, political, and economic decisionmaking apparatus does not yield positive results for them. They see change—any change—as likely to yield an improvement.

Finally, the social movement must have a plan—a set of tactics and an overall strategy it can use to confront the existing power structure. An effective set of tactics and strategies will disrupt the existing order; educate others about inequities, injustices, and civil wrongs; provide some sense of hope or efficacy for movement participants; and push the system—if at times imperceptibly—toward change.

Each of the groups considered in this book has participated to some extent in a social movement in an attempt to improve its situation. But the level, scope, and forms of activity have varied across groups. We now discuss the movements of the respective groups.

Hundreds of black youths are marched away from the Dallas County (Selma), Alabama, courthouse following their arrests the previous day for participating in mass demonstrations as part of the civil rights movement (February 1965). Photo courtesy UPI/Bettmann.

The Black Civil Rights Movement

The black civil rights movement of the 1950s and 1960s is the best-known and most studied of such movements, and in many ways it has served as a model for other groups. As with most movements, it was not one overall movement led from the top but instead constituted a collection of local movements that when added together produced massive social change. In recognition of the localized nature of the black civil rights movement, this section examines two small but vital parts of this movement as illustrations of the way it operated and what it was and was not able to achieve.

Baton Rouge. The Baton Rouge bus boycott, which began on June 19, 1953, is often used as the starting point of the modern black civil rights movement. The boycott sought to have the city enforce its ordinance allowing black riders to be seated in city buses on a first-come, first-served basis—in essence, to

force the city to make reality match rhetoric. The city refused to discipline drivers who failed to enforce the ordinance, so Reverend T. J. Jemison, minister of
Mt. Zion Baptist Church—the city's largest black church—broadcast a radio
appeal for blacks to boycott the city bus system.

The United Defense League (UDL) was formed to direct the mass boycott.
This confederation of organizations held mass rallies, which drew up to three
thousand people, each of the seven nights of the boycott. A movement "police
department" was organized to patrol the black community and to provide se-
curity for movement leaders. A free car pool was organized with volunteer drivers to help boycotting blacks get to and from work. Even the black community's drunks and winos were organized to "open up the car doors of movement
participants as they arrived" at the mass meetings (Jemison, quoted in Morris
1984:19).

Such an effort, of course, is not free of cost. Reverend Jemison asked for and
received permission to redirect $650 he had been given for a business trip to
help support the boycott. Following his example, his church gave an additional
$1,500 to the effort. Other churches in the community followed, donating
$3,800 to give the movement its initial capital. The nightly mass meetings pro-
vided an opportunity to collect operating expenses. As a result, all of the volunteer drivers' expenses were covered, and the expenses of the movement's police department, as well as the costs of miscellaneous goods and services
necessary to run the boycott, were paid as they were incurred.

The dominant white power stucture in Baton Rouge quickly offered a compromise, reserving only the two front side seats for whites and the long bench
seat in the rear of the bus for blacks and leaving all other seats open on a first-
come, first-served basis. After much debate, and with the approval of a mass
meeting of eight thousand blacks, on June 25, 1953, Reverend Jemison announced the end of the boycott and the dismantling of the free car pool.

Although the subsequent Montgomery bus boycott became more famous,
probably because the recalcitrance of the white power structure there resulted
in a more extended and complex effort, the Baton Rouge boycott is instructive.
First, this boycott drew on the black churches for the masses of people needed
to implement and carry out the boycott, communications networks, leadership, and money. But the successful operation of the boycott also necessitated
the creation of an umbrella organization. Without the UDL, there was too
much danger that the purposes of the individual churches would have super-
seded those of the movement.

Second, in Jemison the movement had an educated, articulate leader who
had the ability to recognize the potential for effective social action and to organize and motivate people to take advantage of that opportunity. In a pattern

that was repeated with Dr. Martin Luther King Jr. in Montgomery, Reverend Jemison was a relative newcomer to Baton Rouge and was unencumbered by any history of personal or organizational conflicts with other potential leaders or by any residual level of distrust.

Third, in the Baton Rouge movement the movement leader was an insider in an existing social organization—the largest black church in town—whose resources the movement needed to tap. The advantage this gave the movement was best exemplified by the ease with which Jemison redirected the $650 from the cancelled business trip to the movement coffers. His dual status as both a movement and a church leader placed him a unique position to make an almost effortless, yet vitally important, contribution to the initiation of the movement.

Fourth, there is limited evidence that external resources were tapped (Jemison reported that "a few whites" contributed; see Morris 1984:23), but the brevity of the boycott made these resources less necessary than would have been the case in a prolonged effort. It is important to note, though, that if the movement had been dependent on external resources, it is doubtful that they could have been amassed quickly enough to allow the leadership to mobilize against this grievance.

Finally, the tactic chosen in this case—an economic boycott—was well suited for its task of disrupting the status quo. It allowed—in fact, required—the concerted effort of the masses, giving them a feeling of solidarity while simultaneously inflicting great financial losses on the bus company. This tactic demonstrated the economic clout of the black community to both whites and blacks and also served to broaden the conflict and perhaps to recruit some unwilling, or unwitting, allies. Individuals who had never thought about the seating arrangements on buses, or who, if they had thought about the issue, might have preferred the status quo, may have been willing to tolerate change if their insistence on continued segregation would have meant the loss of bus service or the loss of a job if the bus service had been forced out of existence.

The Baton Rouge bus boycott was only the opening skirmish in the black civil rights movement, but it provided some valuable lessons. The leaders of other, later bus boycotts—Martin Luther King Jr. and Ralph Abernathy in Montgomery (1955–1956), Reverend C. K. Steele in Tallahassee (1956), Reverend A. L. Davis in New Orleans (1957)—were all church-based movement leaders who were keenly aware of the experience of Reverend Jemison in Baton Rouge (Morris 1984).

Of course, the black civil rights movement continued to evolve, new issues were addressed, other leaders emerged. One major area in which the Baton Rouge boycott is not very instructive is in promoting a movement over time.

The experience in Mississippi from summer 1961 through summer 1964 sheds more light on the way the black civil rights movement was able to accomplish what it did.

Mississippi. It is an understatement to say that Mississippi was the stronghold of segregation. As late as 1964, a black attorney who was active in the civil rights movement saw the movement as a "no-fail" situation because "it was impossible for things to have grown worse" (Holt 1966:13).

The black civil rights movement came to Mississippi in 1961 in the form of Freedom Riders, individuals who challenged the state's refusal to desegregate buses and bus stations and who viewed the state through bus windows and jail bars. Late that summer field secretaries from the Student Nonviolent Coordinating Committee (SNCC) also arrived, led by Robert Moses, a Harvard-educated schoolteacher from Harlem. Moses sought to organize black Mississippians based on the idea that they would need to be self-reliant when SNCC left. Rather than taking an obvious leadership role, Moses worked to develop local leaders and to discourage "outside" involvement. His fear was that outsiders who played a major role in the movement would leave at some point without having equipped indigenous leaders for the continuing struggle.

The development of leadership is a slow process, and there is a risk of stalling or stopping the movement if such development is arrested. Continued and increasing white resistance threatened to do just that. With the assassination of the National Association for the Advancement of Colored People (NAACP) field secretary Medger Evers in June 1963 and the continuing violence against civil rights workers with no protection from federal authorities (local and state authorities were often involved in perpetrating the violence or allowing it to continue), Moses began to reconsider his opposition to outside, episodic assistance. In particular, he thought the presence of northern white students might insulate civil rights workers from the most blatant discrimination and might raise northern white consciousness about the racist system that existed in the south. It had become clear to Moses that violence against, and even murders of, Mississippi blacks had been insufficient to arouse national sympathies, much less to inspire protest or action.

Local white officials generally argued that blacks did not vote because they did not want to, because they were apathetic. The first tentative use of white students occurred during a fall 1963 "Freedom Vote," which was designed to reveal the state's hypocrisy and to puncture the apathy myth. Essentially, the idea was to put forth a slate of candidates and to have black voters cast "votes," not at the normal polling places but at less threatening locations and not for any official candidates but for individuals who supported the civil rights movement; further, the blacks knew these votes would not count. If black Mississippians bothered to cast "ballots" under these conditions, the apathy myth could be dispelled.

Allard Lowenstein, a white activist and attorney, organized white students—mainly from Stanford and Yale—to assist in this project. The project accomplished four things. First, with a turnout of over eighty thousand black "voters," no one could seriously argue that black Mississippians were apathetic. Second, and as a result of the first accomplishment, local blacks gained confidence. Not only had they taken a courageous step but so had many of their fellow black citizens. Third, white Mississippians became hysterical over both the idea of a Freedom Vote and the presence of the white students in support of the black civil rights movement. America's best and brightest students were threatened, beaten, shot at, and arrested for the heinous crime of attempting to attend a performance of the Jackson Philharmonic as part of an interracial group. Thus, and fourth, the student volunteers came to understand clearly what life was like in Mississippi, and they communicated this reality outside of the state. The white volunteers wrote to their parents, friends, and representatives in Congress; national attention became focused on Mississippi, and news coverage of the movement increased. The symbolic exercise, therefore, was not meaningless (Chafe 1993).

Based on the Freedom Vote experience, Robert Moses became convinced that bringing in more students from prominent white northern families would either restrain white violence or highlight it for national attention, thus increasing pressure on federal authorities to become involved. An umbrella organization, the Council of Federated Organizations (COFO), was formed to coordinate the civil rights movement efforts. Under COFO auspices, more than one thousand college student volunteers were brought to Mississippi for the 1964 Summer Project. The underlying logic was correct but disheartening. The movement had discovered a tactic that would help it to expand the audience for its struggle and, it was hoped, bring federal intervention on its behalf. The bad news was that the tactic was predicated on the notion that threatening, beating, and shooting at affluent white northern students was a serious offense but that doing the same to black Mississippians was not.

This logic proved all too true. At the very beginning of the Summer Project, three participants—James Chaney, Michael Schwerner, and Andrew Goodman—disappeared while on a trip to investigate the bombing of a black church. Their disappearance prompted a massive investigation by the Federal Bureau of Investigation (FBI) that eventually led to the discovery of the men's bodies.

The important lesson for the movement was that the murder of white civil rights workers (Schwerner and Goodman) resulted in federal attention whereas the numerous attacks on black Mississippians that had been reported previously had not done so.

Although the Summer Project did not change Mississippi overnight, it provided an important first step in the process. For example, "freedom schools" enhanced the academic skills of black children, better preparing them for future political and economic participation. And building on the Freedom Vote, a racially integrated Mississippi Freedom Democratic Party, which pledged allegiance to the national Democratic Party ticket, was formed to challenge the still segregated regular Mississippi Democratic Party. Although it was unsuccessful in achieving its goal of replacing the "regulars" as the official Democratic Party, the project's efforts foretold a major increase in black political participation in the state that had been the most resistant to any such participation of any state in the nation. Perhaps because of the length of their effort, or perhaps because of the more resistant environment, the movement leaders in Mississippi—unlike those in Baton Rouge—used outside resources to further their cause. The lessons of the black civil rights movement were not lost on other racial and ethnic minority groups.

The Chicano Movement

Social movements among Latinos have been limited, and there has been no overarching pan-Hispanic effort. Young Puerto Ricans in New York and Chicago have participated in a Puerto Rican nationalist movement. César Chávez emerged as a leader of the National Farm Workers Association, which joined with Filipinos to protest pay inequities in the agricultural labor force. But the most wide-ranging, significant Latino movement was the Chicano power movement of the 1960s among Mexican Americans in the Southwest.

The Chicano movement was influenced both directly and indirectly by the black civil rights movement. The direct influence came through the participation of a few Mexican Americans in that movement. Individuals such as Maria Varela and Elizabeth Sutherland Martinez gained both valuable experience and a realization that the black movement was not concerned with the plight of Mexican Americans. Indirectly, however, the Chicano movement emerged from the general activism of the 1960s, which was spearheaded by the black civil rights movement.

At the core of the Chicano movement were Mexican American students who sought more attention for the needs of their people. They wanted to move beyond the efforts of the more conservative Mexican American interest groups. The movement's most dramatic early political success came in Crystal City, Texas, in 1963 when the Political Association of Spanish Speaking Peoples (PASSO) was formed and coalesced with a predominantly Mexican American local chapter of the Teamsters Union to defeat all of the white candidates for the City Council, replacing them with Mexican Americans. This "Crystal City Revolt" was important because it demonstrated the possibilities for local Mexican American political mobilization. This was the first time Mexican Americans had taken political control of a municipal government in the U.S. Southwest. Furthermore, it highlighted the important role young people were to play in the movement.

This role was further highlighted in the March 1968 Mexican American student walkout at Lincoln High School in East Los Angeles. Acting on an idea of Sal Castro, a teacher at the school, over one thousand students staged a week-and-a-half-long strike that was "the first major mass protest explicitly against racism undertaken by Mexican Americans in the history of the United States" (Muñoz 1989:64). This action served as a catalyst to increase political awareness, revitalize existing community organizations, generate new political organizations, and mobilize young Mexican Americans, who became the heart of the Chicano movement.

Unlike the black civil rights movement, the Chicano movement relied less on established organizational resources and more on the energies of young people. By doing so, it found an energetic reservoir of leaders and skilled organizers— including Rodolfo "Corky" González, José Angel Gutiérrez, and Reies López Tijerina—who minimized the need to tap outside resources. Furthermore, by emphasizing the need to win local political and economic control of Mexican American communities, the movement adopted a strategy in which there was a possibility of a visible payoff in an effort to attract new supporters.

The Asian American Movement

The Asian American movement is a clear example of a civil rights movement that was spawned by the black civil rights movement. Until the time of the black movement, each group of Asians in the United States had organized, litigated, and participated in politics when such participation was permitted, but they had done so as Japanese Americans, Chinese Americans, Filipino Americans, Korean Americans, or whatever their country of ancestry rather than as Asian Americans. The example of the black civil rights movement, which heightened sensitivity to racism, in combination with the anti–Vietnam war movement changed that situation. A generation of middle-class college students was suddenly aware of its "Asianness" as it questioned the nature of the Vietnam War. The students were in a unique position to raise questions about the racial implications of U.S. military policy. Thus, much like the Chicano movement, the Asian American movement was youth-oriented and drew less on established organizations than did the black movement.

Perhaps because of the attempt to bridge such a broad spectrum of diversity, no single national leader or strategy emerged. Leaders were prominent only within a specific geographic area or a particular Asian ethnic group. Thus, it is not surprising that no single plan of action was ever formulated. The unifying principle of the various localized movements seems to have been the pursuit of equality (Wei 1993).

The American Indian Movement

The 1960s and 1970s also marked the reemergence of American Indian activism from the seventy-year hiatus that had followed the Wounded Knee Massacre of December 28, 1890. The group that came to symbolize this renewed activism was the American Indian Movement (AIM), a group formed in Minneapolis in 1968 to deal with the problems of urban Indians, especially police brutality. Within two years AIM had expanded its concerns and addressed tribal and Indian issues regardless of the Indians' place of residence.

Leadership of AIM came not from established groups but from Clyde Bellecourt and Dennis Banks, two of the cofounders of the movement, and Russell Means—the most outspoken of the AIM leaders, who became a symbol of American Indian resistance. This leadership allowed AIM to attract bright, energetic young Indians from all parts of the country.

AIM became best known for its participation in dramatic events to highlight injustices. For example, in 1972 AIM was a major actor in the takeover of the headquarters of the Bureau of Indian Affairs (BIA) in Washington, D.C. And in 1973, AIM activists protested tribal government corruption on the Pine Ridge Reservation, U.S. violations of the 1868 Fort Laramie Treaty, and continuing federal controls over American Indians by seizing the village of Wounded Knee and holding it for ten weeks against a force of hundreds of federal officers. But AIM's use of confrontation triggered the concerted opposition of the BIA, the FBI, and other federal agencies. These agencies engaged in an effective, organized campaign of surveillance, infiltration, and intimidation against American Indian activists—including AIM—which diverted their energies from pursuing policy changes to squabbling internally.

Summary

One of the goals of each of these movements has been to attain political power. Casting a vote is the most basic formal act of participation in a polity. We now consider the contemporary status of voting rights for minority groups.

Voting Rights Law

The simple act of voting has important symbolic and potentially important practical ramifications. The right to cast a ballot separates the insiders (citizens) from the outsiders (noncitizens) and dependents (the underaged). When aggregated, votes determine who the nation's public policymakers, the people who allocate public resources, will be. In short, the vote is seen as a tool for protecting other rights and achieving other goals—as a means rather than an end.

For most Americans the right to vote is assumed, and Americans assume all other citizens have the same right. After all, in the wake of the Civil War, the Constitution was amended to ban intentional discrimination by public officials based on race or previous condition of servitude (the Fourteenth Amendment) and to prohibit the denial or abridgement of the right to vote by officials at all levels of government on the basis of race, color, or previous condition of servitude (the Fifteenth Amendment). But within a few years the Supreme Court declared much of the legislation designed to enforce the Fifteenth Amendment unconstitutional, and Congress repealed other such legislation. Thus, when federal supervision of southern elections ended in 1877, the states were effectively free to structure and operate their electoral processes as they saw fit.

What followed was the systematic disenfranchisement of the black electorate. Through a variety of devices—discriminatorily administered literacy tests, poll taxes, white primaries—southern states passed some of the most effective legislation ever enacted. For example, between 1896 and 1900, the number of black Louisianans registered to vote dropped from 130,334 to 5,320. Likewise, at the end of the nineteenth century only 9 percent of Mississippi's black voting-age population was registered to vote; three decades earlier the figure had been 70 percent (U.S. Commission on Civil Rights 1968).

In the early part of the twentieth century, some legal progress was made in attacking various methods of disenfranchisement. In 1915 the Supreme Court, in *Guinn v. United States,* declared unconstitutional the **grandfather clause**—a device used by southern states to deny the vote to those whose grandparents were slaves—which circumvented the Fifteenth Amendment. In 1944, in *Smith v. Allwright,* the Court invalidated Texas's **white primary** as a violation of the

Fifteenth Amendment. This primary had been based on the logic that the state's Democratic Party was a private organization and, thus, that its means of nominating candidates—the "white primary"—was not covered by the equal protection clause of the Fourteenth Amendment. The Democratic Party was the dominant party in Texas, and the individual who won the primary was the predetermined winner of the general election. If the Democratic Party were a private organization, and if only members of the party could vote in the primary, black voters were effectively blocked from participation. In spite of these victories, the Supreme Court rarely changed day-to-day realities for black citizens.

It was against this backdrop that the black civil rights movement pressed for the right to vote as a top priority. The belief was that the ballot could be a tool for achieving other changes sought by the movement.

The federal legislation that was passed at least partially in response to the black civil rights movement was the Voting Rights Act (VRA) of 1965, which was amended in 1970, 1975, 1982, and 1992. Basically, the act, as amended:

1. prohibits "tests or devices" that had been used in the past to disenfranchise racial minorities—for example, literacy tests, education requirements, tests of good character, racial gerrymandering, and English-only elections in jurisdictions in which a single linguistic minority constitutes more than 5 percent of the voting-age population
2. requires that "covered" jurisdictions gain federal assent for any changes in election laws or procedures to assure that such changes do not abridge the right to vote on the basis of race, color, or language minority status
3. makes clear that if the effect of a practice is discriminatory, it is unlawful, regardless of the intent of its originator

The second, "preclearance," provision applies in only those political jurisdictions in which fewer than one-half of those who were eligible to vote were registered or voted in the 1964, 1968, or 1972 presidential elections *and* in which a discriminatory "test or device" was used in registration or voting. Thus, the states of Alabama, Alaska, Arizona, Georgia, Louisiana, Mississippi, South Carolina, Texas, and Virginia, as well as four counties in California, five counties in Florida, two towns in Michigan, ten towns in New Hampshire, three counties in New York, forty counties in North Carolina, and two counties in South Dakota are covered jurisdictions.

Legislation has been fairly effective in dealing with vote denial. Although gaps still exist between the political participation rates of the various racial and ethnic populations and the rate of the white population, these gaps have narrowed since the passage of the VRA. And, as is detailed in Chapter 4, the number of successful office seekers from groups previously denied the vote is increasing—particularly for blacks, somewhat less so for Hispanics, and less noticeably for Asian Americans and Indians.

More work remains, however, in the area of **vote dilution.** Vote dilution involves "the impairment of the equal opportunity of minority voters to participate in the political process and to elect candidates of their choice" (McDonald and powell 1993:27). Drawing on Supreme Court decisions that mandate that voting power must be apportioned equally based on population (the one person, one vote decisions), the logic has been extended to mandate that voters have the right to cast ballots that have the potential to elect candidates of their choice. At various times, at-large elections, racially gerrymandered districting schemes that unnecessarily fragment or unnecessarily concentrate minority group voters, laws that prohibit single-shot voting, discriminatory annexations or deannexations, and the abolition of elected or appointed offices or the changing of the means of selection have been used to dilute minority voting strength. These practices are not necessarily dilutive, but when they are combined with other social and historical circumstances, they may create an unequal opportunity for minority group and white voters to elect their preferred candidates.

The determination of whether a jurisdiction is engaging in minority vote dilution requires an examination of the "totality of circumstances." The circumstances that courts examine include racial bloc voting; a history of discrimination; depressed minority socioeconomic status; a paucity of elected minority officials; the use of racial campaign appeals; the existence of formal or informal "slating" groups, which are groups of candidates who band together or who are endorsed as a group by other organizations; and the employment of devices that enhance the possibility for discrimination, such as numbered positions.

Although much of the voting rights legislation was designed to vindicate the suffrage rights of blacks, other groups have also used the law to attempt to enhance their own political power. For example, American Indians used litigation pursuant to modern voting rights legislation in such attempts. Indians have the same right to vote as all other citizens, and election districts in which they vote must be apportioned under the one-person, one-vote principle. All three nonblack minority groups—Hispanics, Asian Americans, and American Indians—are recognized as language minority groups under the VRA, and election administrators must take that into account in affected jurisdictions.

A common remedy applied when vote dilution is found or when legislators are reapportioning or redistricting following the census is to draw districts in which a majority of the residents are nonwhite—"majority minority" districts. Both the creation of such districts and the shape of some of them are matters of continuing controversy. Such controversy is part of the ongoing struggle over whether and, if so, how to merge the reality of racial minorities' political status with the rhetoric of American democracy, and its resolution will have a tremendous impact on the strategies chosen by minority political activists. At its heart, this controversy centers on the notion of representation and what it means. The structure of our electoral process, and of who wins and loses in the process, affects who will raise the questions and what positions will be taken.

University of Pennsylvania law professor and President Clinton's failed nominee for assistant attorney general for civil rights Lani Guinier's ideas on representation and power are not as outlandish as her opponents and the media portrayed them to be (Guinier 1994). Her questioning of whether it is fair in a majoritarian system for a majority—50 percent plus one—in any given election to hold 100 percent of the power is gaining currency. What about the other 50 percent minus one? Should they, because they are in the minority, be excluded from the governing body? It should be understood that whereas Guinier is concerned with the electoral representation of racial minorities, in her view *minority* refers not only to racial minorities but to gender minorities and to Republican or Democrat minorities as well. She also questions whether concentrating racial minorities in majority minority districts is the best approach to rectifying the exclusion of such minorities from the political process. One of her solutions to this imbalance is the concept of cumulative voting.

Cumulative voting, a technique used until recently by the State of Illinois in its legislative races, is a mechanism that benefits numerical minorities, whether they are blacks, Latinos, Asians, Indians, women, Democrats, or Republicans. The concept is simple. At present, if there are seven seats on the city council, each voter votes for one individual in each of seven contests. In essence, each voter has seven votes but can vote for only one candidate in each contest. Under cumulative voting, each voter has seven votes and can assign them however he or she wants. The voter can give five votes to one candidate and one each to two others or can give all seven votes to one candidate. In this manner, numerical minorities could give all of their votes to a particular candidate, thus increasing their chances of electing members of their own group. Cumulative voting systems have allowed the Sisseton Sioux Indians in South Dakota to elect a representative to the local school board and in Chilton County, Alabama, blacks to elect a black to the County Council along with two white Republicans who, until the implementation of cumulative voting, had never been able to overcome the Democratic registration and voting majorities. Recently (1994), a federal judge ordered the institution of a cumulative voting system in Worcester County on Maryland's Eastern Shore in an effort to overcome the inability of blacks to elect members to the Board of County Commissioners.

Although cumulative voting is often mentioned in relation to the four groups that are the subject of this book, it would also benefit whites who are increasingly becoming numerical minorities in many urban centers. Clearly, a serious yet highly charged discussion of the concepts of majority and the access of numerical minorities will take place in the future.

Conclusion

In addition to the constitutional and legal disadvantages that established the rhetoric-versus-reality gap for racial minorities in the United States, this chapter shows that the numerical and socioeconomic realities do not bode well for each group's individual success in American politics. Racial minorities, as with any other numerical minority, start at a disadvantage. This disadvantage is made worse rather than better by the facts that—with some notable exceptions—racial minority groups, on average, have lower percentages of their populations that are old enough to vote, are less well educated, and are poorer than the dominant white majority. Yet there is substantial variation across and within different racial and ethnic groups, which makes the resolution of the coalition-versus-competition dilemma difficult. In some local areas these limitations do not apply, and, as is seen in Chapter 3, political success has been attained in these regions.

Political success has not been attained without struggle. Civil rights movements have been necessary for each group openly to challenge the system in which it was not only at a disadvantage but in which the rules were structured to keep it that way. One of the goals of each of these movements has been to achieve the right to vote, which it hopes it can use as a tool for winning political victories and protecting the fruits of those victories. The Voting Rights Act, as amended, has provided some protection for each of the groups. We now address the way members of these groups have been able to play a role in the U.S. political system.

3

··

America's Racial Minorities in the Contemporary Political System: Actors

Six black Secret Service agents, part of a unit guarding President Clinton, are denied service at a restaurant that is part of a national chain.

Annapolis, Md., April 1, 1993

....

J AMES MADISON, in *Federalist No. 10,* envisioned the United States as a so-ciety in which conflict rather than consensus would predominate. The citi-zenry would be divided into many groups, parties, and factions that would compete for benefits they felt to be rightly theirs. For Madison, the chief cause of these divisions was economic in origin, but, as we well know, race has emerged as a major dividing factor in American society. Madison's con-cept of U.S. society is represented in political science by pluralist theory. **Pluralism,** the reigning paradigm in political science, states in part that if citizens participate in the political process by voting and other means, the political system will produce electoral and policy outcomes favored by the participants.

Yet many of pluralism's assumptions do not favor the participation of, or ac-knowledge the barriers to, participation in the political process by America's racial minorities. Pluralism assumes that many centers of power exist and that different groups have access to a variety of power centers; thus, if a group is blocked from one center of power, it will always have access to another. Therefore, although groups may differ in their levels or types of political resources—for ex-ample, population size versus financial means—on balance the government will play a neutral role, and the resource differential will be balanced through the competition process. Pluralism also assumes that every group has equal access to the political process and that not every group will win all of the time but will win or lose depending on the issue and on its ability to use political resources.

Despite its preeminence in political science, pluralism has numerous critics. Pluralism assumes that interests will become diversified across economic, so-cial, and political issues, resulting in little need for racial and ethnic groups to organize around group-based issues. Race and ethnicity will thus be obscured as these other issues take precedence. Pluralism also states that once groups re-alize their subjective interests, they will become incorporated into the political system. Critics argue that these notions of interest diversification and incorpo-ration dismiss the fact that racial minorities are treated as groups; no individ-ual achievement improves the status of the individual or changes the position of the group (Pinderhughes 1987:38).

Another criticism is that pluralism has a class bias; upper-income individuals are better situated to compete for political outcomes. Despite pluralism's contention that political resources are counterbalanced, with one group's financial resources being neutralized by another group's population base, pluralism tilts political outcomes in favor of those with economic and political resources. As E. E. Schattschneider (1960:34) observes, "The flaw in the pluralist heaven is that the heavenly chorus sings with a strong upper-class accent."

There is a great deal of conflict in the scholarly literature over the utility of the pluralist framework in explaining the political behaviors of and outcomes for America's racial minorities. Nevertheless, African Americans, Latinos, American Indians, and Asian Americans are players—albeit often unequal players—in the U.S. political system. This chapter explores approaches to the second dilemma—what is to be done—by examining ways in which racial and ethnic minorities participate in the political system. The aspects of political attitudes and participation addressed are (1) **group identity** or **cohesion**—the extent of feelings of solidarity with other members of the group—and perceptions of discrimination; (2) **political ideology,** the underlying beliefs and attitudes of a group that shape its opinions and actions on political issues; (3) **partisan identification,** the attachment to and intensity of feeling for a particular political party; (4) **voting behavior,** the way people vote in elections and the forces that influence these votes; and (5) **interest group activities,** actions taken by organized groups seeking to influence public officials and policies.

For each of the areas, when applicable, discussion is broken down along gender lines so that differences in the attitudes and behaviors of women and men within a group, as well as those between groups, are highlighted. These distinctions are important for a variety of reasons. We often hear about the political behavior and feelings of groups, but group feelings and actions may vary in intensity or even in kind when broken down into responses by men versus women. The salience and importance of gender for women in framing their political attitudes and behaviors may result in different attitudes and behaviors from those of men. Further, we cannot assume that gender issues will resonate similarly for all women. It is reasonable to expect that the beliefs of black women may differ not only from those of black men but also from those of Latinas, Indian women, and Asian women. The same expectation holds true for various combinations of women. Moreover, women from one racial or ethnic minority may have views similar to those of men in other ethnic or racial categories. As has been and will continue to be demonstrated throughout this book, race and its effects on the political system may be different for different racial groups.

The best data sources for identifying the political attitudes of blacks and Latinos are the National Black Election Study, 1984–1988 (NBES), and the

Latino National Political Survey, 1990 (LNPS). These sources are national probability samples of the appropriate populations and represent the most comprehensive basis to date for determining the political attitudes of these groups. Data on Asian American and American Indian political attitudes are much more limited. To date, we have no national surveys exclusively devoted to these two populations, although a small number of Asians (n=154) were part of a 1993 national survey conducted for the National Conference of Christians and Jews (NCCJ). Thus, we must rely on the results from a small number of local surveys from various cities and areas around the country.

Group Identity
and Perceptions of Discrimination

Actual or perceived group cohesion (group solidarity) has been identified in political science research as being strongly associated with increased levels of political participation among racial and ethnic minority groups in the United States (Olsen 1970; Verba and Nie 1972). The more individuals identify with other members of a group, the more they are likely to participate in politics and to coalesce around candidates and policy issues they perceive as being beneficial to the group. One of the measures of group cohesion among racial and ethnic minorities is the degree of perceived discrimination against both the individual and one's group. Another measure of group cohesion is the degree of closeness an individual feels to other people in the group with respect to ideas and feelings about issues.

According to the 1984 NBES, 90 percent of blacks surveyed believed discrimination was still a problem for African Americans, with 68 percent believing strongly that racial discrimination was still a problem (Gurin, Hatchett, and Jackson 1989:75–81). Additionally, as reported in another source, a majority of blacks indicated that they had experienced discrimination in education, housing, employment, and wages (Sigelman and Welch 1991). The same pattern was evident in the 1988 NBES data (Tate 1993).

Regarding closeness, 93 percent of the black respondents in the 1984 NBES data reported being close to other blacks in terms of feelings and ideas (Gurin, Hatchett, and Jackson 1989:75–81), and a majority felt that what happens to the group affects them personally. As Table 3.1 exhibits, fully three-fourths of blacks surveyed felt that what happens to black people will shape their lives (Tate 1993:25).

The level of cohesiveness among Latinos, as measured on these dimensions, is very different from the pattern found among African Americans. The LNPS

....

TABLE 3.1

Proportion of Blacks Perceiving That They Share a Common Fate with Other Blacks[a]

	1984 (%)	1988 (%)
Yes	73.5 (796)[b]	77.4 (339)
No	26.5 (287)	22.6 (99)
Total	100 (1,083)	100 (438)

[a]Preelection sample.
[b]Figures in parentheses represent the number of respondents.
Source: Authors' computations from the 1984 and 1988 National Black Election Studies.

found that regardless of national origin, the majority of Latinos believed they had not personally been discriminated against because of their ethnicity. Mexicans were more likely than Cubans to report instances of discrimination. Yet when queried about their perceptions of discrimination, overwhelming majorities of Mexican Americans and Puerto Ricans perceived a lot or some discrimination against their ethnic origin group; additionally, both groups were also inclined to perceive a lot or some discrimination against the other group and against Cubans. Cubans were the least likely to perceive discrimination against Mexican Americans and Puerto Ricans, although a majority still perceived such discrimination. Less than a majority of Cubans perceived a lot or some discrimination against their own group; in fact, fully one-third of the Cuban respondents said they perceived no discrimination against Cubans (de la Garza et al. 1992:91–96).

This finding may reflect the geographic concentration and political power of Cubans in Dade County, Florida. Cubans clearly evidence a different pattern of perceptions than do Mexican Americans and Puerto Ricans. This may partially result from the fact that "Mexicans, Puerto Ricans, and Cubans have little interaction with each other, most do not recognize that they have much in common culturally, and they do not profess strong affection for each other" (de la Garza et al. 1992:14).

As seen in Table 3.2, when Hispanics were questioned about their perception of discrimination against African Americans and Asian Americans, some interesting patterns emerged. Clear majorities of Mexican Americans and Puerto Ricans perceived that discrimination is a problem for African Americans and Asian Americans. Yet one-fifth of Cubans believed discrimina-

TABLE 3.2

Perception of Discrimination Against African Americans and Asians by Latino National Origin Groups

	Mexican (%)	Puerto Rican (%)	Cuban (%)
Degree of discrimination against African Americans			
A lot	43.6 (383)[a]	57.5 (336)	29.9 (93)
Some	39.9 (350)	28.4 (166)	35.0 (109)
A little	12.9 (113)	9.0 (52)	14.3 (44)
None	3.6 (32)	5.1 (30)	20.9 (65)
Total	100 (877)	100 (584)	100 (312)
Degree of discrimination against Asians			
A lot	15.5 (134)	14.0 (81)	4.6 (14)
Some	43.9 (379)	37.9 (219)	35.2 (109)
A little	26.9 (232)	30.1 (174)	23.9 (74)
None	13.5 (119)	18.1 (104)	36.3 (112)
Total	100 (864)	100 (577)	100 (308)

[a]Figures in parentheses represent the number of respondents.

Source: Rodolfo O. de la Garza et al., 1992. *Latino Voices: Mexican, Puerto Rican, and Cuban Perspectives on American Politics* (Boulder: Westview Press), Tables 7.8 and 7.9, p. 93.

tion against blacks is nonexistent in the United States, and one-third indicated that discrimination does not exist against Asian Americans.

As mentioned earlier, national data that exclusively address Asian and American Indian attitudes are not available; thus, we must extrapolate from more localized data sources on the political attitudes and behaviors of these two groups. Data collected in 1984 on blacks, Latinos, and Asians in California suggest that almost one-half, 47 percent, of the Asian respondents said they had personally been discriminated against, but only 22 percent said the discrimination was job-related. However, more than half, 57 percent, felt most or at least some Americans are prejudiced against Asians.

Perceptions of discrimination have a generational dimension. Second-generation Asian Americans are far more likely than are first-generation individuals to perceive discrimination (Cain and Kiewiet 1986). Nevertheless, despite the identification of discrimination as a problem for Asians, another analysis of the same data finds that Asians in California do not score as high on measures of group political cohesiveness as do blacks and Latinos (Uhlaner, Cain, and Kiewiet 1989). This lack of political cohesion may reflect Asians' history of discrimination and exclusion from the American political system. Also, the lack of geographical concentration of Asian Americans may make the development of group cohesiveness more difficult than is the case for African Americans and Latinos. Given the stronger feelings of second-generation Asians compared with first-generation Asians, it is possible that Asians will develop a stronger sense of their racial and political identity in the future.

High levels of group cohesion may translate into increased levels of political participation, especially registering to vote and actually voting, by racial minority groups. Blacks have higher levels of group cohesion and share more of a common destiny than do Latinos and Asians. As we will see later in this chapter in the section "Voting Behavior," lower levels of voter registration and actual voting among Asians and Latinos may be partly explained by the lack of group cohesion, although other factors also contribute to this outcome.

Political Ideology

In popular culture and the news media, racial minorities are often described as ideologically and politically "liberal" on a conservative-to-liberal continuum. Yet those who study black and Latino political attitudes argue that it is inappropriate to use the standard political ideology labels of liberal, moderate, and conservative, which were developed from national studies that contained few nonwhites, and apply them to the black and Latino populations. This simple application of labels misses the complexity and variability of attitudes within the various racial communities. Moreover, the application of the labels implies that there is an agreed-upon definition of their meaning and that individuals who identify themselves by these labels are able to define what they mean (Hero 1992; Smith and Seltzer 1992; Tate 1993).

Are we safe in saying that if an individual or a predominant portion of a group believes the federal government should take a more active role in reducing unemployment, providing services for the poor, and improving the socioeconomic position of blacks and other racial minorities, that individual or group is liberal? By the same token, are we safe in saying that if an individual or the majority of a group supports prayer in public schools, the individual or group is conservative? Based on popular notions of liberal and conservative, the answer would be "yes" to both questions. Yet we commonly find such responses within African American public opinion, which raises doubts about the assignment of stereotypic labels such as liberal and conservative.

• •

TABLE 3.3

Black Ideological Identification[a]

Ideology	1984 (%)	1988 (%)
Strongly liberal	21.8 (154)[b]	18.5 (63)
Not very strongly liberal	12.9 (91)	18.0 (61)
Slightly liberal	16.5 (116)	18.0 (61)
Moderate	7.0 (49)	1.8 (6)
Slightly conservative	16.6 (117)	22.1 (75)
Not very strongly conservative	11.3 (80)	10.2 (35)
Strongly conservative	13.9 (98)	11.4 (39)
Total	100 (705)	100 (340)

[a]Postelection sample.
[b]Figures in parentheses represent the number of respondents.
Source: Authors' computations from the 1984 and 1988 National Black Election Studies.

Contrary to popular wisdom, as Table 3.3 shows, blacks are spread across the ideological spectrum, with only an approximately ten-percentage-point gap between the number of blacks self-identifying as some degree of liberal and those identifying as some degree of conservative. But the meaning behind these labels is unclear. When asked to define what they meant by liberal or conservative when identifying themselves as such, some respondents were unable to do so. Moreover, higher-income blacks were no more likely than lower-income blacks to identify themselves as conservatives, but older blacks were far more likely than younger blacks to identify themselves as liberal. Regardless of self-identified ideological labels, blacks' policy preferences are generally fairly liberal across a variety of issues, but, with the exception of capital punishment, they are relatively conservative on a range of social issues (Tate 1993:31–32, 38).

The meanings of the terms *liberal* and *conservative* do not resonate well with Latinos or accurately reflect the attitudes of various Latino groups (Hero 1992). Table 3.4 displays the range of ideological orientations among Latinos. Mexican Americans are almost equally likely to describe themselves as some degree of liberal, as moderate, and as some variant of conservative. Puerto Ricans and Cubans, however, are more likely to self-describe as some degree of conservative than as liberal or moderate. Regardless of their self-identified ideological label, large majorities of all three groups support what could be characterized as core elements of a liberal domestic agenda (de la Garza et al. 1992).

TABLE 3.4

Latino Ideological Identification

Ideology	Mexican (%)	Puerto Rican (%)	Cuban (%)
Very liberal	4.9 (42)[a]	7.0 (40)	3.6 (11)
Liberal	11.6 (100)	12.3 (71)	13.0 (40)
Slightly liberal	12.1 (104)	9.2 (53)	6.3 (19)
Moderate	35.4 (305)	24.7 (142)	22.5 (69)
Slightly conservative	14.8 (128)	16.3 (93)	14.3 (44)
Conservative	15.4 (133)	22.7 (130)	34.2 (106)
Very conservative	5.8 (50)	7.8 (45)	6.0 (18)
Total	100 (863)	100 (574)	100 (308)

[a]Figures in parentheses represent the number of respondents.

Source: Rodolfo O. de la Garza et al., 1992. *Latino Voices: Mexican, Puerto Rican, and Cuban Perspectives on American Politics* (Boulder: Westview Press), p. 84.

The 1984 Cain and Kiewiet survey of political attitudes of California's three principal minority groups—blacks, Latinos, and Asian Americans—provides a glimpse of the ideological orientations of Asian Americans. Although no question appears to ask respondents to identify themselves as liberal, moderate, or conservative, overall, on the standard questions that determine liberal and conservative positions, Asians generally support a liberal domestic agenda—increased support for welfare programs, support of the equal rights amendment, support of a ban on handguns. Moreover, they are far more likely than are blacks and Latinos in California to take a pro-choice position. Data from the 1992 Los Angeles County Social Survey, although they do not subdivide the Asian population, find that one-quarter of Asians identify themselves as liberal, slightly more than half as moderate, and slightly more than one-fifth as conservative (Bobo et al. 1992). The 1993 NCCJ national survey results are almost identical to those from Los Angeles: One-quarter of Asians identify themselves as liberal, half as moderates, and slightly more than one-fifth as conservatives.

Yet as with the other groups, simply using responses to these questions to determine the ideological orientations of the groups would be very misleading and would miss the complexity of the orientations of the range of Asian American groups. For instance, Chinese Americans are far more conservative than are either the Japanese or Koreans. Of all of the Asian ethnic groupings,

Filipinos, who are overwhelmingly Christian, are more likely to favor prayer in public schools than are the other groups; they are also the strongest supporters of increased military expenditures. Also, of the groups, Koreans are the most supportive of bilingualism and are the most strongly opposed to employer sanctions on hiring illegal immigrants.

In addition to differences among national origin Asian American groups, generational differences appear. First-generation Asian Americans are more likely than those who have been in the United States for a longer time to favor bilingual programs in both education and voting, amnesty for undocumented immigrants, gun control, and school prayer (Cain and Kiewiet 1986).

Somewhat as is true with the Hispanic subgroups, positions on foreign policy issues differ among Asian American groups. The politics of different homelands generates different positions on what U.S. foreign policy positions should be (Cain 1988).

Unfortunately, data on the ideological leanings of American Indians are rare. The one extant study (Ritt 1979) concludes that Indians are ideologically moderate, but this conclusion is based on only 151 American Indian respondents to a national survey. Thus, we must necessarily be circumspect in discussing this group's ideology.

This section has revealed the complexity and range of the ideological identifications of blacks, Latinos, Asians, and, to a lesser extent, Indians. This range of orientations has implications for one strategy of the second dilemma—it makes the formation of interminority group coalitions more difficult. As Chapter 5 discusses, ideology is one of the bases on which interracial coalitions are formed. Shared racial minority group status in the United States does not mean that all minority groups occupy the same end of the ideological spectrum. Blacks, Latinos, and Asians are dispersed all along the ideological continuum, but the meanings of the terms *liberal, moderate,* and *conservative* for these groups differ from the popular culture definition of the terms.

Partisan Identification

As each presidential election nears, the media point to the heavily Democratic orientation and voting within the African American community. Many assume that because blacks vote heavily Democratic, all racial minority groups do likewise. Despite the acknowledgment of this orientation among African American voters, the media never ask the reasons for the orientation and how it came about. The Republican Party, in attempting to appeal to black voters, conveniently ignores the history of the relationship between blacks and the party dating from the party's inception in 1856. Most students of American politics and the public at large believe it was the policies of the Democratic Party rather than the pressure from the Republican Party that resulted in the present configuration of black partisan identification. Moreover, the media never explore the issues of the strength of blacks' commitment to the Democratic Party and whether other racial minority groups have different points of view.

Blacks

Although space does not allow a recitation of the complex history of the relationship between blacks and the political parties in the United States, a little of that history must be reviewed before we can place the current identification of African Americans with the Democratic Party in perspective. From its inception in 1856 around the issue of the abolition of slavery, blacks were heavily involved in the Republican Party. Before the end of Reconstruction, sixteen blacks were elected to Congress, all as Republicans. Blacks were actively involved in the party organization, with John R. Lynch, a state legislator from Mississippi, serving as temporary chair of the 1884 Republican Convention. At the 1892 Republican Convention, 13 percent of the delegates were black (Gurin, Hatchett, and Jackson 1989).

After the compromise of 1877, in which Rutherford B. Hayes promised to remove federal troops from the South and to allow the former Confederate states to deal with the "Negro problem" in their own way if he were elected president, the Democratic Party became the party of white supremacy and the Republican Party became the party of blacks. In attempts to rebuild the Republican Party in the South, successive Republican presidents pursued a strategy aimed at drawing more southern whites into the party while at the same time pushing out or alienating black Republicans. The conflicts between what became known as the **Lily White Republicans** and the **Black and Tan Republicans**—the anti– and pro–civil rights wings of the party, respectively—continued until the 1956 election. Between 1877 and the complete shift of blacks to the Democratic Party in the 1960 elections, numerous pejorative acts and perfidious behaviors toward black Republicans by white Republicans at the national, state, and local levels resulted in the change of blacks' allegiance.

It was not just the push of the Republican Party but was also the pull of the Democratic Party that resulted in a shift of allegiance by blacks. The neglect and hostility of Republican administrations led some prominent blacks, including W.E.B. DuBois, to support Woodrow Wilson in the 1912 presidential election. However, Wilson's subsequent segregation of the federal government and the city of Washington, D.C., and his limited attention to black concerns resulted in blacks returning to the Republican Party in subsequent elections. The perception that Herbert Hoover was pursuing an overtly racist strategy in his administration policies and his explicit overtures to Lily White Republicans, coupled with the Depression and the election of Franklin D. Roosevelt in 1932, set the stage for the beginning of the black party realignment.

Although the implementation of many of Roosevelt's New Deal policies was tinged with racial discrimination and many blacks were still uncertain about Roosevelt's commitment to addressing issues of concern to blacks, many blacks were persuaded enough to vote Democratic in large numbers. Roosevelt's informal formation of a group of black government advisers, commonly referred to as the Kitchen Cabinet—which included prominent individuals such as Robert C. Weaver, Ralph J. Bunche, Mary McLeod Bethune, and Rayford W. Logan, among others—was a first for any presidential administration.[1] Moreover, the visibility of Roosevelt's wife, Eleanor, on issues of importance to the broader black community raised blacks' confidence in Roosevelt's commitment to them. Thus, by Roosevelt's 1944 reelection, blacks voted overwhelmingly Democratic and provided the margin of victory in seven states—Pennsylvania, Maryland, Michigan, Missouri, New York, Illinois, and New Jersey (Gurin, Hatchett, and Jackson 1989:36).

After Roosevelt's death, however, Harry Truman found black loyalty to the Democratic Party was tied to Franklin Roosevelt and realized that he could not automatically count on black votes in the 1948 election. Both Truman and the Republican candidate, Thomas Dewey, knew they would need black votes in the major urban areas to win. Dewey, as governor of New York, had a very good record on issues of concern to blacks. Prior to the 1948 election, Truman had made his civil rights recommendations, based on a report from a commission he had established, to Congress. In addition, a civil rights plank was inserted into the Democratic platform at the 1948 Democratic Convention, which resulted in the walkout of southern Democrats—led by then-Governor Strom Thurmond—and in the formation of the Dixiecrats. The controversy surrounding Truman and his civil rights initiatives led many to assume that Dewey would win the election; however, Truman was victorious.

In the 1952 election, in protest of the influence of the Dixiecrats and the connection between the Dixiecrats and the Democratic Party in the South, many southern blacks voted for Dwight Eisenhower. Eisenhower's appointment of Earl Warren as chief justice of the Supreme Court and the subsequent

TABLE 3.5

Black Partisan Identification[a]

Partisan Identification	1984 (%)	1988 (%)
Strong Democrat	45.8 (521)[b]	57.0 (260)
Weak Democrat	23.5 (267)	21.5 (98)
Independent/leaning toward Democrat	14.2 (162)	10.3 (47)
Independent	4.8 (55)	2.9 (13)
Republican—all strengths	7.8 (88)	6.3 (29)
Other/apolitical	3.8 (44)	2.0 (9)
Total	100 (1,137)	100 (456)

[a]Preelection sample.
[b]Figures in parentheses represent the number of respondents.
Source: Authors' computations from the 1984 and 1988 National Black Election Studies.

decision in *Brown v. Board of Education* in 1954 led many blacks to credit Eisenhower with the victory.[2] An estimated 38 percent of the black vote went to Eisenhower in the 1956 election (Gurin, Hatchett, and Jackson 1989). During his second term, however, Eisenhower's administration was viewed as less committed to civil rights and equality, as was evidenced by Eisenhower's reluctance to implement the 1957 Civil Rights Act and to take a strong stand to enforce school desegregation in Little Rock. As a result, in the 1960 presidential election between John F. Kennedy and Richard M. Nixon, the black vote shifted in large numbers to the Democrats, where it has remained ever since.

In the 1984 NBES data, 83.5 percent of blacks surveyed considered themselves Democrats, yet the degree of partisanship varied. As Table 3.5 demonstrates, slightly less than half of blacks reported themselves as strong Democrats; in 1988, considerably more blacks identified themselves as such. Both the 1984 and 1988 data suggest a gender split within the black electorate—black women were more likely to identify strongly with the Democratic Party than were black men; the latter were more likely to be weak or independent Democratic supporters, political independents, or Republicans (Tate 1993:64).

There also appears to be a generational split—older blacks tend to be more strongly Democratic than are younger blacks. Given the unfavorable evaluations of Presidents Ronald Reagan and George Bush within the black community, "it is unlikely that younger blacks might be more inclined toward the Republican party

TABLE 3.6

Latino Partisan Identification

Partisan Identification	Mexican (%)	Puerto Rican (%)	Cuban (%)
Strong Democrat	31.0 (252)[a]	37.2 (205)	14.4 (45)
Not strong Democrat	28.6 (232)	26.4 (145)	5.1 (16)
Closer to Democrat	7.2 (59)	7.4 (40)	6.0 (18)
Independent/other	11.5 (94)	11.5 (63)	5.7 (18)
Closer to Republican	5.5 (45)	3.6 (20)	4.8 (15)
Not strong Republican	11.6 (94)	7.2 (40)	16.2 (50)
Strong Republican	4.4 (36)	6.7 (37)	47.8 (147)
Total	100 (811)	100 (550)	100 (309)

[a]Figures in parentheses represent the number of respondents.

Source: Rodolfo O. de la Garza et al., 1992. *Latino Voices: Mexican, Puerto Rican, and Cuban Perspectives on American Politics* (Boulder: Westview Press, 1992), p. 127.

than past generations of blacks. Young black voters may be less partisan simply because they lack political experience, and thus may be less likely to identify strongly with parties" (Tate 1993:65). It has also been suggested that Jesse Jackson's treatment by Walter Mondale's forces at the 1984 Democratic Convention may also have contributed to younger blacks' disillusionment with the Democratic Party.

Latinos

The history of Latinos and the two political parties is not as well documented as that of African Americans. Overall, Latinos are strongly Democratic in their partisan identification, but they do not equal blacks in their strength of identification with the Democratic Party. As data from the LNPS survey in Table 3.6 demonstrate, among Mexican Americans two-thirds indicated that they are Democrats of varying strengths. Given Puerto Ricans' tendency to self-identify as conservatives, popular wisdom would predict a more Republican identification. Once again, the data run counter to conventional wisdom. Nearly three-fourths of Puerto Ricans identified themselves as Democrats of varying strengths.

Cubans departed significantly from this pattern. More than two-thirds of Cubans identified themselves as Republicans. In fact, more Cubans identified themselves as strong Republicans than the proportion of Mexicans and Puerto

Ricans who identified as strong Democrats. Once again, however, we must caution that Cuban identification with the Republican Party stems more from foreign policy concerns, particularly U.S. relations with Cuba, than from concern with social policy issues. The LNPS demonstrates that the majority of Cubans favor increased government spending on health, crime, drug control, education, the environment, child services, and bilingual education. In essence, a majority of Cubans support what could be characterized as core elements of a liberal domestic agenda, even though they are more likely to self-identify as conservative (de la Garza et al. 1992:14).

Little research exists on the political behaviors, attitudes, and experiences of Latinas (women), but the few extant studies suggest some subtle gender differences within the Latino groups. On partisan identification, one study that used national exit poll data for the 1980, 1984, and 1988 presidential elections found Latinas to be more liberal and more Democratic than Latinos (Welch and Sigelman 1992).

Asians

Until recently, research had indicated that in the aggregate, Asian Americans appear to be more Republican than Democratic, with Chinese Americans being more strongly Republican than other groups (Cain and Kiewiet 1986; Cain, Kiewiet, and Uhlaner 1991; Stokes 1988). However, partisan attachment is weak, and either party could benefit from Asian American support.

Data from the 1992 Los Angeles County Social Survey, although not subdividing the Asian population into national origins, found that more Asians— 36.3 percent—classified themselves as political independents than as Democrats, 28.7 percent, or Republicans, 29.5 percent. The 1993 NCCJ data present a similar picture. More than one-third—37 percent—of Asians nationally considered themselves political independents, whereas 40 percent identified themselves as Democrats and 18 percent as Republicans. These findings appear to be consistent with the observation that a high proportion of Asian Americans consider themselves political independents rather than members of either political party.

It is also instructive to look at results from the 1984 and 1989 UCLA Asian Pacific American Voter Registration Project for the city of Monterey Park in Los Angeles County, as reported in Table 3.7. Monterey Park, with a 1990 population of 60,738, is the only majority (57.5 percent) Asian American city in the continental United States. (Several cities in Hawaii have Asian American majorities.) In 1989, among Chinese American residents of Monterey Park, al-

Illustrating Cuban group identification, around ten thousand Cuban Americans protest the continued detainment of fellow Cubans at Guantanamo at a rally in Little Havana. Many Cubans are comparing the tent city at the military base with the German concentration camps of World War II (October 1994). Photo by Colin Braley/Reuter; courtesy UPI/Bettmann.

most equal percentages identified as either Democrats or Republicans; more than one-quarter considered themselves political independents. It should be noted that the percentage of Chinese Americans identifying with the Democratic Party in 1989 declined from the comparable figure in 1984.

Voter registration during Chinese New Year, Monterey Park, California, 1992. Photo courtesy Steven J. Gold.

Among Japanese Americans in Monterey Park, slightly more than half identified with the Democratic Party, and only 12.7 percent considered themselves political independents. Once again, between 1984 and 1989 the Democrats suffered a slight decline in the percentage of Japanese Americans identifying with the party. The number identifying as political independents increased slightly from 1984.

Asian Pacifics—defined as Vietnamese, Hawaiians, Guamanians, and Samoans—were similar to the Japanese in their party affiliations. Just over half considered themselves Democrats, and one-fifth indicated no party affiliation. Chinese Americans are far more likely to be Republican than are Japanese Americans, but Chinese Americans are also more likely to be political independents (Nakanishi 1991:42–43). Asian Americans as a whole are more likely than either blacks or Latinos to be political independents.

American Indians

Few studies exist of the political behavior of American Indians in nontribal elections. The existing studies indicate that Indian peoples are not strongly tied to either political party but tend to lean toward the Democrats, although

TABLE 3.7

Asian Pacific American Registered Voters, Monterey Park, 1984 and 1989

	Number Registered	Democrats	Republicans	Other Party	No Party
1984 Chinese	3,152	1,360	972	23	797
Americans	(100)[a]	(43.1)	(30.8)	(0.7)	(25.3)
1989 Chinese	5,356	1,868	1,989	100	1,399
Americans	(100)	(34.9)	(37.1)	(1.9)	(26.1)
1984–1989 Net gain	+2,204	+508	+1,017	+77	+602
1984 Japanese	2,586	1,429	838	21	298
Americans	(100)	(55.3)	(32.4)	(0.8)	(11.5)
1989 Japanese	2,919	1,516	991	42	370
Americans	(100)	(51.9)	(33.9)	(1.4)	(12.7)
1984–1989 Net gain	+343	+87	+153	+21	+72
1984 Asian Pacific	6,441	3,265	1,944	54	1,178
Americans	(100)	(50.7)	(30.2)	(0.8)	(18.3)
1989 Asian Pacific	8,988	3,754	3,198	168	1,868
Americans	(100)	(41.8)	(35.6)	(1.9)	(20.8)
1984–1989 Net gain	+2,547	+489	+1,254	+114	+690

[a]Numbers in parentheses represent the percentage in each category.

Source: Donald T. Nakanishi, 1991. "The Next Swing Vote: Asian Pacific Americans and California Politics." In Byran O. Jackson and Michael B. Preston, editors, *Racial and Ethnic Politics in California* (Berkeley: Institute of Governmental Studies), p. 43.

significant differences in party affiliation are found across tribes. For example, over time the Navajos have shifted from Republican to Democratic and, during the Reagan years, slightly back to the Republicans in national elections; yet they remain fiercely Democratic in Arizona state politics. Since the 1956 presidential election, the Pagagos have consistently voted Democratic (McCool 1982; Ritt 1979). An examination of the partisan preferences of American Indian voters in the Upper Midwest (Wisconsin, Minnesota, and North and South Dakota) in elections from 1982 through 1992 reveals a strong preference for Democrats (Doherty 1994).

One of the factors that has determined Indian party affiliations at the national level has been an administration's stance on Indian issues. During Richard Nixon's administration, many Indians, such as the Navajos, voted Republican because Nixon was viewed as having a strong stance regarding American Indian policy. But they shifted to Jimmy Carter during his years in office because he was also viewed as being "good for Indians." These limited data suggest that categorizing American Indians as either primarily Democrats or Republicans is impossible without taking into account reservation compared with nonreservation Indians and a party's stance on federal Indian policy.

Voting Behavior

Prior to the Voting Rights Act, only 6.7 percent of blacks in Mississippi were registered to vote; by 1967, 59.8 percent of voting-age blacks were registered. It is estimated that in the seven states originally covered by the act, black registration increased from 29.3 percent in March 1965 to 56.6 percent in 1971–1972. Moreover, "the Justice Department estimated that in the five years after passage, almost as many blacks registered in Alabama, Mississippi, Georgia, Louisiana, North Carolina, and South Carolina as in the entire century before 1965" (Davidson 1992:21). Table 3.8 shows the 1992 registration and voting figures for the twenty U.S. states with the highest proportion of blacks and Latinos. Because "most American national elections are won by 5 percent or less," blacks and Latinos have the potential to be a significant force in determining the outcome of these elections (Williams 1987:101). Moreover, in some states the ability of blacks, Latinos, Asians and American Indians to decide electoral outcomes is very strong.

In 1992, 185,684 million Americans were eligible to vote. African Americans accounted for 11.3 percent of the total voting-age population and Latinos for 7.9 percent of that population. This figure is deceptive because the Census Bureau's categorization of Hispanic includes individuals of any race; thus, there is an overlap between the figures for Hispanics and whites and blacks. Asians constitute 2.7 percent of the total voting-age population. Unfortunately, the Census Bureau does not maintain such figures on American Indians.

In 1968 the gap between black and white voter registration rates was 9.2 percentage points; this had narrowed to only 3.3 percentage points in 1984

TABLE 3.8

Registration and Voting by Race for Twenty States with Highest Black and Latino Proportions of the Electorate, 1992

State	% of Total Electorate		% of Voting-Age Population Registered			% of Voting-Age Population Reported Voting		
	Black	Latino	White	Black	Latino	White	Black	Latino
Mississippi	32.7	—	80.2	78.5	—	69.4	61.1	—
Georgia	31.9	—	67.3	53.9	—	58.7	47.1	—
South Carolina	26.9	—	69.2	62.0	—	61.0	48.8	—
Alabama	25.8	—	79.3	71.8	—	65.9	58.1	—
Louisiana	24.3	—	76.2	82.3	—	68.3	71.5	—
North Carolina	22.2	—	70.8	64.0	—	62.4	54.1	—
Maryland	22.1	2.6	74.7	66.4	38.7[a]	69.6	60.2	38.7[a]
Virginia	17.4	—	67.2	64.5	—	57.9	62.9	—
Arkansas	16.7	—	67.8	62.4	—	60.7	46.4	—
Delaware	16.3	—	73.9	57.6	—	69.8	51.8	—
New York	15.3	8.7	66.1	49.7	38.3	61.1	43.4	32.6
Tennessee	14.2	—	63.2	77.4	—	54.8	62.9	—
Illinois	13.9	7.4	72.8	75.2	34.6	66.3	65.3	26.4
Florida	13.6	13.0	64.5	54.7	35.0	57.9	46.3	30.5
New Jersey	13.2	9.7	71.0	62.7	36.8	65.1	49.9	30.6
Michigan	12.7	—	75.3	76.0	—	66.8	65.6	—

(continues)

Table 3.8 (Cont.)

State	% of Total Electorate		% of Voting-Age Population Registered			% of Voting-Age Population Reported Voting		
	Black	Latino	White	Black	Latino	White	Black	Latino
Texas	11.1	22.9	66.1	63.5	42.9	57.2	50.1	33.1
Ohio	10.0	–	70.4	65.6	–	65.2	58.9	–
Connecticut	9.1	5.2	80.0	51.5	49.7	75.0	45.1	42.6
Indiana	9.0	–	68.4	64.4	–	64.1	51.4	–
New Mexico	–	31.0	68.0	–	56.8	63.8	–	51.3
California	–	24.4	60.5	–	25.4	55.9	–	20.0
Arizona	–	16.5	71.8	–	44.7	66.1	–	35.3
Nevada	–	9.8	64.1	–	26.6[a]	58.9	–	24.4[a]
Colorado	–	8.9	77.2	–	66.5	71.5	–	62.2
Oregon	–	4.4	75.8	–	41.2[a]	70.5	–	36.1[a]
Idaho	–	4.1	72.0	–	33.3[a]	67.0	–	26.7[a]
Wyoming	–	3.6	68.9	–	50.0[a]	65.1	–	50.0[a]
Rhode Island	–	3.0	76.0	–	26.1[a]	71.2	–	26.1[a]
Utah	–	2.8	79.3	–	51.6[a]	73.0	–	45.2[a]
Massachusetts	–	2.8	74.2	–	22.7	67.4	–	14.4
Kansas	–	2.5	78.2	–	57.8[a]	73.1	–	44.4[a]
Oklahoma	–	2.4	75.5	–	35.2[a]	69.3	–	33.3

[a]Figures are based on computations using raw numbers; the sample size was too small for the census to provide a precise estimate of the percentage.

Source: Jerry T. Jennings, *Voting and Registration in the Election of November 1992*, 1993. Current Population Reports, Population Characteristics P20-466 (Washington, D.C.: U.S. Bureau of the Census).

....

TABLE 3.9

Registration and Voting by Race, National Sample
(White, Black, Latino, and Asian, 1992)

Race	% of VAP[a]	% of VAP Registered	% of VAP Reported Voting
White	85.0	70.1	63.6
Black	11.3	63.9	54.0
Latino[b]	7.9	35.0	28.9
Asian	2.8	31.2	27.3

[a]Voting-age population.
[b]Latinos may be of any race; consequently, there is some overlap between the Latino and black and white categories.

Source: Jerry T. Jennings, Voting and Registration in the Election of November 1992, 1993. Current Population Reports, Population Characteristics P20–466 (Washington, D.C.: U.S. Bureau of the Census).

(Williams 1987). Yet as Table 3.9 demonstrates, by 1992 the gap had widened again to 6.2 percentage points—70.1 percent of white voting-age residents were registered to vote compared with 63.9 percent of blacks. The gap between white and Latino and Asian voter registration rates was considerably wider, with a difference of 35.1 percentage points between whites and Latinos and 39.2 percentage points between whites and Asians. Stated differently, only 35 percent of Latinos and 31.2 percent of Asians who were of voting age were registered to vote. What explains the increase in the gap between white and black voters, and why are the numbers of Latino and Asian Americans registered to vote so small?

Since 1964 black registration rates have followed general national trends, going up in the 1960s, down in the 1970s, and up again in the 1980s (Williams 1987). The 1992 drop in black registration from the rates in 1984 and 1988 seems to parallel similar drops in white registration for the 1984 to 1988 time period. Yet white registration in 1992, at 70.1 percent, was higher than the 67.9-percent registration rate in 1988. Jesse Jackson's 1984 presidential campaign and the resultant voter registration drives apparently increased black voter registration, but Jackson's 1988 run, although more successful in terms of primary outcomes, may not have had the same effect on national black registration efforts (Tate 1993).

Latinos and Asians have considerably lower registration rates than do African Americans. Latino registration rates have also dropped since 1984 when the percentage stood at 40.1 percent of the voting-age population, declining to 35.5 percent in 1988 and declining further to 35.1 percent in 1992. Latinos are disproportionately younger, poorer, and less educated than the general population, which may suggest that the labyrinth of laws and administrative procedures that exist might have a greater suppressive effect on Latino registration than the 9-percent effect estimated for the population in general (Calvo and Rosenstone 1989; Hero 1992). Other reasons for lower registration might include difficulty with the English language (Calvo and Rosenstone 1989; Meier and Stewart 1991) and difficulty in understanding U.S. politics and the U.S. political system (Vigil 1987:43). Because 1992 was the first year the Census Bureau included Asian Americans in the survey, it is not possible to determine trends in Asian American registration.

The Census Bureau does not maintain statistics for Indian peoples; thus, it is difficult to determine their levels of registration. One study of American Indians in the Upper Midwest concluded that they evince lower levels of registration than whites of similar socioeconomic status (Doherty 1994).

Although 63.9 percent of the black voting-age population was registered to vote in 1992, only 54 percent of that population reported voting in the 1992 elections (see Table 3.9). This represents a 9.6-percentage-point gap between black and white voting rates in 1992. The voting levels for Latinos and Asians were once again substantially lower than those for African Americans. Only 28.9 percent of Latinos and 27.3 percent of Asians who were registered to vote actually voted. This represents a gap between Latino and white and Asian and white voting rates of 34.7 percentage points and 36.3 percentage points, respectively. The differences between black and Latino and black and Asian rates were 25.1 percentage points and 26.7 percentage points, respectively. The limited data available on American Indian voting suggest that for the six elections from 1982 through 1992, turnout averaged approximately 40 percent, but these data are too limited to merit comparison with those available for other groups.

Of particular interest are the differences in registration and voting rates between men and women in each of the three groups shown in Table 3.10. In 1992, black women and Latinas had higher registration rates than did black men and Latinos. Asian men were slightly more likely than women to have registered to vote. When we compare black women and Latinas, black women were the only group that held a registration advantage that actually maintained that advantage in voting—a higher percentage of black women voted than did black men. Although they had lower registration rates, a higher proportion of registered Latinos voted than did Latinas.

TABLE 3.10

Registration and Voting by Race and Sex, National Sample (Black, Latino, and Asian, 1992)

	Black		Latino		Asian	
Category	Male	Female	Male	Female	Male	Female
% VAP[a]	5.1	6.3	3.9	4.0	1.3	1.5
% VAP registered	60.8	66.4	32.1	37.8	32.0	30.6
% VAP reported voting	50.8	56.7	37.8	30.9	28.1	26.7

[a]Voting-age population.

Source: Jerry T. Jennings, *Voting and Registration in the Election of November 1992*, 1993. Current Population Reports, Population Characteristics P20-466 (Washington, D.C.: U.S. Bureau of the Census).

The reasons for higher levels of registration and voting among black women than among black men may stem from the higher levels of education and the labor force distribution of black women in more white-collar and fewer blue-collar jobs than is true for the black male labor force, although black women have higher turnout rates than black men within the same occupation, income, education, and employment status group. Survey data on group consciousness reveal that another possible reason for the differences may be that black women perceive discrimination on the basis of both race and gender. This dual consciousness, therefore, may foster participation of black women to a greater degree than racial consciousness alone stimulates that of black men (Williams 1987).

Interest Group Activities

As we mentioned at the beginning of this chapter, one of the principal components of pluralist theory is competition between interest groups. Although this theory presents some problems for the study of racial minority group politics, interest groups that focus on issues of importance to blacks, Latinos, Asians, and American Indians have been essential to the progress made toward the incorporation of these groups into the American political system. There are far more groups than we have space to cover; therefore, we will highlight several of the major groups—particularly those that have used litigation as a tactic—along with those that are the best known for each of the groups under consideration.

Racial and ethnic minority groups have frequently turned to the courts in an attempt to improve their positions because victories in the courts are more likely to be determined by an appeal to what is right than merely to what is politically popular. For African Americans—and, indeed, as a model for all other racial and ethnic groups—the **NAACP Legal Defense and Educational Fund** (LDF)—a group of attorneys dedicated to affirming and expanding the rights of blacks—founded in 1939, has been the pathbreaking group. The LDF's strategy was to "secure decisions, rulings, and public opinion on the broad principle instead of being devoted to mere miscellaneous cases" (founder Charles Houston, quoted in Vose 1959:23). The LDF, using test cases and class action suits, became known as *the* group through which to attack segregation. Its most famous victory came in *Brown v. Board of Education of Topeka* (1954 and 1955; this case is discussed further in Chapter 4), which overturned *Plessy v. Ferguson* (1896), the case that had established the separate but equal doctrine.

The LDF and its litigation approach to removing the barriers to full participation in the political process by blacks have served as a model for Latinos. With the guidance of LDF attorneys and funding from the Ford Foundation, the Mexican American Legal Defense and Education Fund (MALDEF) was established in 1968. MALDEF functions for Mexican Americans in much the same way the LDF has historically functioned for African Americans. In 1972, the Puerto Rican Legal Defense and Education Fund (PRLDEF) was created in New York City to play a similar role for Puerto Ricans. Additionally, as is characteristic of the diversity that exists within the Asian American community, there are various lawyers' interest groups—the Asian Law Caucus, based in San Francisco; the Asian American Legal Defense and Educational Fund in New York; and the Asian Pacific American Legal Center, based in Los Angeles—loosely united under the aegis of the National Asian Pacific American Legal Consortium.

The Native American Rights Fund (NARF), located in Boulder, Colorado, was founded in 1970 with the help of the Ford Foundation. It was the first national program to provide legal aid to Indians. Although NARF was officially organized in 1970, it actually began as an outgrowth of California Rural Legal Assistance (CRLA). It soon became clear that Indians had unique legal problems that required special expertise; thus, the Indian Services Division of CRLA was organized. The division became a separate organization, the California Indian Legal Services (CILS), in 1968, and CILS received a grant from the Ford Foundation in 1970 with which to establish NARF (James 1973). Most of NARF's attorneys and staff are Indians, although non-Indians are present in a number of positions, and its board of directors is composed of Indian leaders from across the country.

NARF has five priority areas: (1) the preservation of tribal existence, (2) the protection of tribal natural resources, (3) the promotion of human rights, (4) the accountability of governments to Native Americans, and (5) the development of Indian law (Native American Rights Fund 1993). NARF has been involved in a number of legal cases challenging barriers to Indian rights and political participation and challenging states and the federal government to honor treaties with Indian nations and peoples. NARF has either filed or submitted amicus curiae briefs in numerous cases and has been successful in over two hundred cases.

NARF's litigation on behalf of the Catawba Tribe of South Carolina (*Catawba Indian Tribe of South Carolina v. U.S.* 1993) was settled when President Clinton signed Public Law No. 103-116, the Catawba Indian Land Claim Settlement Act of 1993. In another action, NARF won a suit against the Bureau of Indian Affairs on behalf of the Cheyenne-Arapaho Tribes of Oklahoma (*Cheyenne-Arapaho Tribes of Oklahoma v. U.S.* 1992) for failing to protect Indian interests in the pricing of minerals removed from Indian lands. NARF has also protected voting rights of Indians in several states including South Dakota, New York, and Alaska.

In the area of nonlitigation-oriented interest groups, there is a plethora of African American interest groups, the longest lasting of which are the NAACP, founded in 1909 and the parent of the LDF; the National Urban League, founded in 1910; and the Southern Christian Leadership Conference (SCLC), organized in 1957. Others, such as the Student Nonviolent Coordinating Committee and the Congress of Racial Equality, were extremely important during the civil rights movement of the 1960s but are either diminished in their activity or are moribund today.

Some of the more prominent Latino interest groups are the **League of United Latin American Citizens** (LULAC), a group of vocal, middle-class Mexican American citizens formed in 1929 in south Texas, and the National Council of La Raza (NCLR). LULAC was established to fight discrimination against Mexican Americans in Texas. From its inception through the 1960s, LULAC was actively engaged in protest and litigation for equal and civil rights for Mexican Americans. It has grown from a small organization in several south Texas cities to a national organization "with active councils in twenty-eight states, a national headquarters in Washington, D.C., and a professional staff" (Márquez 1989:355–356).

NCLR, previously the Southwest Council of La Raza (founded in 1968), was initially oriented toward community organization and mobilization, but over the years it has developed into an umbrella organization for numerous local Latino organizations. It has voter education and registration programs and a research office that conducts studies and disseminates information on issues of concern to the broader Latino community. NCLR has recently focused its efforts on economic development and small-business investment (Hero 1992:77).

Asian American and American Indian interest groups have also been active. The Japanese American Citizens League (JACL), founded in 1930, is the best established and largest national Asian American organization. JACL was instrumental in bringing the issue of reparations for Japanese interned during World War II to the political agenda and, in 1988, in pushing Congress to pass legislation providing for an apology and a payment of $20,000 to each of the survivors of the internment camps. When President Reagan signed the legislation, he admitted that the United States had committed "a grave wrong" (Takaki 1993:401).

Another Asian American interest group is the West San Gabriel Valley Asian Pacific American Democratic Club (WSGVAPADC), more local in nature than the JACL. WSGVAPADC was formed in 1985 to represent the political views of Asian Americans residing in the western portion of the San Gabriel Valley (principally Monterey Park). Its membership is composed primarily of Chinese and Japanese, and its activities have included conducting voter registration drives, assisting Democratic candidates for public office, and lobbying against English-only initiatives. On several occasions the group has worked closely with LULAC and several white interest groups (Saito 1992:160–168).

Indians organize along tribal lines when action involves members of one tribe in pursuit of tribal goals. But when the issue is of concern to more than one tribe, Indians organize along pan-tribal lines. Therefore, because many American Indian tribes enjoy some level of autonomy, they can and do act as interest groups. Many have lobbied the government and have brought cases to the federal courts, seeking to vindicate rights. Moreover, tribes hold the primary responsibility for Indian community development. There are also formal government agencies, such as the Bureau of Indian Affairs (BIA) and the National Council on Indian Opportunity (created by Lyndon Johnson), which are designed to look after the interest of Indians but do not usually follow through on their mandates. Over the decades, there has been sustained and increasingly vocal opposition to the BIA by both reservation Indians and urban Indians (Nagel 1982).

An example of a pan-tribal organization is the Alaska Federation of Natives, formed in 1966, which successfully filed land claims against the state amounting to 360 million acres, or a little more than the state's entire land area. Other pan-tribal Indian interest groups include the National Indian Youth Council (founded in 1961), the National Tribal Chairman's Association (circa 1960), the National Congress of American Indians (1944), the Institute for the Development of Indian Law (1971), and the Native American Rights Fund (1970).

Conclusion

Madison's assumption that conflict would prevail over consensus has proven to be well-founded. Blacks, Latinos, Asians, and American Indians share some similar political attitudes and participation dimensions, but they differ dramatically on others. Clearly, racial minorities do not all think alike. This chapter also highlights the fact that in the political game, each of the racial and ethnic minorities has been at a disadvantage, despite its efforts to be active in the polity. Still, some successes are noted. In Chapter 4 we explore the way these groups have been treated by the political system, a revisiting of the first dilemma.

4

....

America's Racial Minorities and the Policymaking Process

An official accidentally reveals at a public meeting that white families are being charged $1,500 to hook up to the county's water supply, but American Indian families are charged $9,400 for the same service.

Tripp County, S.D., early 1990s

P UBLIC POLICIES are what governments choose to do or not to do. These policies do not just happen; they are the outputs of the political process and of
government institutions. Political scientists and public policy scholars speak of
public policymaking as a process that consists of five interrelated stages—
agenda setting, formulation, adoption, implementation, and evaluation.

Agenda setting is the process by which issues are identified and by which
conflicts and concerns gain prominence and exposure so they are brought to
the public arena for debate and possible government action (Cobb and Elder
1983). This stage occurs both within and outside of government institutions.
Formulation is the stage at which policy issues are translated into actual proposals from which an alternative may be chosen for adoption, usually by a legislative body. Given the bargaining process that occurs in legislative bodies, political feasibility and ideological stances may become more important
considerations than problem solving. Ideology may produce agreed-on policies that ultimately do not work (Lindblom 1980:39).

Policy adoption involves choosing between proposed alternatives to address
the problem. In collective policymaking bodies such as legislatures and appellate courts, adoption requires building majority coalitions. After policy is
adopted, it then moves to the implementation stage, the stage at which the policy is put into action. This activity is usually the domain of federal, state, or local government agencies. The implementation process is very fluid and is subject to numerous internal and external influences; therefore, the manner in
which a policy is implemented or the shape the policy assumes may or may not
resemble the intent of the individuals who formulated the policy. The final
stage, evaluation, is the process of determining whether the policy had its intended effect and what unintended consequences, both positive and negative,
may have occurred.

This chapter begins with a discussion of what is probably the most important stage of the public policymaking process for racial and ethnic minorities—agenda setting. Because historically minority group members have been
excluded from policymaking bodies, minorities' interests have often not been
voiced. The chapter then details the contemporary situation in the major

87

branches of government, highlighting the increased representation of members of racial and ethnic minority groups.

Next, a detailed explication of the impact of **federalism** on public policymaking is presented. Federalism, which involves the division of powers among the various layers of government—national, state, county, municipal—presents opportunities for access to the public policy process but barriers to effective, efficient policymaking. Although most people believe the action and power reside in national political activity and offices, the reality is that most of the decisions that affect the everyday lives of American citizens are made on the state and local levels. Scholars who study state politics argue that states are "where the action is." These various levels of government require that, depending on the policy issue, racial minorities address their attention to a multiplicity of governmental units because a victory at one level can be undermined or overturned at another.

Finally, a specific policy area, equal educational opportunity, is discussed to give a concrete example of the linkages between structural aspects of American government and what the government has actually done in this important area. This discussion also provides important substantive information about the current issues and the current status of law and policy in this vital civil rights policy area.

Agenda Setting

If an issue is never considered, it is impossible for the government to act upon it. Those who control the government agenda control the debate, the types of policies that are formulated, and the structure of the implementation process. The models of agenda setting are, in brief, (1) outside initiative, (2) mobilization, and (3) inside access (Cobb, Ross, and Ross 1976). In the **outside initiative model**, groups outside of government push for their issues to be heard by the decisionmakers, usually through mass mobilization such as demonstrations. The general issue is then translated into more specific demands and is expanded to include a broader number of groups, thus gaining attention as part of the public agenda.

In the **mobilization model**, issues are placed on the agenda by individuals either inside the government or with direct access to government, but the issues must be expanded to the public to gain its support. With the **inside access model** items are placed on the agenda by individuals inside the government and are expanded only to those groups that place pressure on decisionmakers to move the problem forward. Issues are not expanded to the public, either because the policymakers do not require legitimation of the idea or do not want the public to know about it.

All of these models are based on pluralist theory, and the limited research on racial minorities and agenda setting has found that minorities have little access to or influence on the policy agenda-setting process (McClain 1993b). The only model minorities have thus far been successful in utilizing in their attempts to influence the agenda has been the outside initiative model, of which the modern civil rights movement is a prime example.

As is clear from this brief discussion of the policy process and agenda setting, individuals within the structures of government have tremendous influence on the policy outputs from those structures. It becomes necessary, therefore, for groups to have a significant presence in these institutions if they are to affect the policy process. The major national institutions of government—the office of the president, the Supreme Court, Congress, and the bureaucracy—play prominent roles in acting on or not acting on the issues that affect racial minorities. Furthermore, the fact that each of the national institutions is duplicated in some form at the state and local levels has often meant that racial minority groups' citizens have been caught between different levels of the federal system. Policies of both the U.S. and state governments have directly affected the ability of racial minorities to gain access to and participate in the political process.

Minority Representation

Since the passage of the Voting Rights Act in 1965, there has been a significant increase in the number of black and Latino elected officials. As of January 1993, 8,015 African Americans held office at all levels of government; of that number, 29 percent were black females. The number of black women elected to office is growing at a faster rate than that of black men (Joint Center for Political and Economic Studies 1993). Before the passage of the Voting Rights Act, it was estimated that there were fewer than 500 black elected officials.

The VRA has also been important for the election of Latinos to national, state, and local offices. According to the National Association of Latino Elected and Appointed Officials, in 1993 there were 5,170 Latino elected and appointed officials, of which 1,554 (30.1 percent) were female. Numbers of Asian American and American Indian elected officials, excluding tribal government officials, are more difficult to identify, but there are several visible officeholders, one of whom is discussed later in this section.

The Presidency

No member of a racial or an ethnic minority has ever held the office of president of the United States, the highest office in the political system. This fact is important because although the executive branch is only one of the three branches of government, the president has an extraordinary ability to shape public policy through executive powers, as well as from the "bully pulpit" of the office. Historically, presidents have used their executive powers and powers of persuasion both to include and exclude racial minorities from the political process.

In 1830, President Andrew Jackson used his influence and authority to push his Indian Removal Bill through Congress. Jackson was successful in instituting a program of removing Indians from the southern states to provide land for expanded cotton production. Although a Supreme Court decision, *Worcester v. Georgia* (1832), ensured the sovereignty of the Cherokees, President Jackson refused to follow the decision and initiated what has been called "the Trail of Tears." The Five Civilized Tribes—Cherokee, Chickasaw, Choctaw, Creek, and Seminole—were removed from the southeastern states and forced westward to Oklahoma, then the center of what was called Indian Territory.

In 1941, President Franklin Roosevelt issued Executive Order 8802, which banned discrimination in the defense industries and the federal government on the basis of race, creed, color, or national origin, after a threatened march on Washington by blacks to protest racial discrimination in the defense industry. The executive order also created a Committee on Fair Employment Practices. Yet in 1943, Roosevelt signed Executive Order 9066, which created zones in the United States in which the military had the power to exclude people. Under this order, over 112,000 Japanese Americans who were residing in these zones were forcefully removed to "relocation" camps. Of note is the fact that German Americans and Italian Americans, whose ancestors also came from countries with which the United States was fighting in World War II, were not subjected to the same exclusion from these zones.

Lyndon B. Johnson used his knowledge of Congress and his political skill to persuade Congress to pass the Civil Rights Act of 1964 and the Voting Rights Act of 1965. More recently, President Bill Clinton invited representatives from the 545 federally recognized Indian tribes to meet at the White House to discuss Indian issues. (This number continually changes. At the end of the 103rd Congress in December 1994, the number of federally recognized tribes had risen to 551.) This was the first time since 1822 that Indians had been invited to meet officially with a U.S. president to discuss issues of concern to them.

A group of Bainbridge Island, Washington, Japanese American citizens are escorted by the Army to a Seattle dock where they are placed on trains and sent to Manzanar, California, for internment (March 1942). Friends and relatives on the bridge, soon to be evacuated, bid them farewell. Photo courtesy UPI/Bettmann.

This high-profile visit indicated a shift in the U.S. government's approach to Indian affairs.

Presidential Appointments. Presidents also send signals about their commitment to particular constituencies through the appointments they make. Four of President Clinton's initial cabinet officers were African American—Ronald Brown, secretary of commerce; Hazel O'Leary, secretary of energy; Jesse Brown, secretary for veterans's affairs; and Michael Espy, secretary of agriculture. (Although his is not offically a cabinet-level office, President Clinton informally recognizes Lee Brown, director of the Office of Drug Policy, as a cabinet-level official.) This is the largest number of blacks to serve in cabinet posts in any administration to date. President Clinton also has two Latinos as cabinet officers–Henry Cisneros, former mayor of San Antonio, Texas, is secretary of housing and urban development, and Federico Peña, former mayor of Denver,

Wallace Coffey, chairman of the Comanche Tribe of Lawson, Oklahoma, offers his hand to President Clinton following a meeting between the president and representatives of all the federally recognized tribes (April 1994). Photo courtesy Reuters/ Bettmann.

Colorado, is secretary of transportation. As with African Americans, this is the largest number of Latinos ever to serve in the cabinet.

Clinton's appointments to the lifetime positions on the federal courts have marked a "revolutionary" increase in minority group representation among a group of policymakers that prior to 1961 had included only one black male and one male who had a Mexican father (as well as two white females). As of July 1, 1994, Clinton had increased the black proportion of the federal judiciary from 5.4 percent (at the time of his election) to 7.8 percent and the Hispanic proportion from 4.0 to 4.6 percent. Asian representation remained at 0.6 percent. Clinton has also appointed the first American Indian federal judge, Billy Michael Burrage of Oklahoma (Goldman and Saranson 1994).

Given the power of the president's office and the symbolism involved in running for the position, it was only a matter of time before a nonwhite candidate would make a serious attempt to gain the office.[1] We end our discussion of the presidency by examining the 1984 and 1988 presidential candidacies of Jesse Jackson. Jackson's situation is part of the second dilemma—what do racial minorities do to gain access to the political system?

Jesse Jackson's Presidential Campaigns: 1984 and 1988. Blacks represent the largest single voting bloc within the Democratic Party, and by the early 1980s they were well integrated into the affairs of the party. Despite their integration and their placement on committees of the Democratic National Committee, many—including Jesse Jackson—questioned the level of influence blacks had within the party. There was also the emergent feeling among the black electorate that the Democratic Party was not seriously committed to furthering the advancement of blacks. This feeling, combined with the Reagan administration's negative policies and attitudes toward blacks and the perception that the Democratic Party had failed to oppose many of Reagan's initiatives, caused Jesse Jackson to seek the Democratic presidential nomination in 1984 (Tate 1993).

Jackson hoped to be the voice for those outside of the political system and to increase both his and, by inference, black influence on the policies and positions of the party. Jackson's 1984 candidacy was seen as a challenge to the Democratic Party and its leadership; it also represented a challenge and a problem to the black leadership establishment—that is, black elected officials and national civil rights leaders. His 1984 candidacy was opposed by most black elected officials—many of whom were already committed to other candidates at the point of Jackson's announcement—including most big-city black mayors and a majority of the **Congressional Black Caucus**—a group of black members of Congress who seek to exert influence and promote issues of interest to African Americans—as well as the leaders of the NAACP and the National Urban League. Jackson was also plagued by doubts regarding his ability to carry out a credible campaign, and there were fears that his candidacy would split the black vote and lead to the nomination of a conservative Democratic candidate (Smith 1990: 216).

During the 1984 campaign, Jackson pushed a progressive agenda through the concept of a **Rainbow Coalition**—a joint effort of peoples of all colors—that he hoped might become the majority in the Democratic Party. This premise was based on the assumption that the black vote, which constituted 20 percent of the Democratic Party voter coalition, could be mobilized to form the base of the Rainbow Coalition and that enough nonblacks (whites, Latinos, Asians, and American Indians) would join in a coalition with blacks to form a multiethnic "Rainbow" majority.

Jackson finished in third place, with 18 percent of the vote and 9 percent of the convention delegates, in the 1984 presidential primary and nominating process, and he received few concessions from the Democratic Party. All of his minority policy planks were defeated by the Walter Mondale forces at the national convention, and Mondale refused to meet or negotiate with Jackson until after the convention. "In 1984 Jackson's 'victories,' including his highly celebrated speech at the 1984 national convention, were largely symbolic" (Tate 1993:61).

Jackson's campaign for the presidency in 1988 contrasted sharply with the 1984 effort. Jackson gained the support of virtually the entire black leadership establishment: a majority of big-city black mayors, members of the Congressional Black Caucus, and leaders of the national civil rights organizations. "With the exception of Los Angeles Mayor Thomas Bradley and Atlanta's Andrew Young, who declared himself neutral (the latter ostensibly because of his role as convention city host); Detroit Mayor Coleman Young, who supported Mike Dukakis; and Missouri's Congressman Alan Wheat, who supported his home-state colleague, Richard Gephardt, it is difficult to think of a major national black leader that did not support Jackson's 1988 campaign" (Smith 1990:216).

In 1988 Jackson won the presidential primaries in the District of Columbia, Alabama, Georgia, Louisiana, Mississippi, and Virginia, and he won caucuses in Alaska, Delaware, Michigan, South Carolina, and Puerto Rico. By the time of the Democratic Convention, Jackson was second in a field of eight Democratic contenders; he garnered 29 percent of the primary vote compared to Dukakis's 43 percent and collected 1,105 delegates compared to Dukakis's 2,309 (Smith 1990:228). Jackson chose to focus on what political scientists call **valence issues**—issues that have universal appeal, such as anti-crime and antipoverty issues—during the 1988 campaign, and he is credited by Democrats as well as Republicans with being the campaign's most effective advocate on the issues of drug use and teens' personal responsibility regarding sex and pregnancy.

Jackson's two presidential campaigns were historic, and they marked a change in the public role blacks were ready to play in presidential politics. First, they demonstrated that black voters were prepared to support and mobilize behind one of their own, as evidenced by significantly increased black voter registration and participation in both 1984 and 1988. Second, despite the inability of Jackson's delegates to play a balance-of-power role in the choice of the party nominee in either 1984 or 1988, Jackson's two campaigns were successful in inserting progressive ideas and policy initiatives into the campaign debates on domestic and foreign policy issues—a perspective that may not have been articulated without his presence.

Congress

The U.S. Senate and the House of Representatives are the national legislative bodies. They are responsible not only for making laws but also for determining budget allocations to the entire federal government. Clearly, this body has significant influence over, and importance to, the issues of concern to racial minorities.

Levels of Representation. In 1971, black members of the House of Representatives and the one black in the Senate formed the Congressional Black Caucus in an attempt to increase the influence of blacks in the House, as well as to provide research and information support for members. The 1992 elections—the first following the reapportionment and redistricting occasioned by the 1990 census—resulted in a substantial increase in the group's membership. Carol Moseley-Braun of Illinois was elected to the Senate, the first black woman (and the first black Democrat) to serve in that body. She was the first black in the Senate since the defeat of Edward Brooke, a Massachusetts Republican, in 1978. In the 1994 elections thirty-seven blacks (listed in Table 4.1) were elected to the House of Representatives—of which nine are women and two are Republicans—plus one black female Democratic nonvoting delegate from the District of Columbia. Blacks now make up 8.5 percent of the House of Representatives.

Currently, no Latinos are serving in the U.S. Senate; the last was Joseph Montoya, a Democrat from New Mexico, who was defeated in 1976. The number of Latinos in the House jumped from ten to nineteen after the 1992 elections but dropped to seventeen (listed in Table 4.2) after the 1994 elections; Latinos now constitute 3.9 percent of House members. Three of the seventeen members are Latinas, and three are Republicans. Table 4.2 also shows the ethnic origin of the Hispanic members of Congress. Eleven of the seventeen are Mexican Americans, with the other six split evenly between Cubans and Puerto Ricans. There is also a nonvoting delegate from Puerto Rico. In 1977, Latino representatives established the **Congressional Hispanic Caucus** along lines similar to the Congressional Black Caucus (see Glossary).

There is one Asian American senator, Daniel Inouye (D-Hawaii), and one native Hawaiian, Daniel Akaka (D), who is often counted as an Asian

TABLE 4.1

Black Members of the 104th Congress, 1995–1997

Name	State	Party
Senate		
Carol Moseley-Braun	Illinois	Democrat
House of Representatives		
John Conyers	Michigan	Democrat
Barbara Collins	Michigan	Democrat
Louis Stokes	Ohio	Democrat
William Clay	Missouri	Democrat
Ron Dellums	California	Democrat
Walter Tucker	California	Democrat
Maxine Waters	California	Democrat
Julian Dixon	California	Democrat
Charles Rangel	New York	Democrat
Major Owens	New York	Democrat
Edolphus Towns	New York	Democrat
Floyd Flake	New York	Democrat
Cardiss Collins	Illinois	Democrat
Bobby Rush	Illinois	Democrat
Mel Reynolds	Illinois	Democrat
John Lewis	Georgia	Democrat
Sanford Bishop	Georgia	Democrat
Cynthia McKinney	Georgia	Democrat
Kweisi Mfume	Maryland	Democrat
Albert Wynn	Maryland	Democrat
Donald Payne	New Jersey	Democrat
Shelia Jackson Lee	Texas	Democrat
Eddie B. Johnson	Texas	Democrat
Gary Franks	Connecticut	Republican
William Jefferson	Louisiana	Democrat
Cleo Fields	Louisiana	Democrat
Chaka Fattah	Pennsylvania	Democrat
Earl Hilliard	Alabama	Democrat
Corrine Brown	Florida	Democrat
Alcee Hastings	Florida	Democrat
Carrie Meek	Florida	Democrat
Bennie Thompson	Mississippi	Democrat
Eva Clayton	North Carolina	Democrat
Melvin Watt	North Carolina	Democrat
James Clyburn	South Carolina	Democrat
Robert Scott	Virginia	Democrat
J. C. Watts	Oklahoma	Republican
Nonvoting delegate in the House		
Eleanor Holmes Norton	Washington, D.C.	Democrat

Source: Compiled by authors.

TABLE 4.2

Latino Members of the 104th Congress, 1995–1997

Name	Ethnic Origin	State	Party
Senate			
None			
House of Representatives			
Ed Pastor	Mexican	Arizona	Democrat
Xavier Beccera	Mexican	California	Democrat
Matthew Martinez	Mexican	California	Democrat
Lucile Roybal-Allard	Mexican	California	Democrat
Esteban Torres	Mexican	California	Democrat
Ileana Ros-Lehtinen	Cuban	Florida	Republican
Lincoln Dias-Balart	Cuban	Florida	Republican
Luis Gutierrez	Puerto Rican	Illinois	Democrat
Nydia Velasquez	Puerto Rican	New York	Democrat
Jose Serrano	Puerto Rican	New York	Democrat
Robert Menendez	Cuban	New Jersey	Democrat
Frank Tejeda	Mexican	Texas	Democrat
Solomon Ortiz	Mexican	Texas	Democrat
Henry Bonilla	Mexican	Texas	Republican
Henry Gonzales	Mexican	Texas	Democrat
E. K. de la Garza	Mexican	Texas	Democrat
Bill Richardson	Mexican	New Mexico	Democrat
Nonvoting delegate in the House			
Carlos Romero-Barcelo	Puerto Rican	Puerto Rico	Democrat/ Partido Nuevo Progresista[a]

[a]Partido Nuevo Progresista (PNP) is a pro-statehood party formed after a 1967 vote showed strong, but still minority, support for seeking the addition of Puerto Rico as the fifty-first state.

Source: Compiled by the authors.

American legislator. There are four Asian American members of the House of Representatives—three Democrats and one Republican—plus two nonvoting Democratic delegates, one each from Guam and American Samoa (see list in Table 4.3). In May 1994, the **Congressional Asian Pacific American Caucus** was formed, with all seven Democrats joining; the Republican, Representative Jay Kim (California) has not yet joined. Representative Patsy T. Mink (D-Hawaii) was quoted as saying that the Caucus was formed because the Asian Pacific members of Congress have felt that "we have not been consulted on im-

TABLE 4.3

Asian–Pacific Island Members of the 104th Congress, 1995–1997

Name	Ethnic Origin	State	Party
Senate			
Daniel K. Akaka	Native Hawaiian	Hawaii	Democrat
Daniel Inouye	Japanese	Hawaii	Democrat
House of Representatives			
Robert Matsui	Japanese	California	Democrat
Norm Mineta	Japanese	California	Democrat
Jay Kim	Korean	California	Republican
Patsy T. Mink	Japanese	Hawaii	Democrat
Nonvoting delegates in the House			
Robert Underwood	Chamorro	Guam	Democrat
Eni Faleomavaega	Samoan	American Samoa	Democrat

Source: Compiled by the authors.

portant steps taken by this [Clinton] administration and ones in the past" (*Washington Post*, May 22, 1994, A10)

Although the number of all of the minorities in Congress is small, none is smaller than the number of American Indians serving—one. (See Table 4.4 for a historical listing of American Indians who have served in the U.S. Senate and House of Representatives.) It may be informative, therefore, to profile the only American Indian in the Senate.

Ben Nighthorse Campbell. Senator Ben Nighthorse Campbell of Colorado was elected to the House of Representatives in 1987. He is the only member of Congress who wears a ponytail and a bolo tie. The son of a Portuguese mother and a Northern Cheyenne father, Campbell was not raised on a reservation but in California with his sister in an orphanage and a series of foster homes. The lack of a stable home situation caused him to spend a lot of time on the streets, where fighting was prevalent. As a youth he picked fruit in the Sacramento Valley, where he was befriended by Japanese children who taught him judo so he could defend himself (Clifford 1992; Nolan 1992).

Campbell fell in love with judo and perfected his skills. After graduating from San Jose State University in 1957, he moved to Japan for four years to

TABLE 4.4

American Indians Who Have Served in the U.S. Senate and House of Representatives

Name	Tribe	State	Service Years
Senate			
Matthew Stanley Quay	Abenaki or Delaware	Pennsylvania	1887–1899, 1901–1904
Charles Curtis[a]	Kaw-Osage	Kansas	1907–1913, 1915–1929
Robert L. Owen	Cherokee	Oklahoma	1907–1925
B. Nighthorse Campbell	Northern Cheyenne	Colorado	1992–
House of Representatives			
Charles Curtis	Kaw-Osage	Kansas	1893–1907
Charles D. Carter	Choctaw	Oklahoma	1907–1927
W. W. Hastings	Cherokee	Oklahoma	1915–1921, 1923–1935
William G. Stigler	Choctaw	Oklahoma	1944–1952
Benjamin Reifel	Rosebud Sioux	South Dakota	1961–1971
B. Nighthorse Campbell	Northern Cheyenne	Colorado	1987–1992

[a]Curtis served as Herbert Hoover's vice president for the period 1929–1933 and thus served as president of the Senate during that time.

Source: This information was drawn from a table developed by Gerald Wilkinson, National Indian Youth Council, provided to the authors by the office of Senator Ben Nighthorse Campbell, and data from the Congressional Research Service. This table is correct to the best of our knowledge. The Congressional Research Service indicates that the American Indian background of Quay is rumored but has not been verified.

study intensively, making additional money by acting small parts in Japanese films. Campbell won a gold medal at the Pan American Games in 1963 and captained the 1964 U.S. Olympic judo team in Tokyo. He later coached the U.S. international team (Clifford 1992).

While in Japan, Campbell also refined his Indian jewelry-making technique, and upon his return to the United States he began to market his jewelry. Sold under the name Ben Nighthorse, Campbell's Indian jewelry has made him a millionaire, with some of his pieces selling for as much as twenty thousand dollars (Clifford 1992).

Campbell served in the Colorado State Legislature from 1983 to 1986, when he ran for the U.S. House of Representatives. He was elected to the U.S. Senate in

1992. He is a fiscal conservative (he favors a balanced budget amendment and a capital gains tax cut) and a social liberal (he is fiercely pro-choice). One of his notable accomplishments in Congress has been to facilitate the changing of the name of the Custer National Monument to the Little Bighorn National Monument. There will also be a monument to the Indians who died at Little Bighorn—including Campbell's great-grandfather, a Cheyenne who rode with Crazy Horse. Campbell's commitment to correcting the history of the Little Bighorn began in 1976 when, as a member of a group of Indians who came to commemorate the one-hundredth anniversary of the battle, he was denied entrance to the battlefield. Everyone except the Indians was allowed to enter (Clifford 1992).

Campbell is also a rancher; as a member of the House he served on the House Interior Committee. His votes often placed him in conflict with environmentalists, who see him as supporting the extraction, rather than the conservation, of natural resources from public lands. Yet it is difficult to pigeonhole Campbell because he also voted in support of environmental positions when he thought they were correct in their intentions (Clifford 1992). The difficulty in categorizing Campbell was dramatically demonstrated on March 3, 1995, when he surprised everyone by announcing a switch from the Democratic to the Republican Party, while at the same time reporting that "he would continue to vote as he has in the past, which has been with the Democrats and President Clinton 78 percent of the time" (Seelye 1995:8). As Campbell said on the occasion of his switch, "I've always been considered a moderate, to the consternation of the left wing of the Democratic Party. I imagine my continued moderacy will be now to the consternation of the right wing of the Republican Party" (Seelye 1995:8). Campbell's change of partisan affiliation is generally attributed to personal conflicts within his state's Democratic Party, rather than any ideological shift.

The Supreme Court

The Supreme Court is often viewed as merely the final authority on constitutional issues, determining whether previous and current judicial decisions and legislative acts are constitutional. The Court, however, plays a much greater role because in many instances its decisions may establish new public policy. We can, therefore, view the Supreme Court as a participant in the policymaking process. For racial minority groups, the Supreme Court has been extremely important in their abilities to gain equal rights and constitutional protections. The Court is a particularly important access point for racial and ethnic minorities because victories can be won by appealing to policymakers to do what is consistent with the Constitution rather than merely what the majority wants.

U.S. Senator Ben Nighthorse Campbell, a Northern Cheyenne, is the only American Indian currently serving in the U.S. Congress.

The Supreme Court has been especially important in establishing the legal framework within which racial minorities in the United States have had to exist. Although many of the most significant decisions—both favorable and unfavorable to minority litigants—have been made in cases involving African Americans, several decisions have also been made in cases brought by other groups. It should be understood that regardless of the minority group that brings the suit, the decision often has implications for the other groups as well.

Racial diversity on the Court has been and continues to be a significant political issue each time a seat becomes available. The first black to serve on the Court was Appeals Court judge, former U.S. solicitor general, and director/counsel of the NAACP-LDF Thurgood Marshall, who was nominated by President Johnson in 1967. Marshall's confirmation hearings were held up by southern senators, particularly Strom Thurmond of South Carolina, who adamantly opposed the appointment of a black to the Court. Marshall was a liberal member of the Court led by Chief Justice Earl Warren, which issued many of the decisions that opened up the political process for racial minorities.

Marshall retired from the Court in 1991, at which time President George Bush nominated the far-right black conservative Clarence Thomas to fill the vacancy. Thomas's nomination and the subsequent opposition by a sizable segment of black Americans highlight the fact that the race of a nominee does not ensure the support of other members of the racial group. Policy positions and attitudes may be even more important to racial minorities than similarities in color. Clarence Thomas's positions on a variety of issues—for example, equal protection, privacy rights, equal employment opportunity, and access to education—run counter to what many perceive to be the best interests of black America. Thus, whereas Anita Hill's accusations of sexual harassment and the televising of the second set of confirmation hearings drew attention to Thomas's nomination, many blacks, organized groups, and individuals testified in opposition to his nomination during the first set of hearings. Marshall and Thomas are the only two racial minorities to have served on the Court to date. (Two white females, Sandra Day O'Connor and Ruth Bader Ginsberg, currently serve on the Court.)

The Bureaucracy

Although it is technically part of the executive branch, any president quickly learns that he does not control the bureaucracy. People working within agencies cannot be strictly supervised; therefore, even when the law is very specific, they must necessarily exercise discretion. For example, within U.S. urban areas the maximum speed limit is 55 miles per hour. Yet each of us has witnessed people breaking that law, and at times such transgressions are observed by law enforcement officers. If these local bureaucrats (police officers work within a bureaucracy and thus are bureaucrats) can affect the implementation of a specific policy such as speed limits, imagine the possibilities when they are charged with regulating in the public interest, detecting and prohibiting discrimination, or evaluating the work performance of subordinates—tasks assigned routinely to federal bureaucrats.

Because bureaucrats are appointed rather than elected, many people who are concerned about the representativeness of bodies such as Congress, or even with more visible nonelected bodies such as the Supreme Court, pay little attention to the composition of the bureaucracy. However, the representativeness of the bureaucracy can be important for a variety of reasons. First, such representativeness is a symbol of the openness of government. People may believe a government is legitimate if it employs people who are similar to them. Second, to the extent that people's attitudes are shaped by their socialization, a bureaucracy composed of a cross section of the nation's population will help to ensure that a full range of viewpoints will be articulated somewhere within the government. Third, to the extent that attitudes affect behavior, a more **representative bureaucracy**—one in which the demographic characteristics of the personnel mirror those of the population—may produce a more responsive bureaucracy. For example, there is evidence that black and Hispanic schoolchildren fare better when a greater number of black and Hispanic teachers, respectively, are present in their school systems (Meier and Stewart 1991; Meier, Stewart, and England 1989). Finally, citizens may be more willing to participate in government programs if the service providers are similar to them. For instance, there is evidence that HIV-infected patients, people desperately in need of bureaucratic services, clearly prefer to be served by people who share their race, gender, and sexual orientation (Thielemann and Stewart 1995).

Of course, the correspondence between the characteristics of the bureaucracy and those of the general population is not perfect. Studies from around the world, including the United States, consistently show that the middle class is overrepresented in the bureaucracy. This should not be surprising because members of the lower class generally lack the skills to perform bureaucratic tasks, and members of the upper class would not commonly engage in such activities. Further, these studies show that compared to other countries, on a variety of dimensions the United States has the world's most representative bureaucracy. To make another comparison, the federal bureaucracy much more closely mirrors the characteristics of the general population than does the "representative" legislative branch.

TABLE 4.5

Representation of Racial-National Origin Groups in Federal Civilian Workforce and Civilian Labor Force, September 1993 (in percent)

	Federal Civilian Workforce	Civilian Labor Force
Blacks	16.8	10.5
Hispanics	5.6	9.0
Asian Americans	3.6	2.9
American Indians	1.7	0.7
Whites	72.3	76.9
Totals	100.0	100.0

Source: U.S. Office of Personnel Management, 1994. *Annual Report to Congress on the Federal Equal Opportunity Recruitment Program* (Fiscal Year 1993). CE-104, January (Washington, D.C.: Career Entry Group, Office of Affirmative Recruiting and Employment), p. 6.

Beyond these generalizations, what specifically can be said about the representation of the nation's racial and ethnic minorities in the federal bureaucracy? Table 4.5 shows racial and ethnic group representation in federal civilian employment vis-à-vis that in the civilian labor force. Beyond the specifics, three points should be made. First, when compared to the general population proportions reported in Tables 2.1 and 2.2, blacks and Asian Americans are actually overrepresented in the federal bureaucracy. Second, the other groups fare poorly using the same standard. Third, blacks, Asian Americans, and American Indians are better represented among those employed in the public sector than among those who work in the private sector.

Even minority groups that are relatively well represented may not be distributed equitably within the federal bureaucracy. Table 4.6 shows the distribution of each minority racial and ethnic group across the federal pay grades. Each minority group is overrepresented at the lowest categories presented and at the two highest categories. In between, the pattern is mixed. At the next to the lowest categories, every group except Asian Americans is overrepresented. At the middle category, blacks and American Indians are notably underrepresented, Hispanics are almost perfectly represented, and Asian Americans are overrepresented.

TABLE 4.6

Distribution of Racial–National Origin Groups in Federal Civilian Workforce by Pay Grades, September 1993 (in percent)

Federal Pay Grade[a]	Total	Blacks	Hispanics	Asian Americans	American Indians
1–4	7.5	14.0	10.1	7.9	14.8
5–8	29.8	45.2	35.9	26.4	39.7
9–12	41.6	31.6	41.9	45.9	34.9
13–15	20.5	9.0	11.8	19.7	10.3
SES/SL[b]	0.6	0.2	0.2	0.2	0.3
Totals	100.0	100.0	100.0	100.0	100.0

[a]Minimum-maximum salaries for each category are as follows: 1–4, $11,903–$21,307; 5–8, $18,340–$32,710; 9–12, $27,789–$52,385; 13–15, $47,920–$86,589; SES/SL, $79,931–$115,700.

[b]Senior Executive Service and Senior Level

Source: U.S. Office of Personnel Management, 1994. *Annual Report to Congress on the Federal Equal Opportunity Recruitment Program* (Fiscal Year 1993). CE–104, January (Washington, D.C.: Career Entry Group, Office of Affirmative Recruiting and Employment), pp. 12, 15, 18, 21.

In sum, it appears that the federal bureaucracy—despite its problems—is more open to minority employment than the private sector, which bodes well for an improvement in the way minorities are treated by the government. In addition, the trends appear to be positive for minorities moving into higher levels of the bureaucracy, which is one of the most viable avenues available for upward mobility. But we must remember that effective public policymaking also requires action in the states.

Federalism

The final structural feature of American government to be discussed, one that has had a major impact on racial and ethnic minorities, is the division of powers between the national and state governments—federalism. Although the two levels share some powers—concurrent powers—it is in the areas in which the powers do not overlap that minorities have most been affected. Multiple levels of government create multiple access points, which is both good and bad. People who want change have ample opportunity to petition the government; so, too, do people who oppose change. The result is that the outcome of policy disputes depends as much on the locus of decisions—jurisdictional issues—as it does on the merits of policy proposals.

Much of the struggle over policies that affect racial and ethnic minorities in the United States hinges on the federal structure. As was seen in the earlier discussions of the Constitution and voting rights, the fact that policy decisions have been made in the states assured that those engaged in discrimination would be judging themselves. The Supreme Court, in a series of decisions, permitted this situation to exist. In the *Slaughterhouse Cases* (1873) the Court ruled that U.S. citizens had dual citizenship, national and local, and that the Fourteenth Amendment defended citizens' rights only against laws adopted by the national government and not against state governments' incursions. The decision in *U.S. v. Reese* (1876) interpreted the Fifteenth Amendment as allowing states to impose various criteria, including literacy tests, on prospective voters. In the *Civil Rights Cases* (1883) the Court voided the 1875 Civil Rights Act, ruling that the national government could not interfere with the private actions of individuals within states. And in *U.S. v. Harris* (1883) the Court struck down the Ku Klux Klan Act because it applied to the "private activities" of individuals. Taken together, these decisions allowed states to infringe on the civil rights of citizens, especially minority citizens.

It was not until the 1960s that states' rights arguments against minority civil rights were apparently overridden. Basing its authority on the commerce clause of the Constitution, the Civil Rights Act of 1964 asserted authority over what had previously been thought to be part of the "private" sector, access to "public" accommodations—buses, waiting rooms, restaurants, and hotels. Furthermore, as detailed later, increased reliance of local educational systems on federal funding gave the national government heretofore unknown leverage in achieving school desegregation in the states that had maintained de jure discrimination.

The post-1964 era was qualitatively different in terms of civil rights policy than the decades that preceded it. Richard Nixon represents an important breakpoint because he showed that one could win the presidency by not being overtly racist but by allowing civil rights opponents to believe he agreed with them. The trend that started with Nixon reached its fruition with the Reagan and Bush administrations, during which enforcement responsibilities were left to the states. Who are the state policymakers?

State Elective Office

At the state level, as of 1993 the largest numbers of black elected officials were found in ten states—Mississippi (751), Alabama (699), Louisiana (636), Georgia (545), Texas (472), North Carolina (468), Illinois (465), South Carolina (450), Arkansas (380), and Michigan (333). With the exception of Illinois and Michigan, the other states are covered by the Voting Rights Act. L. Douglas Wilder, whose term ended in January 1994, served as governor of Virginia, and the 1994 elections brought the total of blacks elected to statewide office to 18 (down from a high of 21), which includes the comptroller of New York state (a Democrat) and the secretary of state of Colorado (a Republican). In addition to Governor Wilder, African Americans who have held statewide offices include Merv Dymally and George Brown, former lieutenant governors of California and Colorado, respectively; Roland Burris, comptroller of Illinois and currently state attorney general; James Lewis, treasurer of New Mexico; and Ed Brooke, Republican senator from Massachusetts.

Latinos have also had success in electing individuals to statewide offices. As of 1994, the largest numbers of Latino elected officials were found in nine states—Texas (2,215), Illinois (881), California (796), New Mexico (716), Arizona (341), Colorado (201), New York (83), Florida (64), and New Jersey (37). The state with the highest number of Latina elected officials is Illinois, where 68.1 percent of the 881 Latino elected officials are female. Latinos have served as governors of New Mexico (Democrats Ezequiel Cabeza de Baca, 1917, Tony Anaya, 1983–1987, Jerry Apodaca, 1975–1979, and Democrat-turned-Republican Octavian Ambrosio Larrazolo, 1919–1921), Arizona (Democrat Raul Castro, 1975–1977), and Florida (Republican Robert Martinez, 1987–1991); the current state attorney general in Texas, Dan Morales, is also Latino.

Asians–Pacific Americans have served as the governor of Hawaii, the lieutenant governors of Delaware and Hawaii, the secretary of state in California, and in fifty-four state legislative seats in Hawaii. To date, Asian electoral successes have been regional rather than national (Nakanishi 1991).

American Indian successes at the statewide level have been even more rare than those of Asians. Larry EchoHawk, a Democrat and a Pawnee Indian, has served in the Idaho state legislature and as attorney general but failed in his 1994 run for governor of that state. American Indians serve in the state legislatures of New Mexico (four in the House, two in the Senate), Arizona (two and one, respectively), Oklahoma (one in the Senate), Washington (one in the House), South Dakota (two in the House and one in the Senate), Minnesota (one in the Senate), Montana (two in the House), North Carolina (one in the House), and Alaska (four in each).

Table 4.7 shows the state distribution, tribal and party affiliations, and first year in office of American Indian–Alaskan Native state legislators. Although we lacked the data in Chapter 3 decisively to categorize American Indians as either Democrats or Republicans, such is not the case for those elected to state legislative offices, an overwhelming majority of which are Democrats. The tribe with the largest number of representatives is the Navajo, but this may be a function of the fact that the Navajo Nation is located in parts of four states, two of which are Arizona and New Mexico.

How does this representation work within the federal system to produce public policy? We now turn to an example of this.

Equal Educational Opportunity

The struggle over equal educational opportunity provides a good example of the way the policymaking process within the federal system produces and thwarts policy change. Denial of such opportunity has been and continues to be a serious problem for members of the nation's racial and ethnic minority groups because it has important implications for one's chances for social mobility. The "American dream" of hard work being rewarded with higher income—which allows one access to better-quality housing, health care, and recreational opportunities—has always been, and is now even more, predicated on training or education. The way this works is not a mystery. Access to many jobs and to the professions, positions with greater responsibility and higher pay, is limited to those with higher levels of educational attainment. Unfortunately, education systems do not have a strong record of providing effective education for racial and ethnic minorities. Schools serve as "sorting machines" (Spring 1989), separating students into different categories based on a number of criteria—including race and ethnicity—and providing different groups of students with educations of different quality.

Blacks

When the U.S. Supreme Court accepted the "separate but equal" interpretation of the Equal Protection Clause of the Constitution (*Plessy v. Ferguson* 1896) and then soon made a decision that ignored the "but equal" part of the phrase in public education (*Cumming v. County Board of Education* 1899), racially segregated schools were legitimized. What followed was a long war, waged in courtrooms primarily by the legal arm of the NAACP, the NAACP Legal Defense and Educational Fund—the "Ink Fund"—in an attempt to overturn this momentous decision.

TABLE 4.7

American Indian–Alaska Native State Legislators, 1995

State	Body	Name	Tribe	Party	First Year in Office
Arizona	House	Jack Jackson	Navajo	Democrat	1985
		Ben Hamley	Navajo	Democrat	1972
	Senate	James Henderson	Navajo	Democrat	1982
Alaska	House	Lyman Hoffman	Yupic-Eskimo	Democrat	1986
		Eileen MacLean	Inupiag-Eskimo	Democrat	1988
		Irene Nicholai	Athabascan	Democrat	1992
		Bill Williams	Tlingit	Democrat	1980
	Senate	Al Adams	Inupaic	Democrat	1980
		George Jackow	Athabascan	Democrat	1993
		Georgiana Lincoln	Athabascan	Democrat	1992
		Fred Zahroff	Russian-Aleut	Democrat	1984
Minnesota	Senate	Harold Finn	Ojibwa	Democrat	1990
Montana	House	Jay Stovall	Crow	Republican	1993
		George Heavy Runner	Blackfoot	Democrat	1994
New Mexico	House	Leo Watchman	Navajo	Democrat	1993
		Tom Atcitty	Navajo	Democrat	1981
		Linda Morgan	Navajo	Democrat	1989
		James R. Madalena	Jemez Pueblo	Democrat	1985
	Senate	John Pinto	Navajo	Democrat	1977
		Leonard Tsosie	Navajo	Democrat	1993
North Carolina	House	Ronnie Sutton	Lumbee	Democrat	1991
Oklahoma	Senate	Kelley Haney	Seminole Creek	Democrat	1987
South Dakota	House	Ron Volesky	Standing Rock Sioux	Democrat	1980
		Richard Hagen	Ogalala Sioux	Democrat	1982
	Senate	Paul Valandra	Rosebud Sioux	Democrat	1990
Washington	House	Stan Flemming	Cherokee	Democrat	1992

Source: Compiled by the authors.

The Ink Fund, operating in an environment of uncertainty about how far courts were willing to go in reinterpreting the law and functioning with limited resources, adopted an incremental strategy. Litigation was seen as a means of minimizing costs while pursuing a benefit—education—that would improve the economic position of blacks, sometimes immediately and, at the least, in the long run. Litigation was also viewed as a way of testing and shaping public opinion that could facilitate policy change, of increasing the costs of maintaining segregation, and of mobilizing the black community. Any positive decision could be declared a victory in an attempt to assist in the mobilization effort (Tushnet 1987:2–14, 33–69).

Strategically, the Ink Fund focused on three types of cases—desegregation of public graduate and professional schools, salary equalization suits, and facility equalization suits. Attorneys won Supreme Court declarations that a black applicant to the University of Missouri Law School had the same right to an opportunity for legal education as whites within the state (*Missouri ex rel. Gaines v. Canada* 1938) and that the pay differential between black and white teachers in the Norfolk public school system violated even *Plessy* (*Alston v. School Board of Norfolk* 1940); in spite of these victories, separate but equal remained the law. The Ink Fund effectively used courts as alternatives to legislatures in the pursuit of policy change (Tushnet 1987:32–42, 59–81).

But the limited types of cases pursued by the Ink Fund meant that at some point the organization would have to change strategies. With case law in these areas having been developed as extensively as possible, unless the organization established and pursued new goals the basic problem—*Plessy*—would remain. Realization of this fact led to the adoption of a direct challenge to segregation that resulted in the Supreme Court's reversal of the *Plessy* decision in *Brown v. Board of Education* (1954, 1955). In this case, the Court consolidated appeals from Kansas, South Carolina, and Virginia; accelerated an appeal from Delaware; and declared unanimously that separate schools, segregated by race, were "inherently unequal." The Ink Fund and the U.S. Supreme Court had combined to construct a new definition of equality and to make that new definition public policy (Tushnet 1987:142–161).

At that point, policymaking in the area of equal educational opportunity shifted from a focus on overturning a loathsome judicial precedent to implementing a favorable one. Initial euphoria led to overly optimistic predictions about the speed with which segregated school systems could be dismantled. Thurgood Marshall, the victorious attorney in the *Brown* case, thought it might take "up to five years" for segregation to be eradicated, but he was sure that by the "100th Anniversary of the Emancipation Proclamation [in 1963]

... segregation in all its forms [will have been] eliminated" (quoted in Cruse 1987:25–26).

Reality, of course, was quite different. Encouraged by an implementation decree that called for desegregation with "all deliberate speed" and "at the ear-liest possible date," opponents of the Court's order expended massive amounts of energy deliberating and virtually no time moving quickly. Many could not envision a possible implementation date. Furthermore, the vast majority of deliberations focused on ways to evade the intent of the *Brown* decision rather than on ways to comply with that intent.

In the face of this resistance, implementation efforts were inconsistent. In federal district courts, the scenes of most of the desegregation battles, results varied. For example, whereas Judge Frank Johnson (Alabama) sought to im-plement *Brown* conscientiously, refusing to let the Court's "authority and dig-nity ... be bent and swayed by ... politically-generated whirlwinds" (*In re Wallace* 1959:121), that same year Judge T. Whitfield Davidson (Texas) lec-tured black plaintiffs from the bench, saying that "the white man has a right to maintain his racial integrity and it can't be done so easily in integrated schools" (quoted in Peltason 1971:119). When the Fifth Circuit Court of Appeals, which heard most of the desegregation cases, remanded cases to these lower courts, the judges often found ways to further subvert the intent of *Brown*. By March 1961, for instance, district judges' opinions in the Dallas school desegregation case had already been reversed six times. Clearly, the appellate courts had diffi-culty establishing uniform standards at the trial court level.

Nor was support from the executive or legislative branches immediately forth-coming. President Eisenhower declared that he would not presume "that the judi-cial branch of government is incapable of implementing the Supreme Court's de-cision" (quoted in Peltason 1971:50); when he sent troops to Little Rock to help desegregate the schools there, his action was more unusual than it was typical. Presidential actions are generally explicable in terms of electoral rationality: "When presidential candidates faced an electoral imperative to seek blacks' votes, blacks finally began to gain allies in their struggle against a segregated second-class citizenship enforced by the laws of many states" (Robertson and Judd 1989:168).

Congress was even less supportive than the executive branch. Nearly all of the southern members, fearful of electoral repercussions if the *Brown* decision were implemented, signed the infamous **Southern Manifesto,** a declaration de-crying the decision (Lewis 1965:39). Only when its typical inertia was out-weighed by a combination of shifting public opinion—prompted at least in part by media coverage of the civil rights movement—the assassination of President Kennedy, the strong leadership of a southern-born President Lyndon

Johnson, and an influx of new members swept into office in the 1964 elections did Congress overcome its usual timidity and enact significant legislation (Sundquist 1968).

This legislation took the form of the 1964 Civil Rights Act (see Orfield 1969). With this legislation, some of the responsibility for desegregation efforts shifted to the bureaucracy, to what was then the Department of Health, Education, and Welfare (HEW), which provided the department with a little noticed but powerful tool—the power to cut off federal funds to school districts that practiced discrimination. That power, in conjunction with increased federal funds flowing to local school districts following the passage of the Elementary and Secondary Education Act of 1965, gave HEW the leverage it needed to begin to make significant changes. The Office for Civil Rights (OCR), the agency within HEW charged with enforcement responsibilities, and the federal courts gradually tightened the ratchet on school districts so that by fall 1970 school districts in the South were more desegregated than those in any other part of the country. This massive change occurred because of bureaucratic and judicial pressure, and it happened in spite of President Nixon's electoral "southern" strategy (Panetta and Gall 1971; *Alexander v. Holmes* 1969; *Green v. New Kent County School Board* 1968; *U.S. v. Georgia* 1969).

In our federal system, because the national government does not actually operate an education system, the ultimate responsibility for providing equal educational opportunity lies with local school officials. For elected local officials the calculus in the desegregation process was similar to that for other elected officials. For example, elected school superintendents in Georgia resisted desegregation more vigorously than did their appointed counterparts for fear they would lose their positions (Rodgers and Bullock 1976:64–65).

Hispanics

In the Hispanic community equal educational opportunity issues generally paralleled those of black Americans but were resolved much later. As relatively late arrivals in the United States, Puerto Ricans and Cubans were not the pathbreakers in Hispanic equal educational opportunity battles. That role was played by Mexican Americans.

Mexican Americans, although not subject to separate but equal laws in quite the same way as blacks, were routinely denied access to education or received only an inferior segregated education. "Mexican-only" schools, established by local school boards, were present in Texas at the advent of the twentieth century (Rangel and Alcala 1972). In California, segregated Mexican schools were established as soon as a locale had enough students to hold classes.

As the twentieth century progressed, the policy of limited education evolved into one of Americanization—of transforming Mexican Americans into "Americans." Although these assimilationist pressures came from the state level, local officials often took actions that were at odds with these forces. Compulsory school attendance laws were often ignored if Mexican American children were involved. These children were counted in the school census that was used to obtain funds from the state of Texas, but local school districts did not need to spend money on truant children. Even if Mexican American children did attend schools, funds were not apportioned on an even remotely equitable basis. The provision of unequal education was possible because most school districts established separate classes for Mexican Americans within Anglo-dominated schools. Such segregation was based on local school board policies rather than on constitutional or statutory grounds, as was the case with blacks (San Miguel 1987:33–37, 47–55).

In some areas that had few Mexican American students, segregating students was too expensive and awkward. Even in districts with officially segregated schools, segregation was not total (Wollenberg 1978:111–117). Integration might be allowed on the basis of "apparent prosperity, cleanliness, the aggressiveness of parents, and the quota of Mexican-Americans already in the mixed school" (Tuck 1946:185–186). Segregation was less common at the secondary school level because (1) the Americanization rationale no longer held (if students were to be Americanized, the process should have occurred in the elementary grades), (2) many school districts could not afford two secondary schools, and (3) the Mexican American dropout rate was so high that few Hispanic students stayed in school that long (Wollenberg 1978:117–118).

Even in the 1950s many Mexican American students were offered a segregated education, either through separate schools or within formally desegregated schools. Postwar protests by Mexican Americans and the 1947 repeal of the California statute that made it legal to segregate an ethnic group had no impact on segregation (although Mexican Americans were not specifically mentioned in the code [Cooke 1971]; see *Romero v. Weakley* 1955:836). Intraschool segregation was taken to such lengths, for example, that Mexican American and Anglo junior high school graduates sometimes held ceremonies on separate days (Weinberg 1977:286).

For Hispanics, the litigation campaign challenging segregated schools was spearheaded by the League of United Latin American Citizens (LULAC). LULAC's initial challenge against segregation was a class action suit brought against the Del Rio, Texas, Independent School District, alleging that Mexican American students were being denied equal protection under the law as stated in the U.S. Constitution by being placed in segregated facilities (*Independent School District v. Salvatierra* 1930). For the first time in history "the courts were asked . . . to determine the constitutionality of the actions of a local school district with respect to the education of Mexican Americans" (San Miguel 1987:78). The court agreed that Mexican Americans could not be segregated simply because of their ethnicity but found that the school board was not engaged in this practice. The school board could continue to segregate Mexican Americans on the grounds of irregular attendance and, more important, language, which the court found permissible on educational grounds. Thus, its first foray into the courts was unsuccessful, and LULAC resolved to emphasize other tactics (San Miguel 1987:81).

Litigation was not used again until 1945, when LULAC came to the aid of several Mexican Americans who were challenging the segregation of Spanish-speaking pupils in Orange County, California. LULAC alleged denial of equal protection, and a favorable ruling was obtained and upheld in the Circuit Court of Appeals (Mendez v. Westminster School District 1946, 1947). For the first time in history a federal court found segregation of Mexican Americans in public schools to be a violation of state law and a denial of the equal protection clause of the U.S. Constitution. This latter finding meant the decision was relevant to Mexican Americans elsewhere. Thus, the attorney general of Texas issued an opinion banning segregation of Mexican American students except for "language deficiencies and other individual needs and aptitudes demonstrated by examination or properly conducted tests . . . through the first three grades" (quoted in San Miguel 1987:120). The amount of actual change, however, varied. In Texas, with the absence of implementation guidelines, segregation continued. In California, many school systems desegregated, but de facto segregation in large urban areas led one observer to suggest that Mexican American students in California were more segregated in 1973 than they had been prior to Mendez in 1947 (Wollenberg 1978:132–134).

The legal battle shifted back to Texas in 1948. LULAC, in conjunction with a newly organized group of Hispanic World War II veterans, the American G.I. Forum, supported a lawsuit by several Mexican American parents charging officials in several central Texas school districts with unconstitutional segregation. The decision in this case, *Delgado et al. v. Bastrop Independent School District of Bastrop County et al.* (1948), enjoined local school officials from segregating Mexican American students. The decision in *Delgado* went beyond the one in *Mendez* to clarify that segregation of Mexican American students, even in the absence of articulated regulations or policies, was not permissible. The decision also held state school officials responsible for "condoning or aiding" the segregation of Mexican Americans. Unlike the aftermath of *Mendez,* implementation guidelines were issued by the state superintendent of public instruction,[2] but the results were much the same—massive noncompliance. When pressure from the Mexican American community convinced the state superintendent to withdraw the accreditation of the noncompliant Del Rio school district, the state legislature abolished that position and appointed another person to the newly created position of commissioner of education. It should be no surprise that the new commissioner was less than energetic about dismantling the dual schools for Mexican Americans and Anglos; in fact, his first decision was to reverse the disaccreditation of the Del Rio schools (San Miguel 1987:125–130).[3]

Throughout the 1950s—particularly after the *Brown* decision struck down segregation of blacks—cases were brought before the judiciary, occasionally resulting in a favorable decision or settlement. In *Hernandez v. Driscoll Consolidated Independent School District* (1957), the court found that Hispanics had been unconstitutionally assigned to separate classes on the basis of ancestry, but it allowed them to be assigned to such classes if they lacked English-language skills.[4] The actual dismantling of dual schools for Anglos and Mexican Americans was rare, and litigation was again temporarily abandoned as a tactic by Hispanic interest groups because of its perceived futility (Rangel and Alcala 1972:345).

Litigation was revived as a major tactic in support of equal educational opportunity for Mexican Americans with the formation of the **Mexican American Legal Defense and Education Fund (MALDEF)** in 1968 (O'Connor and Epstein 1984). MALDEF participated in litigation that covered a wide range of issues, but education was an important focus.

The type of education litigation most frequently undertaken sought to eliminate segregated schools. Segregation was a necessary focus for MALDEF because OCR, the federal government's school desegregation enforcement agency, had originally treated Hispanics as whites for desegregation purposes; thus, they could remain segregated without arousing federal interest. In addition, local school districts could send both black and Hispanic students to the same schools to achieve some "desegregation," leaving other schools all Anglo (Rangel and Alcala 1972:365–372).

This policy changed formally in 1970 when Stanley Pottinger of OCR announced that the agency would henceforth be concerned with discrimination on the basis of national origin. As this applied to school districts, the memo

stated: "Where inability to speak and understand the English language excludes national origin minority group children from effective participation in
the educational program offered by a school district, the district must take affirmative steps to rectify the language deficiency in order to open its instructional program to these students" (quoted in Weinberg 1977:287).

A second weapon MALDEF needed in the fight against segregation was provided by the courts in *Cisneros v. Corpus Christi Independent School District*
(1970). In this case, which was not filed by MALDEF, the plaintiffs asked the
court to apply the principles of *Brown* to Mexican Americans. Such a finding
would require that Mexican Americans be recognized by the courts as a separate class. The U.S. District Court obliged, and for the first time in history
Mexican Americans were declared to be an identifiable group within public
school systems and were protected by the Fourteenth Amendment.

The thrill of victory was short-lived, however, because that same month the
Fifth Circuit Court of Appeals handed down a decision in the Houston desegregation case that allowed local authorities to treat Mexican Americans as
whites for desegregation purposes, leaving Anglos unaffected by the process
(*Ross v. Eckels* 1970). Another decision allowed school officials in Miami to
consider Cubans as whites for desegregation purposes (Orfield 1978:203).
Thus, the task facing MALDEF was to obtain higher court acceptance of the
Cisneros decision. In pursuit of this goal, MALDEF filed amicus curiae briefs
in a number of Mexican American school desegregation cases pending before
the Fifth Circuit. MALDEF's position was basically that "we want to know
where we stand" (quoted in San Miguel 1987:180).

The Fifth Circuit, in appeals from Corpus Christi and Austin cases, found
that Mexican Americans were an identifiable group that had been denied their
constitutional rights in these instances (*Cisneros v. Corpus Christi Independent
School District* 1971; *U.S. v. Texas Education Agency* 1972). MALDEF obtained
a victory, but the waters were still muddy. An intracircuit difference of opinion
existed that had to be resolved.

The resolution came in *Keyes*, the Denver desegregation case decided in
1973. The decision in this case, which had been filed by blacks, required that
the court take a position on the status of Mexican Americans. Denver had
significant populations of blacks, Anglos, and Hispanics, so the court had
either to lump Hispanics with Anglos or to recognize Hispanics as a separate
group. The latter choice would have led to the conclusion that Hispanics
had also been illegally segregated and would have required a plan to desegregate them as well. The U.S. Supreme Court decided that Mexican
Americans were an identifiable minority group and that they were constitu-

tionally entitled to recognition as such for desegregation purposes (*Keyes v. School District No. 1, Denver, Colorado* 1973). School officials in systems found to be unconstitutionally segregated could not treat Hispanics as whites for the purpose of desegregation. Subsequent decisions extended the logic of Keyes to Puerto Ricans in New York and Boston (*Hart v. Community School Board of Brooklyn District #2* 1974:733; *Morgan v. Hennigan* 1974: 415).

The *Keyes* case did not spawn an abundance of Hispanic desegregation. Even though Hispanics as a whole were more segregated than blacks in the mid-1970s (National Institute of Education 1977; Orfield 1978:205–206), MALDEF turned its attention from desegregation to other methods of achieving equal educational opportunities. The remedy MALDEF stressed in its fight was **bilingual education**—the idea that non-English-speaking students should be taught in their native language or be taught English. But the legal groundwork for movement in bilingual education was laid not by Hispanics but by Asians.

Asians

The situation of Asians in U.S. education systems has generally been one of discrimination. For example, the Supreme Court, in *Gong Lum v. Rice* (1927), upheld Mississippi's exclusion of Asian Americans from white schools. School segregation did not exist only to separate blacks from whites but to separate Asians from whites as well.

Given the population concentrations of Asians, their situation can best be exemplified by the history of Chinese Americans in San Francisco schools. As soon as there was a significant number of Chinese taxpayers in San Francisco, the Chinese community pressed local authorities to fund public education for their children. Only when the number of Chinese youths increased to one that could not be ignored did the local school board respond, and then it provided a segregated education. Even under these conditions, Americanization was remarkably successful. But obtaining access for Chinese children to the education system required a constant struggle with state and local legislative and education agencies from the mid-nineteenth century onward (Low 1982).

More dramatic than legislation or administrative action in its impact on policy was a case filed on behalf of Chinese students in San Francisco. In *Lau v. Nichols* (1974), the Supreme Court required that school districts "take affirmative steps to rectify the language deficiency [of national origin minority students] . . . to open [their] instructional program[s] to these students." The

Court found that the failure of school districts to provide non-English-speaking students—in this case twenty-eight hundred Chinese students—with instruction they could understand denied them their right to an equal educational opportunity. The court required that the school district take action but stopped short of mandating bilingual education.

American Indians

U.S. educational policy toward Indians since the nineteenth century had been to create separate boarding schools, removing children from their home areas to see that they received a "proper" education. Although approximately seventy of these schools still exist, policy has changed considerably. In 1969, a Special Senate Subcommittee on Indian Education found that "national policies for educating American Indians are a failure of major proportions. They have not offered Indian children—either in years past or today—an educational opportunity anywhere near equal to that offered the great bulk of American children" (U.S. Senate 1969:163). Although nothing was done immediately to address this situation, the Indian Education Act of 1972 increased funding for Indian education, and the Indian Self-Determination and Education Assistance Act of 1975 and the Education Amendments Act of 1978 sought to promote "Indian control of Indian affairs in all matters relating to education" (25 U.S. Code § 2010). Today, approximately 80 percent of American Indian schoolchildren attend public schools in the communities in which they live.

American Indian children are also covered by the *Lau* decision. Rather than attempting to eliminate the use of tribal languages, in seventeen states bilingual education programs are offered to American Indian children who only speak their tribal language. Even where full-fledged bilingual-bicultural programs have not been required, tutors have been provided for such children (*Guadalupe Organization, Inc. v. Tempe Elementary School District* 1978).

Continuing Issues

With the provision of equal educational opportunity left in the hands of the same local officials who had operated dual school systems, we should not be surprised that discrimination continues. Three issues—bilingual education, resegregation, and second-generation discrimination—demand attention.

Bilingual Education. Even though bilingualism was given its impetus by litigation involving Chinese students, Hispanics are clearly the largest group of potential beneficiaries. The National Center for Education Statistics (1978) reports that 70 percent of the estimated 3.6 million children in the United States with limited English proficiency are Hispanic.

Problems with implementing bilingual education programs quickly became apparent. MALDEF's plan for a bilingual-bicultural educational program in a desegregated Denver school system was rejected as working at cross-purposes with desegregation (*Keyes v. School District No. 1, Denver, Colorado* 1973:480): "Bilingual education . . . is not a *substitute* for desegregation" [emphasis in the original]. Although bilingual programs could be part of a remedy for unconstitutional segregation, the court did not believe they could be a remedy in and of themselves (Fernández and Guskin 1981:113). Thereafter, court decisions generally chose between desegregation—that is, dispersing students throughout a school system—and bilingual programs, which seemed to promote segregation based on language or national origin (for an example of the latter, see *Serna v. Portales Municipal Schools* 1974), although in some cases the court did adopt a bilingual education plan as part of a remedy for segregation (see *Bradley v. Milliken* 1975:1144).

Although MALDEF remained nominally committed to both desegregation and bilingualism (Orfield 1978:211–214), it emphasized the establishment of bilingual classes. Hispanic students boycotting East Los Angeles high schools in 1968 asked for bilingual programs rather than desegregation (Wollenberg 1978:134–135). And when OCR struck at discrimination against Hispanics, bilingualism was often the preferred remedy, even if segregation remained (Orfield 1978:207).

The **Puerto Rican Legal Defense and Education Fund (PRLDEF)**, a relative latecomer to Hispanics' civil rights struggle, never argued for desegregation. Perhaps because language and culture are more salient for Puerto Ricans, and perhaps because Puerto Ricans are concentrated in urban areas where desegregation is impractical because of the scarcity of Anglos, bilingualism was the organization's primary goal from the beginning. PRLDEF sued or intervened in cases in New York City; New Jersey; Boston; Wilmington, Delaware; Buffalo; Philadelphia; and Waterbury, Connecticut. It negotiated an out-of-court settlement to establish the nation's largest bilingual education program in the New York City school system (Orfield 1978:211–217). The general thrust of legal intervention had become even more specific by the late 1970s. When Hispanic legal organizations took action, they usually intervened in cases at the remedy stage for or in defense of bilingual programs.

In the wake of *Lau*, OCR used its regulatory authority to require that school districts test non-English-speaking students and place them in bilingual education programs. Despite provisions designed to prevent the "existence of racially/ethnically identifiable classes" within such programs (Teitelbaum and Hiller 1977:160), segregation remains common. Segregated bilingual programs are prevalent because

1. Affected students normally attend schools that have considerable segregation.
2. Although OCR has brought heavy enforcement pressure on school systems to provide bilingualism, it has done virtually nothing about desegregation.
3. The regulations in the various programs are filled with loopholes that are so large they make a mockery of the policy statements about segregation. The regulations permit segregating groups defined by linguistic ability when local school officials say doing so is educationally necessary.

"In practice there has been almost routine segregation at the local level and no federal enforcement of integration policies" (Orfield 1978:220).

Resegregation. Blatant segregation remained the policy in some "desegregated" school systems—within classrooms (sometimes reinforced by room dividers), on buses, in lunchrooms, and in extracurricular activities (American Friends Service Committee et al. 1970). But these overt practices gradually stopped as a result of litigation or simply because of the inconvenience of maintaining such awkward policies.

However, more recent evidence suggests that resegregation is occurring. Southern schools were the most fully desegregated schools in the nation by fall 1970, and the level of integration remained fairly stable until 1988. But after that date, racial segregation began to increase once again. The segregation of Latino students is also on the rise. During the 1991–1992 school year, almost two-thirds (66 percent) of black students and almost three-fourths (73.4 percent) of Latino students attended predominantly minority schools. Slightly over one-third of both groups (33.9 percent of blacks, 34 percent of Latinos) attended schools with a greater than 90 percent minority enrollment. Put another way, the typical black student attended a school with a 34.4 percent white enrollment; the typical Latino student attended a school with a 31.2 percent white enrollment (Orfield 1993).

Second-Generation Discrimination. Even if schools are desegregated, such desegregation is not necessarily synonymous with the provision of equal educational opportunity. The "quality of desegregation varies as much as [the] quantity" (Hochschild 1984:33). More invidious has been the rise of more subtle means of minimizing interracial contact, which we refer to collectively as second-generation discrimination. Often in conjunction with desegregation, school systems have adopted or expanded the scope of ability grouping of students and have concentrated minority students in lower-level academic groups (Meier, Stewart, and England 1989). Such racial concentration might be justified as remedial action for the provision of inferior education in segregated schools, but the evidence from education research shows that "minority students are highly overrepresented in a situation that perpetuates their disadvantage. . . . [They] are resegregated, provided with an inferior educational experience compared to that of their peers, stigmatized by staff and other students—in short, placed in learning environments that do little to close the gap in minority-majority achievement levels" (Simmons and Brady 1981:132).

Likewise, disciplinary practices can be used for purposes other than maintaining order and authority. Such practices are sometimes "a mere pretense for punishing a child for other reasons," including being black, Hispanic, or poor (Children's Defense Fund 1974:130, also 1975). "Black students are punished for offenses allowed white students or given heavier penalties for similar offenses" (Eyler, Cook, and Ward 1983:144).

Conclusion

This chapter provides a glimpse of the different stages of the public policymaking process and the interaction of the various institutional actors, operating within a federal system, in that process. The crucial hurdle for racial and ethnic minority groups has been getting issues placed on the agenda of a government institution, and the presence of minority group representatives within an institution can facilitate that step. Some progress has been made in increasing minority group representation across institutions at all levels of government.

The case study of equal educational opportunity policy reveals the evolution of the policy problem. The problem was originally defined as constituting the legally mandated racial segregation of black and white students in southern schools. It was presumed that once black and white students entered the same school buildings, the equal educational opportunity problem would be solved. Yet it was discovered that students of other racial and ethnic groups were also denied this opportunity.

The complexity of the American public policymaking system is also illustrated here. The courts, prodded by interest groups, took the lead in defining the problem and articulating a policy, but they found themselves so far ahead of the executive and legislative branches that their decisions could not be implemented. The courts provided a forum in which the pro–civil rights coalition could appeal to "right" rather than to political power. And the conflict could be overt because the U.S. legal system is adversarial yet muted, because the format of the conflict is stylized.

Changes external to the policy subsystem were definitely of major importance in the outcome of the conflict. If E. E. Schattschneider (1960:2) is correct that "the *audience* determines the outcome of a fight" [emphasis in the original], then the mass media served to change immensely the size and composition of that audience. The expansion of the availability and use of mass media meant the audience for the conflict was no longer strictly local and that it was more independently informed than had been the case when similar issues had previously been decided.

Local officials, who had to implement the policy change within the federal system, were able to thwart a momentous Supreme Court decision. Only when the legislature finally adopted a supportive policy, thus empowering the bureaucracy to participate in implementation, did significant policy change occur.

The accomplishments of those who fought the battles are monumental. Yet by defining the policy problem in terms of segregation, a solution was also defined: When schools were desegregated, success would be achieved. Subsequent experience has shown dramatically that segregated schools were only the symptom, not the disease. But in the minds of many, when schools in which de jure discrimination had existed were desegregated, it was time to focus on other policy problems. The results of this evolution of the policy process include an inertia and a lack of consensus about whether equal educational opportunity is being provided in this country and how one would recognize such opportunity if one saw it.

5

···

Coalition or Competition?
Patterns of Interminority
Group Relations

A knife is found plunged into the desk of a Japanese
American shop steward, accompanied by the message
"Go home, Jap."

Stanford, Calif., May 17, 1993

MANIFEST CHANGES have occurred and continue to occur in the demographics of most major cities in the United States. Whereas we once referred to urban political dynamics in terms of whites versus blacks, today Latinos, increasing numbers of Asians, and—to a lesser extent—Indians have been added to the mix. These demographic changes have not only altered the political dynamics of urban politics but have also created a new context for relationships among the various racial groups which may take the form of coalition, conflict, or mutual nonrecognition. The continuing second dilemma faced by racial minorities in American society is represented by the question posed by Rodney King at his first postverdict news conference in the wake of the 1992 Los Angeles riots—"Can we all get along?" What options within the American political system are available to members of minority groups, and what are the consequences of pursuing each of these options? Is it feasible for blacks, Latinos, Asians, and Indians to form coalitions to attain political outcomes? Or is it more common for the goals and objectives of these groups to be in conflict? The debate over biracial coalition politics has been intense and enduring. The looming questions have always been "should minorities go it alone and bargain with the larger society, or do they need to form alliances to counter their minority status? And if they make alliances, with whom should they link their fate" (Sonenshein 1993:3).

This chapter focuses once again on aspects of the second dilemma by examining (1) **coalition politics**—the aggregation of groups to pursue a specific political goal—of blacks, Latinos, and Asian Americans; and (2) the increasing tensions among blacks, Latinos, and Asians and between these groups and the white majority. (Although half of the American Indian population consists of "urban Indians," little research has been conducted on their participation in urban politics.) Additionally, we present a case study of Los Angeles that highlights the various patterns of interminority and majority group relations.

Interminority Group Relations

When differences among groups are found regarding political goals and outcomes, the potential for conflict exists. Political coalitions require that groups have similar goals, desire similar outcomes, and be willing to pursue their objectives in a collaborative and cooperative fashion. Coalitions may be loosely or tightly organized, and cooperation may be tacit or explicit. As with coalitions, the form of competition between groups with differing goals may also vary. Competition may be pursued on an "enemies always" basis or on a "not permanent enemies" stance (Eisinger 1976:17–18).

Group competition accounts for some aspects of the discrimination experienced by minorities. Individuals and groups accrue power and status in a variety of ways; thus, some power contests are understood as involving group against group. Competition exists, therefore, when two or more groups strive for the same finite objectives so that the success of one group may imply a reduced probability that another will attain its goals. We could view group competition in terms of power contests that exist when there is rivalry and when groups have roots in different cultures. Furthermore, the greatest perceived competition may occur among groups that are nearly equal in political power (Blalock 1967). This framework, although it is addressed to majority-minority relations, is also useful in examining relationships among minority groups if we recognize that not only status differences but also status similarities may become bases for conflict.

Coalition or Competition Politics?

The presence of multiple minority groups in major metropolitan cities has led to the assumption that shared racial minority group status generates the potential for political coalitions among the various groups. One of the assumptions of coalition theory has been that the relationship among the various racial minority groups will be one of mutual respect and shared political goals and ideals. Another assumption of coalition theory, however, has been that black political assertiveness is incompatible with the existence of biracial political coalitions between blacks and whites (Sonenshein 1993). Although they were referring to African Americans, Stokely Carmichael and Charles V. Hamilton, in their seminal work, *Black Power* (1967:79–80), offer four bases on which viable biracial coalitions (between whites and blacks) may be formed. These may also apply to coalitions among blacks, Latinos, Asians, and Indians:

(1) Parties entering into a coalition must recognize their respective self-interests, (2) each party must believe it will benefit from a cooperative relationship with the other or others, (3) each party must have its own independent power base and also have control over its own decisionmaking, and (4) each party must recognize that the coalition is formed with specific and identifiable goals in mind. Accordingly, *interests* rather than *ideology* provide the most substantial basis for the most productive biracial coalitions. Arguing that "politics results from a conflict of interests, not of conscience," Carmichael and Hamilton (1967:75) suggest that whites—liberal or otherwise—would desert blacks if their own interests were threatened.

Yet the argument of interests versus ideology is at the heart of the debate over a theory of biracial coalitions. One side of the argument sees interests as the ties that bind biracial coalitions together, coalitions that are, at best, short-lived tactical compromises among self-centered groups. Those who emphasize ideology argue that the essential element of biracial coalitions is common beliefs. This perspective of coalition theory holds that preexisting racial attitudes influence one's perception of racial issues and that these attitudes shape political actions. Thus, coalitions form not from objective self-interests but from shared ideology. The most likely coalition will be one between groups that are close in ideology even when another union would be more advantageous.

The interests-versus-ideology distinction for biracial coalitions is not as clear-cut and dichotomized as it may appear. When black and liberal white—primarily Jewish—interests came into conflict in New York City, liberal sentiments were insufficient to hold the coalition together (Sonenshein 1990). Nevertheless, although ideology alone may not hold coalitions together, without a shared ideology biracial and interracial coalitions are unlikely to form in the first place (Sonenshein 1993).

There are numerous instances of coalitions between blacks and Latinos. Common concerns, such as poverty, during the 1960s formed the foundation for unions between blacks and Latinos, especially Mexican Americans (Estrada et al. 1981), and there is clear evidence of coalition building between blacks and Latinos (see, e.g., Browning, Marshall, and Tabb 1984, 1990; Henry and Muñoz 1991; Sonenshein 1993). In Los Angeles since the early 1970s, the mechanism for minority political incorporation has been a tightly knit coalition of African Americans and liberal whites, primarily Jews, with subsidiary support from Latinos and Asians (Sonenshein 1993).

However, the coalitions between blacks and Latinos began to break apart when policies designed to promote equal access and equity for different groups were sometimes in conflict. For example, blacks were concerned that bilingual education would shift resources from the effort toward desegregation and thus were not supportive of it (Falcón 1988:178). Other policy issues of concern to Latinos that were not perceived as being supported by blacks included the English-only movement, employer sanctions, and the extension of coverage to Latinos in amendments to the Voting Rights Act (National Council of La Raza 1990). Furthermore, Latinos began to question whether affirmative action had benefited them as much as it had blacks, since they felt blacks had secured more municipal jobs than had Latinos (Cohen 1982; Falcon 1988).

The coalition between blacks and liberal whites in Los Angeles was beginning to show signs of strain during the last years of Thomas Bradley's administration because of divergent economic interests among the primary partners and increasing demands on the part of Asians and Latinos for **incorporation**—the extent to which a group is represented in dominant policymaking coalitions—into city politics (Sonenshein 1990). In Los Angeles, Asians and Latinos differ significantly from blacks and whites in terms of ideology and interests (Henry and Muñoz 1991:329). (These ideological differences among blacks, Latinos, and Asians were discussed in Chapter 3.) Although recognizing—as we stressed—that standard labels of liberal, moderate, and conservative are too simplistic to reflect the range of ideological orientations within racial minority groups, we can safely conclude that African Americans, Mexicans, and Puerto Ricans hold more liberal perspectives on a range of issues than do Cubans and Asians. Within the Asian group, Chinese Americans are far more conservative than are either Japanese or Koreans.

A 1993 *Los Angeles Times* survey of southern California residents—whites, blacks, Asians, and Latinos—found that 65 percent of blacks identified whites as being the most prejudiced group, and 45 percent felt Asians were the next most prejudiced group, an increase from the 19 percent of blacks who expressed this feeling in a similar 1989 survey. Moreover, blacks believed that Asians (39 percent), far more than whites (29 percent), were gaining economic power to an extent that is not good for southern California (UCLA Asian American Studies Center 1993:5). When pressed to be specific about which group of Asians was perceived as causing problems, a quarter of both blacks and Latinos felt all Asians were doing so, although 19 percent of blacks identified Koreans as the source of problems and a similar percentage of Latinos mentioned Vietnamese. For the most part, blacks did not view Latinos as being prejudiced (11 percent) nor as gaining more economic power than was good for the area (16 percent). These results support the inference that blacks and Latinos are the most likely coalition partners, followed by Asians and then Anglos (Henry and Muñoz 1991:330). Other analysis has found affinities between blacks and Latinos as compared to whites and Asians (Uhlaner 1991). Evidence such as this demonstrates the difficulties in forming coalitions of racial minorities (Sonenshein 1993:263).

Competition may also arise among the various groups when blacks, Latinos, and Asians each have different goals, when there is distrust or suspicion among the groups, or when the size of one group is such that it no longer needs to form coalitions with other minority groups to gain political success (Falcón 1988; McClain 1993; McClain and Karnig 1990; Meier and Stewart 1991; Warren, Corbett, and Stack 1990). There is increasing evidence that in many communities blacks, Latinos, and Asians compete for scarce jobs, adequate housing, and government services (Falcon 1988; Johnson and Oliver 1989; MacManus and Cassell 1982; Mollenkopf 1990; Oliver and Johnson 1984; Welch, Karnig, and Eribes 1983). Moreover, some survey data suggest that a growing hostility and distrust exist among the three groups (Johnson and Oliver 1989; Oliver and Johnson 1984), with a majority of Mexican Americans not in favor of building coalitions with blacks (see also Ambrecht and Pachon 1974; Browning, Marshall, and Tabb 1984; Grebler, Moore, and Guzman 1970; Henry 1980).

A study using data from the 1980s of all forty-nine U.S. cities with more than twenty-five thousand people and whose populations were at least 10 percent black and 10 percent Latino found that analyses of socioeconomic data—income, education, employment, and percent not in poverty—revealed no harmful competition in general between blacks and Latinos. The results support a positive covariation relationship: When any group (black, Latino, or white) prospers with respect to education, income, employment, and non-poverty, the other groups do significantly better as well. Political outcome data—percent on the city council, proportionality of council representation, black or Latino mayor—present a somewhat different picture. When either blacks or Latinos made political gains, they did so at the expense of whites. Political competition between blacks and Latinos was evident only when controls for white political outcomes were introduced. This suggests that as black and Latino political successes increase, political competition between blacks and Latinos may be triggered, especially as fewer whites reside in minority-dominated cities (McClain 1993a; McClain and Karnig 1990).

Evidence also indicates that competition appears to occur as the size of the black population increases, with negative consequences for Latinos, particularly on several socioeconomic measures. However, increases in the Latino proportion of a city's population do not appear to be related to competition that is harmful to blacks. Moreover, in a small sample of cities in which blacks constitute a plurality or a majority, Latinos seem to fare less well socioeconomically and, in particular, politically (McClain and Karnig 1990).

In the area of municipal employment, black and Latino outcomes are negatively related to white employment outcomes, which indicates a degree of competition for municipal jobs (McClain 1993a). Blacks or Latinos gain at the expense of non-Latino whites. But evidence also indicates that competition in municipal employment appears to occur as the size of the black workforce increases, with consequences for Latinos. The most significant predictor of limits to Latino municipal employment opportunities is the black percentage of the workforce. As the black share increases, Latino opportunities decline. Latino workforce percentage, however, does not appear to have the same effect on black municipal opportunities. Furthermore, in a small sample of cities in which blacks constitute a plurality or a majority, Latinos seem to fare less well in municipal employment outcomes; in cities in which Latinos constitute a plurality or a majority, the consequences for black municipal employment are inconsistent. Clear evidence that blacks suffer deleterious effects in municipal employment outcomes exists in only one city, Miami.

Whereas this summary of research on interminority group relations indicates increasing competition between blacks and Latinos in certain urban areas, we must recognize that both coalitional and competitive behaviors may occur in the same city but between different strata of each group. For example, elites may engage in political coalition building, whereas working-class and lower-class persons may see their interaction with other racial groups as constituting competition for jobs, housing, and city services. Los Angeles, California, is illustrative of this dual pattern of interaction. Moreover, it is also a city in which blacks, Latinos, and Asians are represented in sufficient numbers that their political behaviors have consequences for city politics.

Los Angeles[1]

Los Angeles is prototypical of turn-of-the-century western nonpartisan reform cities. It has been described as an **entrepreneurial city,** a city in which electoral politics is organized so that business interests play a significant role and urban bureaucracies are structured so as not to be dominated by either elected officials or local business interests. Moreover, the nonpartisan tradition of California city politics guarantees that political party organizations play a minimal role in Los Angeles city politics.

Los Angeles was founded in 1781 by Mexican settlers consisting of "two blacks, seven 'mulattoes,' one 'half-breed' and nine 'Indians'" (Sonenshein 1993:21). By 1790, blacks and people of mixed black ancestry were outnumbered by Mexican settlers. African Americans arrived in Los Angeles after the United States gained control of California in 1850, but they did not come in significant numbers until the land boom of the late 1800s opened the city to blacks. Blacks bought property and, until 1915, lived wherever they could afford to buy, many amassing significant wealth through resale to developers at substantial profits. By 1880, the Los Angeles schools had been desegregated, and racial tensions were low (Sonenshein 1993:22). Additionally, by applying pressure on city hall, blacks were able to obtain a few political benefits, including the appointment of one black police officer and one black fireman in the late 1890s. In 1890, an estimated 34 percent of Los Angeles blacks lived in owner-occupied homes. This figure greatly exceeded home-owning rates for Mexicans and Japanese, approximated the level for whites, and far exceeded levels for blacks in other major cities at the time. Yet despite this home-owning level blacks were confined to low-paying, low-status jobs.

Although it had been founded by Mexicans and had been part of Mexican territory, Los Angeles was more accepting of blacks than it was of Mexican Americans. With the increased migration of white midwesterners during the late 1800s, Mexican Americans became increasingly less important in the city's economic and cultural arenas. As a result of the need for unskilled labor and the importation of Mexicans to fill that need, by the early 1900s the Los Angeles Mexican American community was dominated by laborers. As a result, the Mexican American and Mexican populations were less well-off economically than were blacks. Both groups were subjected to massive deportations in 1931, which so decimated the city's Mexican American community that it did not restabilize until the return of its veterans at the end of World War II (Sonenshein 1993:24).

California was particularly antagonistic toward Japanese Americans and Chinese Americans, even more so than it was toward Mexican Americans. As long ago as 1880, California was virulently anti-Asian. Chinese immigration was essentially curtailed with the passage of the Chinese Exclusion Act of 1882, yet Japanese migration to Los Angeles increased steadily until restrictive immigration laws were passed in 1920. "Between 1890 and 1930, the Japanese-American population of Los Angeles County grew from an estimated 1,200 persons to 35,390" (Sonenshein 1993:24). Japanese Americans developed a subeconomy that was parallel to the city's main economy, and they were fairly successful. Yet the hostility toward them did not dissipate; on the contrary, it intensified and climaxed with the internment of Japanese Americans in 1942.

Although blacks and, to a lesser extent, Japanese Americans prospered in terms of home ownership (blacks) and business success (Japanese), access by Los Angeles blacks, Mexican Americans, and Asian Americans to long-term socioeconomic opportunities and political power was severely constrained by changes that were about to occur in the political culture of the city.

Puritanical Conservatism

In the late 1800s a tremendous influx of white midwestern immigrants to Los Angeles brought a desire to build a city "freed from the ethnic heterogeneous influences of eastern and midwestern cities" (Sonenshein 1993:26). "Militant Protestant clergy" were in the vanguard of the creation of a "native, white anglo-saxon Protestant city," a goal that was completed by 1900. By 1920 white Protestants were the ruling class and controlled most of the public offices; moreover, "the new atmosphere was puritanical and ethnocentric" (Sonenshein 1993:26). As a consequence of the new political culture,

> The civic culture and eventually the local economy became increasingly hostile to Blacks and other minorities. The dominant conservative philosophy was augmented by the migration of southern whites to the city after 1910. By now, the increased size of the Black community made it potentially threatening. The southern whites were particularly hostile to Blacks, but the white Protestants also sought to preserve their "small town" city. The result was the development of restrictions on Blacks and other minorities, cutting them off from the next stages of the city's system of generating wealth. (Sonenshein 1993:27)

Conservative reformers who were allied with southern whites openly conspired to restrict minority access to political and economic opportunities through a series of legal maneuvers and political changes. Two city charters, in 1911 and 1915, severely limited elected officials' ability to control city government. This action removed the incentive to develop political party organizations. As many of the reformers remembered, strong political party organizations had provided the mechanism for limited political incorporation of minorities in eastern and midwestern cities. In 1914 there was even an abortive attempt to start a whites-only jitney service so that whites would not have to share public transportation with blacks. Housing restrictions in the forms of restrictive covenants, which bound home owners not to sell their property to minorities, and block agreements, which bound entire neighborhoods, were introduced, and their legality was upheld by the courts. (The Supreme Court did not declare restrictive covenants unconstitutional until 1948.)

Housing restrictions led to the creation of Los Angeles's black ghettos. When thousands of blacks moved into Watts, that city swiftly incorporated into Los Angeles in 1926 to prevent a black-dominated local government. Other communities including Santa Monica, Huntington Beach, Lomita, and Manhattan Beach also made it difficult or impossible for blacks to buy houses. Thus, the natural turnover in neighborhoods—that of poorer blacks moving in as middle-class blacks moved up—did not occur, and blacks, regardless of economic level, found themselves confined to specific areas of Los Angeles. This segregation also produced a severe housing shortage for blacks during World War II, when thousands poured into the city seeking war-related job opportunities.

World War II transformed the city into a major center for the production of aircraft and ships. As this sector grew, the need for skilled labor also increased. The federal government declared Los Angeles an area that had an extreme labor shortage, and people—whites and blacks—flocked to the city. Black labor was now needed, and jobs that had once been denied to them were marginally opened—primarily as a result of President Roosevelt's executive order barring racial discrimination in the defense plants. The deportation of tens of thousands of Mexican immigrants in 1931 and the internment of Japanese Americans in 1942 removed major competitors for jobs and housing.

Postwar Los Angeles returned to the prewar rules and attitudes governing and restricting opportunities for blacks.

The end of the labor shortage became the vehicle for restoring the old rules. Japanese-Americans released from internment obviously wanted to regain their homes and jobs. . . . Returning soldiers clogged the labor force. Mexican workers were imported to Los Angeles once again; by 1950, they outnumbered Blacks. The postwar era allowed for the first time in decades the development of a stable Latino community. . . . The city was returning to minority competition for unskilled jobs, while whites gained most of the skilled jobs. (Sonenshein 1993:30)

As a result of the return to discriminatory hiring practices, between 1950 and 1960 blacks lost many of the occupational gains they had made during the war. Yet at the same time, when restrictive covenants were outlawed blacks were able to expand beyond ghetto boundaries as middle- and upper-class blacks moved into areas vacated by whites who had moved to the suburbs. Consequently, by the 1960s Los Angeles blacks were in a paradoxical situation—relative to blacks in other urban areas in the East and Midwest, they enjoyed higher levels of socioeconomic success and home ownership. Yet relative to white Angelenos, Los Angeles blacks were falling increasingly behind economically. As late as 1960, an estimated 95 percent of the city's refuse workers,

80 percent of its street maintenance workers, and 95 percent of its custodians were black (Sonenshein 1993:23).

Political Structure

A unique aspect of the conservative reformists' plan for hegemony of the political structure of Los Angeles was the passage by the voters in 1925 of **district elections**—a system of district elections for city council members in which candidates are elected by voters in defined geographic parts of the city rather than citywide. Despite a campaign by the city's leaders and the conservative *Los Angeles Times* to overturn the vote, the citizens voted in 1927 to maintain the system. The district electoral system provided the opening, albeit a small one, for minority participation in Los Angeles city politics. However, the political culture was hostile toward minority representation, and even in substantial minority councilmanic districts, it was difficult for blacks and Latinos to be elected. In 1960, the three city council districts that had sizable black populations were represented by white council members. Latinos had slightly more success because of the election of Edward Roybal to the city council in 1949. Interestingly, Roybal won the Ninth Council District through the efforts of a multiracial coalition made up of Latinos, blacks, and liberal Jews (Sonenshein 1993:31). In later years, the city leaders used gerrymandering to ensure that blacks and Latinos were unable to elect representatives from their racial groups to the city council.

Los Angeles city leaders—by blocking minority access and maintaining their myopic view of the city as a white Anglo-Saxon Protestant city—ignored many of the changes that had occurred throughout the nation since World War II. This approach allowed city hall to

> pursue a small-town conservatism of fiscal stringency, strong support for the forces of order, and reluctance to participate in federal social programs. The combination of downtown business and the conservative *Los Angeles Times* was a potent power structure, which restricted political debate. With the backing of the police bureaucracy, this tightly knit leadership could hold back the hands of time. (Sonenshein 1993:31)

This conservative reform culture and the resultant absence of strong political party organizations allowed public bureaucracies to cultivate and develop their own constituencies and to resist public control and oversight. The Los Angeles Police Department (LAPD) is an extreme example of bureaucratic independence and resistance to public control. Over time, particularly under

Chief William Parker in the 1950s, the LAPD "developed the ability to insulate itself completely from political oversight. The department ultimately developed an independent political power base, which it used to restrict the city's politics. . . . In time, the LAPD became one of the city's main roadblocks to social change, resisting the rise to power of Blacks and liberals" (Sonenshein 1993:32). The LAPD has been a source of anger and frustration for the minority communities of Los Angeles and has been at the heart of some of the city's most violent and destructive civil disturbances, from the 1965 Watts riot to the 1991 beating of Rodney King to the 1992 riots, as well as being at the center of several mayoral elections, such as that of Sam Yorty in 1961 and Tom Bradley in 1973.

As inhospitable as the Los Angeles political culture and structure were regarding the inclusion of blacks, Latinos, and Asians into the political process, the very nature of the system provided the foundation for multiethnic politics in the city. "Modern Los Angeles had never been a melting pot; *everybody* who differed from the white conservative model was excluded. Therefore, a Los Angeles–style melting pot had to be created politically" (Sonenshein 1993:35). Thus, minority exclusion provided the basis for coalition politics among blacks, Latinos, and Asians.

Coalition Politics

By 1960, blacks constituted 13.7 percent of the population of Los Angeles—nearly half a million people—and, propelled by the national civil rights movement, were poised to seek access to the city political system. As a result of overt and de facto residential racial segregation, blacks were concentrated in three councilmanic districts—the Eighth, Ninth, and Tenth Districts. The Ninth District was represented by Edward Roybal, who unsuccessfully opposed the city council's 1960 reapportionment plan designed to dilute black voting strength by dividing the city's black population among five districts, thereby protecting incumbents and not allowing the creation of a majority black councilmanic district (Sonenshein 1993:36–38).

Disappointed by the reapportionment plan and upset by Los Angeles Mayor Norris Poulson's lack of responsiveness to the concerns of the black community, particularly brutality by the LAPD, blacks supported Samuel Yorty in the 1961 mayoral race. Yorty fashioned an unlikely coalition of valley home owners and inner-city racial minority groups. Yorty promised white home owners that he would eliminate a complicated trash collection system, which was a volatile issue for them, and promised black and Latino residents that he would fight police brutality and appoint minorities to city commissions. Blacks especially and Latinos provided the margin of victory for Yorty, and he did appoint several minorities to city commissions. However, he failed to make good on his promises to reform the LAPD; in fact, following a conversation with Chief Parker, Yorty never again spoke out against the department, and he gave the department whatever it requested (Sonenshein 1993:38, 40).

Shortly after Yorty's victory, to which they felt they had contributed substantially, blacks set their sights on the vacant Tenth District council seat. The city council was to appoint an individual, and initially Yorty was supportive of the appointment of a black. City council members Edward Roybal and Jewish liberal Rosalind Wyman openly called for such an appointment. Numerous individuals were nominated, including Thomas Bradley, at the time a retired police officer and lawyer who had broad district support. However, a majority of the city council members wanted the seat to go to Joe Hollingsworth, a white Republican businessman, and despite heavy pressure from Roybal they appointed Hollingsworth to the seat. Mayor Yorty signed the ordinance certifying Hollingsworth's appointment, which angered the city's blacks. "The regime seemed intent on preventing black representation" (Sonenshein 1993:41).

Irate black community groups started recall proceedings against Hollingsworth. On two separate occasions, the recall organizers collected the requisite number of signatures to trigger a recall election, but each time they were stymied by the city clerk. On the first occasion, the clerk invalidated enough signatures to reduce the total to less than the minimum number required. On the second attempt, after the organizers had collected more than enough additional signatures to set the recall process in motion, the city clerk invalidated the recall on a technicality he had only recently discovered. Despite a challenge to the State Court of Appeals, the clerk's decision was upheld.

While the Tenth District appointment was being challenged, Roybal—the only minority council member—ran successfully for the U.S. Congress, thereby opening up the seat from the Ninth District. The district's population was about 50 percent black and 50 percent Latino, but Roybal had been successful in representing the interests of both constituencies. Despite the population distribution, Roybal's high visibility and tenure in office had caused the Ninth District to be viewed as a "Latino district." Roybal's resignation and the council's authority to appoint a replacement set into motion competition between blacks and Latinos, and the appointment "had a great influence on the development of black and Latino representation at city hall for the next two decades" (Sonenshein 1993:43).

Two candidates emerged—one black, Gilbert Lindsay, and one Latino, Richard Tafoya, who was Roybal's cousin. Fresh from their defeat in the Tenth District, blacks were determined to gain the Ninth District seat. A black-Latino struggle ensued, with blacks attempting to gain their first seat on the council while Latinos sought to retain the only seat they had been successful in winning. Lindsay was eventually appointed in January 1963, becoming the first African American officeholder. His appointment was the beginning of a twenty-three-year period during which Latinos had no elected officials at city hall. "A particular irony of this battle was that Roybal had been the main opponent of the council's various plans to prevent black council representation" (Sonenshein 1993:44).

As the 1963 municipal elections approached, the Eighth District seat, which was held by a white, was being contested by a black; the Ninth District seat held by Lindsay was being contested by Tafoya; and Tom Bradley was challenging Hollingsworth in the Tenth District. In the March election, Bradley was elected, with runoff elections held in the Eighth and Ninth Districts. Eventually, the black candidates in those two districts won, placing three blacks on the Los Angeles city council.

Despite the competition for the Ninth District seat, Bradley's campaign for the Tenth District seat is identified as the beginning of a multiracial coalition in Los Angeles city politics. Liberal whites—especially Jews—blacks, Asians, and Latinos, particularly Roybal, were instrumental in getting Bradley elected. The multiracial coalition that was forged in 1963 and that was fortified through a series of events over the span of a decade eventually propelled Bradley into the mayor's office in 1973.

The 1965 city elections produced a dynamic composed of Bradley and the multiracial coalition, which was opposed to Mayor Yorty; the other two black city council members were allied with Yorty. Although Yorty won, the entrenchment of the conservative regime in Los Angeles city politics and the exclusion of blacks and liberal whites provided the basis for continued cooperation within Bradley's multiracial coalition.

In August 1965, a traffic arrest by the California Highway Patrol escalated into the first major race riot of the 1960s. The behavior of the LAPD and the attitudes of and responses to the violence and destruction by Mayor Yorty and Police Chief Parker caused Bradley to emerge as their chief critic. Despite black leaders' hope that as a result of the deaths (of thirty-one blacks and three whites) and destruction ($41 million in property damage) that occurred during the riot attention to their concerns would be forthcoming, "the riot was an unqualified disaster for biracial politics, creating a durable and powerful backlash among whites and Latinos" (Sonenshein 1993:78). Surveys revealed blacks' optimism that conditions were improving, a position that was not shared by whites and Latinos.

Large majorities of both groups were profoundly affronted by the violence and expressed strong support for the police. Few thought the riot would improve race relations. Both groups expressed substantial personal fear of attack by Blacks. . . . Some Latino activists expressed resentment at the great attention being paid to Blacks in the wake of the riot, especially in the allocation of anti-poverty funds. The obvious lack of Latino political influence was remarkable considering that Latinos outnumbered Blacks in the county. (Sonenshein 1993:78)

In the aftermath, the riot solidified blacks' resolve to gain more power at city hall.

Bradley's Ascension to the Mayor's Office

In the wake of the changes occurring in the United States, and on the heels of the 1967 election of Richard Hatcher (Gary, Indiana) and Carl Stokes (Cleveland) as black mayors of major cities, Councilman Tom Bradley decided to become a candidate for mayor in the 1969 election. The specter of the Watts riot and the racial polarization that existed in the nation as well as in Los Angeles overshadowed the race between Bradley and the incumbent mayor, Sam Yorty. Bradley hoped to build on the biracial coalition that had helped him win his Tenth District seat, but 1969 proved not to be his year.

In the primary, Bradley led the packed field with 42 percent of the vote, just 8 percentage points short of winning the mayor's office outright. Yorty came in a distant second with 26 percent of the vote. Consequently, Bradley and Yorty moved into the general election. Bradley's primary campaign had assumed that a common ideological bond existed among blacks, Jews, liberal gentiles, and Mexican Americans, and to some extent this had been successful. However, in the general election, where Bradley needed to increase the level of his white support, Yorty was able to successfully exploit the weaknesses in Bradley's coalition strategy.

Yorty set about to impede a coalition among blacks, Latinos, and Jews by highlighting the black-Jewish conflict in the Ocean Hill–Brownsville school district in New York City in 1968. He told middle-class Latinos that because Bradley had pitched his campaign toward poorer Latinos, he would ignore their needs. Yorty also directly exploited white fears of having a black mayor by running ads in the real estate section of valley newspapers with Bradley's picture and the caption "Will Your City Be Safe with This Man?" (Sonenshein 1993:91). In addition, Yorty stoked the embers of the conflict between Bradley and the LAPD, who viewed Bradley—despite his previous police career—as an enemy because of his criticisms of the department and its procedures.

In the general election, the three-way coalition among blacks, liberal whites, and Latinos did not come together as well as Bradley had expected. Yorty won the race with 53 percent of the vote to Bradley's 47 percent. Black support for Bradley was high, and Jewish support was moderate, but two-thirds of Latinos voted for Yorty, as did a similar percentage of whites (Sonenshein 1993:93–94). Despite the loss in 1969, the experience set the stage for Bradley's run for and election to the mayor's office in 1973.

With a more professional and reorganized campaign, Bradley emerged from a three-way primary contest in 1973 in first place, with Sam Yorty second and Jesse Unruh, an unexpected Democratic challenger who cut into Bradley's black and Jewish support, in third place. Once again, Bradley and Yorty faced each other in the 1973 general election. Yorty attempted to use tactics similar to those he had used in 1969, but he was less successful. The LAPD also campaigned heavily against Bradley, threatening that if he were elected there would be mass resignations from the department. Despite these attempts, Bradley easily defeated Yorty with 54 percent of the vote. Bradley's victory was achieved with "high black turnout, solid Jewish support, an increasing Latino base, and little countermobilization by conservative whites" (Sonenshein 1993:108). There was evidence of an emerging black-Latino coalition, and Latinos eventually formed the most loyal and supportive faction of Bradley's coalition. Bradley's win exhibited the depth and strength of multiracial coalition politics in Los Angeles—a coalition that was to consolidate power, bring Asian Americans into its fold, and control city hall from 1973 to 1993 when Bradley stepped down as mayor.

Asian Americans and the Bradley Coalition

Asian Americans became full partners in the Bradley coalition after his initial election in 1973; however, there had always been an Asian presence in his campaign organization. George Takei, known for his role as navigator Sulu in the original *Star Trek* television series, was the chair of a subgroup of Asian Americans in Bradley's 1969 and 1973 mayoral campaigns. Following Bradley's election and Takei's narrow defeat in his quest for Bradley's former Tenth District council seat, Bradley appointed Takei to the board of the Southern California Rapid Transit District.

Of Bradley's initial appointments to city commissions, 10 of 140 appointees were Asian Americans. Asians fared well under Bradley, increasing their share of public-sector jobs and top-level positions. When Bradley entered office in 1973, Asians constituted 4.0 percent of the city workforce; by 1991 that figure was 7.5 percent. Additionally, in 1973 they represented 3.0 percent of officials and administrators, and in 1991 that proportion had risen to 8.0 percent. Increases in professional public-sector jobs also occurred, with Asians holding 8.0 percent of the professional jobs in 1973 and 15.4 percent in 1991 (Sonenshein 1993:152–153). Bradley became a major fund-raiser within the Los Angeles Asian American community. Over time—along with Latinos— Asian Americans remained the most consistent of the pro-Bradley groups.

Demise of the Coalition

Although Bradley won reelection to a fourth term in 1985 with a record 68 percent of the vote and with victories in all fifteen council districts, changes were taking place within his coalition. Economic alignments were changing, and ideological unions between liberal whites and minorities were becoming strained.

> There had always been the potential for conflict between minority and white liberal constituencies in Los Angeles. While ideology provided an important common bond, differences of class interest and personal ambition started to crystallize after 1985. The threads of the coalition's balancing act—an ideological interracial alliance and an economic coalition between minority leaders and downtown business—began to unravel. (Sonenshein 1993:191)

Bradley saw former coalition members and supporters become adversaries. His control over the city council ended when two of his supporters left the council in 1987. Earlier successful strategies, such as being pro-growth, became victims of their own success, giving rise to voices of opposition within the coalition—for example, from those who favored slow growth. Additionally, for the first time in his career, Bradley's sterling image was tarnished by a financial scandal shortly before the 1989 elections. These factors, coupled with a challenge by a black noncoalition member of the city council who siphoned black votes from Bradley, resulted in Bradley's reelection to a fifth term in 1989 with only 54 percent of the vote. The coalition that controlled Los Angeles city politics was splintering. Although it was not disappearing, it was becoming only one of several groups, rather than the dominant group, competing within city politics.

These facts, combined with such events as the beating of Rodney King by the LAPD in 1991 and the rioting in 1992 following the acquittal of the four police officers tried for the beating, contributed to Bradley's 1992 decision not to seek a sixth term in 1993. Yet before leaving office, Bradley was able to pull the coalition together to pass Proposition F in June 1992, which reformed the LAPD by removing civil service protection for the police chief, limiting the chief to one ten-year term, and providing more civil authority over the department. "The winning campaign to implement police reform must be considered one of the greatest victories of the biracial coalition that took power in 1973" (Sonenshein 1993:226).

The 1993 mayoral contest pitted Michael Woo, a Democratic Asian American member of the city council and a member of Bradley's coalition, against Richard Riordan, a maverick millionaire Republican businessman. Bradley's coalition had now broken into several different parts, and Woo's defeat signaled the final demise of the multiracial coalition that had governed Los Angeles for two decades. The end of this coalition does not mean multiracial politics is a thing of the past in Los Angeles; it simply means that the structure Bradley built no longer exists in the same form.

Competition

At the time of the formation of the Bradley multiracial coalition, tensions still existed among black, Latino, and Asian elites over the ability of Latinos and Asians to elect representatives to the city council while blacks solidified their control of three of the fifteen council seats. During councilmanic reapportionment activities in 1985 and 1986, Bradley vetoed a plan that would have eliminated the only Asian American district and created a Latino district. However, the unexpected death of a council member provided an opening to reapportion districts in a manner that satisfied all of the parties of Bradley's coalition. As a result, by 1986 two Latinos and one Asian American served along with the three blacks on the fifteen-member Los Angeles city council.

Whereas the elites amicably resolved their reapportionment differences, tensions were rising among lower-income blacks, Latinos, and Asians. Economic and housing market competition was increasing among these groups in Los Angeles. The city's economy was being restructured by the loss of industry and, hence, of jobs. An estimated seventy thousand heavy-manufacturing jobs were lost as a result of plant closings, automation, and the movement of companies overseas. Because of their concentration in the heavy-manufacturing sector, blacks experienced tremendous job loss and dislocation. In addition, between 1970 and 1980, poor Latino and Asian immigrants began to move into the formerly all-black south-central area of Los Angeles. Latino immigrants were unable to find housing in the Latino barrio of East Los Angeles and began to settle in increasing numbers in the black south-central region (Johnson and Oliver 1989).

The sharing of residential space was not the only incursion blacks in that region experienced. Asian immigrants, especially Koreans, opened businesses of

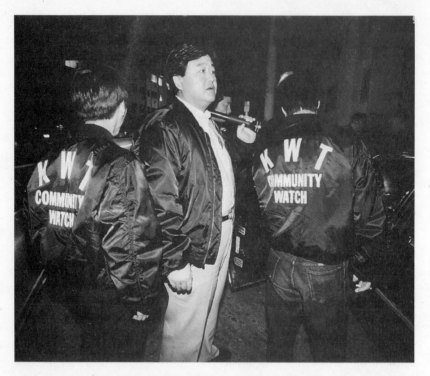

Khi Ahn (*center*), captain of the Koreatown Crime Team, checks out an attempted car theft. The citizens' group regularly patrols the Koreatown section of Los Angeles, a scene of tension even before the riots following the acquittals of the four officers in the first Rodney King beating trial (April 1993). Photo courtesy Reuters/Bettmann.

all types in black areas. In particular, Koreans penetrated the small-business market in south-central Los Angeles. Relations between Korean shop owners and black customers were rocky and filled with tension. Disadvantaged blacks viewed the Korean merchants as "foreigners" who charged high prices, refused to invest in the community in which they conducted business or to hire blacks, and were rude and discourteous to black customers. The killing of a black teenager by a Korean store owner and the proprietor's light sentence for manslaughter in 1991 only intensified the conflict. This antipathy between blacks and Koreans culminated in the targeting of Korean businesses by blacks during the 1992 Los Angeles riots: "The basic bone of contention, especially between Blacks and members of immigrant minority groups, is the issue of jobs. Given their deteriorating position in the American urban economy, there is a growing perception among inner-city Blacks that the new immigration has hurt them economically" (Johnson and Oliver 1989:455).

Conflict has also occurred over housing and social amenities. Blacks in the south-central region have been concerned that the influx of immigrants into their neighborhoods has had a displacement effect. Blacks have charged that landlords prefer to rent to Latinos or Asians because of the presence of multiple wage earners in those families, thus forcing black families to move outside the Los Angeles metropolitan area to areas with lower housing costs. Additionally, blacks have viewed Latino and Asian immigrants as **free riders**, taking advantage of the social services and benefits blacks feel they fought hard for through protests and litigation (Johnson and Oliver 1989:456).

Conclusion

We have used Los Angeles as a case study of the ways in which the second dilemma is manifest. This case shows the way the city's government system was structured to ensure minimal minority participation (shades of the first dilemma) and describes the process by which blacks, Latinos, and Asians were able to gain access to the system. Relations between the three groups and the white majority have taken and continue to take various forms. There have been a number of political successes but also many failures.

Although Los Angeles has been our case study for a discussion of racial minority group coalition or competition politics, elements of these patterns of interaction can be found in other cities as well. Los Angeles is a special case because it is a western nonpartisan city in which political parties play a limited role in local politics. In cities in which political parties are strong and actively involved in city politics, a different dynamic of coalition politics may be present. However, the increasing tension among blacks, Latinos, and Asians in urban politics seems to be present in many cities regardless of government structure and partisan activities. Whereas the competition between whites and various racial minority groups in urban politics is still a reality in some cities, competition among blacks, Latinos, and Asians will continue to increase as the white presence in many urban centers diminishes. Thus, the second dilemma for America's racial minority groups—what options to choose in attempts to gain access to the political process—is continuing and very complex.

6

....

Will We
"All Get Along?"

A white man and an Asian man assault a Latina
college student because she speaks out on behalf of
illegal immigrants.

Davis, Calif., April 21, 1993

T HE EPIGRAPHS that begin each chapter are real, although the names have, to rephrase the ending of the old television series *Dragnet*, been withheld to protect the guilty. For many residents of this country, incidents such as these—especially the train station and restaurant incidents—are thought to be long past. Even when they did occur, most people think they were limited to "backward" rural areas and southern states. In fact, many citizens argue vociferously that "some people" (that is, racial and ethnic minorities) today make far too much of race and ethnicity. They deny the existence of widespread differences in treatment or opportunities based on race or ethnicity as America approaches the twenty-first century. Sadly, these are only a small sample of interracial conflicts that have been documented in the United States. Indeed, for other individuals the events depicted here constitute evidence of the continuing salience of race and ethnicity in the American political fabric and of the differential treatment accorded many U.S. residents based solely on the color of their skin.

When the Rodney King incident and the subsequent verdict galvanized the nation, they simply made undeniable what any conscious human would find difficult to deny—the fact that racial and ethnic conflicts are common in the United States as we move toward the twenty-first century. Yet particularly during the Reagan and Bush administrations, it was popular to think of racism as something long past.

Race has been and is still an enduring piece of the American political fabric. Although the overt signs of segregation and discrimination that were present when we were born are less common today, racism continues and is still practiced. Consequently, gaining an understanding of the politics of America's racial minority groups is essential to our understanding of the American political system in general. One cannot truly be a student of American politics without also being familiar with the politics of race and the political behaviors of America's racial minority groups.

The Dilemmas Revisited

We began this book by identifying the two primary dilemmas racial minority groups have faced and continue to face as participants in the American political process. The first dilemma is the asymmetry of the U.S. commitment to freedom and equality for all and the denial of these rights, first to African Americans and American Indians and then to Latinos and Asian Americans. This contradiction, identified early by Alexis de Tocqueville, has been addressed in part, but problems still exist. African Americans, American Indians, Latinos, and Asian Americans are citizens, and no one questions whether the protections and privileges embodied in the Constitution apply to all citizens. Also, the right to vote is an accepted principle, and denial of the right to vote on the basis of color is prohibited—at least in theory.

Yet the issue of citizenship is still of grave importance for the Latino and Asian American communities. Because of new immigration into the United States of foreign-born Latinos and Asians, some segments of the American electorate see all members of these groups as immigrants. This perception of "immigrant status" has resulted in discrimination against and denial of rights of American citizens of Latino and Asian descent. We are reminded of the video of Cheech Marin's popular song "Born in East LA," in which he is mistakenly swept up by the Immigration and Naturalization Services (INS), fails to convince the INS official that he was born in the United States, is sent to Mexico, and spends the remainder of the video trying to convince officials that he really is a native-born U.S. citizen. Few American citizens, except for Latinos and Asian Americans, are confronted with this part of the first dilemma in the 1990s, although many Americans who change jobs are discovering that they have to prove their identity and employment eligibility to the satisfaction of the INS. With the passage of Proposition 187 in California, which attempts to deny all but emergency services to undocumented aliens, "foreign-looking" individuals may find themselves called upon to prove their citizenship.[1]

A second part of the first dilemma, the right to vote, is still very much at issue. The debate is no longer over whether everyone has the right to vote, although there are still instances of localities blatantly attempting to deny or interfere with the voting rights of racial minorities, but is now over the mechanisms used to protect the right to vote or the dilution of the vote of racial minorities. The issue is complex.

Chapter 2 discusses the Voting Rights Act of 1965 and its subsequent amendments. Debates over the intent, scope, and enforcement of the act continue. Some persons are beginning to use the creation of majority minority districts and lack of competitiveness as a veiled attack on the Voting Rights Act.

But such an attack ignores the plethora of other, "safe" districts created for incumbents of both parties. Given the centrality of race in American politics, it is easy to attack the creation of majority minority districts as being unfair while ignoring the unfairness of the rest of the process. This is not to say that there are not legitimate debates over whether black people should be congregated in one district rather than spread over more than one. But the use of majority minority districts as a prima facie case of "the horrible things we are doing to the political process" only masks the concern with race rather than with the serious issues of what it means to represent and to be represented.

Relatedly, critics of districts drawn to maximize minority representation voice comparisons with the system of apartheid identified with South Africa. Such comparisons reveal an ignorance of history because apartheid's goals were the exclusion of one race from participation in government and the domination of one race by another. When majority minority districts are drawn, their purposes are the opposite of those of apartheid. In such districts, no one is denied the right to register and to vote for the candidate of his or her choice, to run for office, or to exercise any of the other political or civil rights characteristically denied by apartheid.

The second dilemma, what should racial minorities do to increase their access to the political process, is ongoing. As we move toward the year 2000, what do we, the authors, see as the future for racial minorities in American politics? Do we envision more coalitions among racial minority groups, or do we anticipate increased tensions? As the numbers of the various minority groups increase in urban centers and, concomitantly, as the size of the white population decreases, tensions are bound to increase. As we have seen throughout this book, African Americans, Latinos, Asian Americans, and American Indians differ in a number of areas—for example, ideology, partisan identification, policy preferences. Clearly, the old stereotype that "all minorities think alike," a variant of the racist stereotype "they all look alike," has been shown to be totally false. The groups may have some issues in common, but there are just as many issues on which they may disagree.

We must also remember that racial minorities, having been socialized in a society that sees them as inferior to whites, are equally likely to believe in the inferiority of members of racial groups other than their own. Thus, blacks are likely to have stereotypic attitudes toward Asians and Latinos, Asians toward blacks and Latinos, and Latinos toward Asians and blacks. Moreover, immigrants coming to this country have formed their images of African Americans and American Indians from Hollywood films and American television exported by way of satellite and, syndication. As a result of all of these factors,

TABLE 6.1

Groups with Which Blacks, Latinos, and Asians Feel They Have the Most in Common

	Group with Most in Common			
Respondents	Black (%)	Latino (%)	Asian (%)	White (%)
Black	–	45	7	34
Latino	25	–	6	55
Asian	12	27	–	50

Source: National Conference of Christians and Jews, 1993. *Taking America's Pulse: The Full Report of the National Conference Survey on Inter-Group Relations.* New York: National Conference of Christians and Jews.

tensions among the groups will continue to increase and, unless elite members of the communities intervene, will only become worse. Table 6.1 reports the results of a survey that indicate major divergences in how close group members feel to each other. Although more blacks feel closer to Latinos than to any other group, the feeling is not reciprocated. Both Latinos and Asians report feeling closer to whites than to any other racial or ethnic group.

Another direction in which racial minority group politics may move is toward the formation of voting coalitions with other racial minorities. Such movement, however, depends upon the political context within which these groups interact. In cities in which the various groups are numerical minorities and competition for representation appears to be between minorities and whites, the desire to increase the minority share of favorable political outcomes may represent the basis for coalitions. The opposite may be true, however, in cities where a racial minority has become a numerical majority. In those instances, the majority minority no longer needs to form coalitions with others to maintain electoral domination; thus, coalitions may be formed between other racial minorities and whites. At no time should we presume that the extant white power structure will not act in an attempt to maintain its hegemony.

An arena in which access for racial minorities is crucial and to which attention will also be directed in the future is the policy process. Only in recent years has a sufficient number of minority policymakers appeared to allow us to begin to gauge their impact. Obviously, much work remains.

Although the number of minority elected officials contrasts starkly with the small numbers prior to the Voting Rights Act of 1965, the number is still a fraction of what it should be. As more racial minorities are elected to public office—particularly at the state and local level—appointed to significant government decisionmaking positions, and hired in larger numbers as professionals within the public sector, racial minorities' access to the policy process will improve, which will allow the mobilization and inside access models of agenda setting to be utilized. However, until the time when racial minorities have greater input into the policymaking process, they are likely to remain targets, rather than initiators, of public policy.

Looking to the Future

We foresee the nature of partisan politics and racial minority group voting undergoing changes. Blacks are not likely to shift dramatically from the Democratic Party to the Republican Party, primarily because the Republican Party is moving farther away from the issues of importance to the national black community. Moreover, the intolerance of differences that is seen among some Republicans, which was cultivated during the Reagan and Bush administrations and exhibited at the 1992 national convention in Houston, makes it even more unlikely that blacks will find the Republican Party a welcome alternative. Nevertheless, given the trends in the level of partisan identification with the Democratic Party, we foresee a weakening of blacks' attachment to the party and possibly an increase in the numbers who see themselves as political independents. As discussed in Chapter 3, blacks constitute an important voting bloc for the Democrats, and any significant weakening of party attachment is likely to create electoral problems in certain regions of the country.

We also expect that Mexican Americans and Puerto Ricans will essentially remain within the Democratic Party fold but that in some instances and some regions of the country—for example, parts of the Southwest—they will adopt an independent stance or see the outreach by the Republican Party as inviting. On the other hand, we also predict that Cubans will remain primarily Republican, particularly following President Clinton's change in policy toward Cuban émigrés, which removes their favored treatment.

The groups most susceptible to being recruited by the political parties in the future are Asian Americans and American Indians. The group with the highest proportion identifying themselves as political independents is Asian Americans. Their allegiance and voting patterns, as with those of American Indians, appear to depend on the policy positions taken by the parties on issues of concern to the various subgroups. The defection of U.S. Senator Ben Nighthorse Campbell from the Democratic to the Republican party provides a unique opportunity to test Indian identification on voting behavior.

Lest one think the politics and political behaviors of racial minorities are unimportant components of the American political process, the U.S. Census Bureau estimates that by the year 2020, Latinos will constitute 15.7 percent of the population. African Americans, presently the largest minority group, will be second, with 13.9 percent of the populace, with Asian Americans third at 7.0 percent. American Indians, although fourth, will also experience a substantial increase to nine-tenths of 1 percent of the population (Day 1993:xxii). In some regions of the country—for example, California—whites will be in the minority because the combination of racial minority groups will constitute a majority of the population. Thus, despite barriers—past and present—to effective participation of these groups in American politics, racial minority groups will become more, rather than less, important to the American political system. And the increase in the numbers and geographic concentration of specific populations will make these minorities more potent political forces—forces with which both Democrats and Republicans will have to contend.

Conclusion

As we end this book, the answer to Rodney King's plea, "Can we all get along?" remains in doubt. Issues of race were at the heart of the beginnings of this nation, and they remain central to the American political system as we approach the twenty-first century. Barriers to the full participation of racial minorities in that system remain. Many school districts are still effectively segregated, and second-generation discrimination issues are moving to the forefront. Racial prejudice does not appear to be waning. Thus, one should not be so smug as to suggest, as some do, that "all that stuff happened in the past and has nothing to do with the situation today." History has a causal effect on the future, and historical effects linger for several generations and, in some instances, perpetuate themselves.

In spite of these ongoing concerns, progress has clearly been made. The authors—one white, one black; one female, one male; one raised in the Deep South, one raised in the West and North—were born in 1950 and 1951, respectively, into a society that was highly segregated. In our lifetimes we have seen a major transformation in the social, educational, and political opportunities of various racial groups. We have seen grandsons and granddaughters of slaves registering to vote for the first time, the signs that designated "colored" water fountains and restrooms removed, the election of the first big-city black mayors, the election of the first black governor in the state that was at the heart of the Old Confederacy, and integrated churches and police forces in the rural Deep South. Progress has been made, although not equitably or swiftly.

We have also seen David Duke, an allegedly former and perhaps current Ku Klux Klansman, make a serious run for governor of Louisiana; three highly publicized cases of individuals—Charles Stuart in Boston, Susan Smith in South Carolina, and Jesse Anderson (the man who was killed at the same time and in the same prison as Jeffrey Dahmer)—allegedly murder family members but initially blame the crime on an unknown black assailant; a high school principal in Wedowee, Alabama, cancel (then reinstate) a high school prom to prevent interracial couples from attending; teachers label a bored black elementary school student as mentally retarded when he would not (not *could* not) read a passage he had been assigned; and five white high school seniors in Greenwich, Connecticut, insert a coded hate message in their yearbook. Obviously, many issues still need to be resolved, and such resolutions will only come with a great deal of conflict. But given the potential political influence of the minority groups, we try to remain hopeful that progress will continue.

Discussion Questions

Chapter 1

1. The authors state that there is "evidence of the continuing salience of race and ethnicity in the American political fabric." Do you agree with this assessment? Why or why not?

2. Thomas Jefferson, a student of classical liberal theory, opposed slavery but owned slaves. Theoretically, given the tenets of that theory, what justification could Jefferson have devised to explain his holding of slaves? Also from a classical liberal framework, what would be the weaknesses of his rationalization?

3. Citizenship is a primary criterion for participation in the American political system. What are the similarities and differences in the barriers to citizenship faced by African Americans, Latinos, Asian Americans, and American Indians? What are the important landmarks in these groups' efforts to attain citizenship? How was the Constitution changed to accommodate the inclusion of these groups?

4. Following citizenship, the ability to vote is central to participation in the political process. Yet gaining the franchise was not easy for racial minorities. How have the requirements for voting eligibility evolved since the ratification of the Constitution? How did blacks, Latinos, Asians, and American Indians each gain the franchise?

Chapter 2

1. A group's size is important in a majoritarian system, but population means different things depending upon the political issue under consideration. How do demographic characteristics affect actual and potential political power?

2. "Minorities" by definition are at a disadvantage in national politics. But in some areas, groups that are in the minority nationally constitute a near majority or a majority. What are the implications of this pattern for minority politics?

3. Why are some political movements successful whereas others fail? Choose a group that suffers from a disadvantage within the U.S. political system and explain how you would design a political movement to try to alleviate this situation.

4. What kind of protection is afforded to racial and ethnic minorities under contemporary voting rights law, and why was such a law thought to be necessary when it was passed and extended?

5. Do you agree with Lani Guinier's questioning of whether a majoritarian system means that 51 percent of the people control 100 percent of the power?

Chapter 3

1. Why is there a conflict within the scholarly literature over the utility of the pluralist framework for explaining the political behaviors of and outcomes for racial minorities in American politics?

2. What are the elements of group cohesion? And why is group cohesion important to the political participation of racial minorities?

3. How would you characterize the ideological orientations of African Americans, Latinos, American Indians, and Asian Americans? Do you feel the terms *liberal* and *conservative* are appropriate labels for racial minority ideological and political orientations? Why or why not?

4. What is the history of the relationship of blacks to the two political parties? What is the level of partisan identification among the various minority groups? How strongly attached to the two parties are the various racial minority groups?

5. What reasons would you give for the gender differences in voter registration and turnout within the various groups?

6. What has been the effect of Jesse Jackson's two presidential campaigns on the presidential selection process? On the access of racial minorities to the political system? Or has there been little or no change as a result of his campaigns? Give examples for your position.

Chapter 4

1. By what process is public policy made, and what potential and what pitfalls does this process have for members of racial and ethnic minority groups?

2. Why is access to the policy process important for the continued incorporation of racial groups into the political system?

3. Because we are all affected by public policy, we are all "targets" of public policy-making. Why might being such a target be of greater concern to a member of a racial or an ethnic minority group than to a member of a majority group?

4. Which of the major political institutions do you think has the greatest impact on public policies that affect minority group members? Defend your position.

5. Why should anyone be concerned about whether members of racial and ethnic minority groups are represented in the executive, legislative, and judicial branches of government?

6. What are the advantages and disadvantages of the federal system of government for members of racial and ethnic minority groups?

7. Fierce political battles have been fought in attempts to attain equal educational opportunity. Why is this goal considered to be so important? What has been achieved? What is left to be accomplished?

Chapter 5

1. What is your response to the question, should minorities work alone and bargain with the larger society, or do they need to form alliances to counter their minority status?

2. Why is there a popular assumption that blacks, Latinos, Asians, and Indians will form coalitions? Is this assumption accurate? Under what conditions are multiracial alliances feasible?

3. One pattern of interminority group relations is competition. What are the conditions under which racial minorities view themselves as competitors with other minorities?

4. Would we expect the dual patterns of relations among racial minorities in Los Angeles to be present in other cities? Why or why not?

5. What role did Asians play in Bradley's coalition?

Chapter 6

1. What do you see as the future of racial minority group politics?

Glossary

Adoption is the stage in the public policymaking process in which decisions are made among proposed alternatives for dealing with a problem. This activity is most often conducted by the legislative branch of government.

Agenda setting is the phase in the policymaking process in which the particular issues gain exposure that is significant enough to cause policymakers to either choose to act or feel compelled to act on them. The policy output is often determined by which actors are involved in the agenda-setting process. See also **inside access model, mobilization model, and outside initiative model.**

Antimiscegenation laws, which existed in over half the states, banned interracial marriages. Most antimiscegenation laws addressed black and white marriages, although many states included prohibitions on white and Asian marriages and white and Hispanic marriages. Antimiscegenation laws were declared unconstitutional by the Supreme Court's 1967 ruling in *Loving v. Virginia.*

Bilingual education is the concept that purports that non-English-speaking students should be taught in their native language or be taught to speak English. For Latino activists, MALDEF in particular, this issue has surpassed desegregation in importance and, in fact, can conflict with it.

Black and Tan Republicans constituted the wing of the Republican Party that favored Reconstruction and strong enforcement of civil rights laws. The Republicans' nomination of Barry Goldwater in the 1964 presidential election signaled the final demise of this faction.

Citizenship is the status of enjoying to the fullest extent the privileges and immunities granted by a sovereign state. At present the Constitution provides citizenship to all those born or **naturalized** in the United States. In the pre–Civil War United States, citizenship was determined by the state in which one resided, and as a means of furthering racial discrimination virtually every state refused to confer citizenship upon nonwhites. The Fourteenth Amendment (1868), at least on paper, mandated that states could not deny citizenship on the basis of race; however, it took more than a century and countless legislative acts and executive orders before all eligible racial minorities were granted full citizenship.

Classical liberalism is the political and economic theory—normally associated with John Locke and John Stuart Mill, among others—that posits that the individual possesses a sphere of rights free from interference by the state. These rights are both civil and economic in nature. Classical liberalism is the primary political theory underlying the U.S. Constitution. Although it has conferred civil rights on the populace, it was also the justification for perpetuating slavery. The government was not allowed to regulate slavery because slaves were viewed as their owners' property.

Coalition politics constitutes the way in which a collection of disparate groups come together to fight for a specific political purpose that is shared to some degree by all of the groups. In minority politics, coalitions form among the various racial groups, and controversy exists over how well the groups cooperate versus how much they are in competition with each other.

Congressional Black Caucus is a group of black senators and representatives that was formed in 1971 as a means of concentrating black power in Congress. The purpose of the group is to combine forces to promote issues of special concern to African Americans, and it has been influential on certain minority issues. Latinos followed suit in 1977 with the formation of the **Congressional Hispanic Caucus**, and in 1994 Asians in Congress formed the **Congressional Asian Pacific American Caucus.**

Cumulative voting is a voting technique in which each voter can register an intensity of preference. Voters are not required to vote for only one candidate per open seat; they may apply all of their votes to one candidate or choose any other distribution up to the maximum number of positions to be filled. For example, a cumulative voting scheme for a six-person governing body would assign six votes to each voter. A voter, therefore, could vote for six separate candidates, place all six votes for one candidate, apply two votes to one candidate and four votes to another, or any other combination adding up to six. Cumulative voting is important because it allows minority groups—whether racial, religious, or partisan in nature—to concentrate their votes and, thus, to increase their chances for representation. Although controversial, cumulative voting schemes were used by Illinois to elect its state representatives for almost a century, and they have been present in several local jurisdictions throughout the United States.

District elections constitute an electoral system in which the entity in question is divided into a number of subregions, each electing its own official. Conversely, in at-large elections regions are not divided; rather, all officials are elected by the entire entity. For racial minorities, district elections are considered to be advantageous because racial groups can be concentrated into a single district and, thus, elect an official of their own choice. However, with racial gerrymandering, district elections do not guarantee that the group will be able to elect someone of its own choice.

Dominated groups are those groups that have been excluded from participation in the decisionmaking process by which society's resources are distributed. Racial minorities, among others, qualify as dominated groups.

Entrepreneurial city is a city in which electoral politics is arranged so that business interests play a significant role and, in most cases, political party organization plays a very small role. Los Angeles is an example of an entrepreneurial city.

Ethnicity subsumes a set of learned characteristics, often, but not always, associated with nationality. These characteristics, such as language and religion, have frequently been the basis for discrimination against groups.

Evaluation is the final step of the policymaking process in which it is determined whether the policy had the intended effect. The methods employed to assess a particular policy are extremely crucial in the final evaluation.

Federalism constitutes the division of powers between the national government and the state governments. Each level exercises some powers exclusively while sharing others.

Formulation is the stage in the policymaking process at which issues on the agenda are converted to actual proposals to be considered for adoption into policy. The formulation stage is characterized by a number of alternatives to be chosen from in reaching a particular policy goal; therefore, a crucial element of the formulation stage is the composition of the institution(s) making the policy choices.

Free riders are those who do not participate in political action because they know they will receive the benefits without incurring costs. Some black activists claim that other minority groups are free riders because they did not struggle to obtain civil rights as blacks did and yet have received the benefits.

Grandfather Clause was a device used by southern states in the late nineteenth and early twentieth centuries to prevent black suffrage. By denying the right to vote to those whose grandfathers were slaves, the South effectively denied suffrage to virtually all southern blacks. The Grandfather Clause is one of many examples of how the South circumvented Reconstruction. In 1915 the Supreme Court, in *Guinn v. United States*, declared that the grandfather clause was unconstitutional.

Group identity or cohesion, in terms of racial politics, refers to the extent of the solidarity expressed by members of a racial minority. Cohesion can be measured by the proportion of minorities who believe that their group experiences discrimination and by feelings of closeness to other members of the group. Cohesion is important because it is a strong predictor of how effectively a minority group can be mobilized for political action.

Group political consciousness is a measure of how individuals in a racial minority view themselves within that minority group—in particular, what they prefer to be called. It is an important gauge of group cohesion.

Implementation involves putting a policy into action after it has been formulated and adopted. As with the other stages of the policymaking process, implementation is subject to numerous influences that are both internal and external to the implementing agency or agencies; consequently, following implementation a policy may or may not resemble the form in which it was actually developed.

Incorporation is the degree to which groups are represented in the dominant policymaking coalitions within a city. Racial and ethnic minority groups have rarely been incorporated.

Inside access (initiative) model is a type of agenda-setting process in which issues arise within the sphere of government and are not extended to the mass public. Until racial minorities' presence within the policymaking elite is increased, this model is the least applicable to setting the civil rights agenda.

Interest group activities are the actions of organized associations of individuals who share the same views on a particular issue or set of connected issues and attempt to influence related government policies. Racial minorities can be classified as interest groups when they solicit the government on racial policies.

League of United Latin American Citizens (LULAC) is an organization formed by middle-class activists to advance the goals of Latinos. The group has been instrumental in fighting segregation of Latinos in education.

Lily White Republicans represent a wing of the Republican Party that did not favor strong reconstruction or a civil rights platform. By 1964, the Lily White wing had emerged as the leader of the party.

MALDEF. See NAACP LDF.

Mobilization model is a model of agenda setting that considers issues that are initiated by the policymaking elite; yet for interest in the issue to be sustained, policymakers must extend it to the public at large. As with the inside initiative model, the mobilization model's applicability to the civil rights agenda is largely dependent upon the presence of minorities within the policymaking elite.

The National Association for the Advancement of Colored People's Legal Defense and Educational Fund, NAACP LDF, is a group of attorneys whose primary goal is to advance the cause of African Americans by using the legal system. Once fused with the NAACP, the LDF, or Ink Fund, is now an independent organization that has won many significant cases involving African Americans—most notably the *Brown v. Board of Education* (1954, 1955) case, which outlawed segregation in public schools. Today, in addition to fighting racial discrimination, the LDF works on behalf of death-row inmates and the economically disadvantaged. Other minorities have followed the litigation-oriented model of the LDF, particularly the Mexican American Legal Defense and Education Fund (**MALDEF**) and the Puerto Rican Legal Defense and Education Fund (**PRLDEF**).

Naturalization is the process by which nonnative-born people can become citizens of the United States. In the past, restrictive naturalization procedures have been used to keep racial minorities—particularly Asians, Indians, and Latinos—from becoming citizens.

Outside initiative model is an agenda-setting model that considers the process by which issues are brought to the agenda through the nongovernmental ranks. The issue is initiated by a particular group, then moves to the public at large and, finally, reaches the relevant policymakers. This model of agenda setting is the most applicable to the efforts by racial minorities, who have not been present within the policymaking elite, to bring civil rights issues to the agenda.

Partisan identification is the attachment a group or an individual feels to a particular political party. It measures direction toward a particular party and intensity of support. Party identification is a useful indicator in predicting voting behavior. Blacks, Chicanos, and Puerto Ricans are strong Democratic identifiers; Cuban Americans generally identify with the Republican Party; and Asians identify less strongly with either party.

Pluralism is a theory of government that contends that power is group based. Moreover, pluralism claims that since there are multiple points of access within American government, each group possesses equal opportunity when competing with other groups for power and resources. In minority politics, pluralism views each minority group as having the ability to compete adequately for power and resources; however, many scholars criticize pluralism for not taking into account systematic racial discrimination that exists within the system.

Political ideology constitutes the underlying beliefs, intentions, and attitudes of a particular social or political group, which in turn shape the group's actions and opinions on political issues. Ideology is traditionally conceived in terms of liberal, moderate, and conservative; however, numerous scholars find that classification scheme to be unsatisfactory. Furthermore, in relation to minority group politics, scholars have experienced difficulty in attributing a particular ideology to each racial group.

Political incorporation constitutes the extent to which a particular racial minority is able to exert influence within a political system. Incorporation goes beyond mere representation; rather, it is based on quality of leadership and coalition building with other racial groups.

PRLDEF. See **NAACP LDF.**

Public policies are the result of a purposive course of action by government officials attempting to deal with a problem. They represent what government does, as opposed to what it says it is going to do, about public problems.

Racism is the belief that race is the chief determinant of human characteristics and capabilities and that differences among the races provide for the superiority of one race. Racism is the primary condition that leads to discrimination against one race by another.

Rainbow Coalition is a concept first advanced by then presidential candidate Jesse Jackson in the hopes of forging a majority within the Democratic Party. Jackson sought to build a coalition of blacks, Latinos, Asians, American Indians, poor whites, and liberal whites as a means of pushing the party in a leftward direction. In 1984 the Rainbow Coalition met with limited success in influencing the Democratic Party platform; in 1988, following a more professionally managed campaign, Jackson was able to transform the Rainbow Coalition into a slightly more influential force.

Representative bureaucracy is a concept concerned with the degree to which the public workforce shares the demographic characteristics of the population at large. The presumption is that shared characteristics yield shared attitudes. If this is true, a representative bureaucracy should be a responsive bureaucracy.

Second-generation discrimination refers to a subtle form of discrimination against minority students in public education. Many schools group minority students together under the guise of remedial education, yet evidence indicates that this is in reality a form of resegregation—that is, schools are merely finding ways to keep minority groups separate and to provide them with an inferior education.

Separate but equal doctrine constitutes the interpretation of the Equal Protection Clause of the Fourteenth Amendment articulated in *Plessy v. Ferguson* (1986), which allows for racially segregated facilities as long as they are of equal quality. In reality, however, the facilities for blacks have been inferior to those for whites.

Social movements are efforts by disadvantaged groups to empower themselves. Prerequisites to the formation of social movements include an existing structure of social organizations, a leadership pool, the ability to tap outside resources, and skillful planning.

Socioeconomic status is a measure used in the social sciences that gauges the social and economic condition of a particular group or individual. Some of the indicators include educational attainment, income, unemployment rate, and poverty. For racial minority groups, socioeconomic status is a good predictor of political activity and of the ability of the group to overcome discrimination.

Southern Manifesto was the statement issued by most white southern politicians immediately following the *Brown v. Board of Education* (1954, 1955) decision, which outlawed segregation. The statement decried the decision and indicated that the South would be willing to fight its implementation. The Southern Manifesto was one of the first indications that the South would resist integration regardless of national policy.

Suffrage is, simply, the right to vote. Traditionally, the jurisdiction conferring the right to vote, or the franchise, has been the individual state. The states have used their ability to determine suffrage as a means of discriminating against women and racial minorities. Constitutional amendments (Fifteen, Nineteen, Twenty-Four, and Twenty-Six) and federal legislation (e.g., the Voting Rights Act of 1965) have been enacted to ensure universal suffrage to all citizens over age eighteen regardless of race, gender, or financial status.

Three-fifths compromise was the settlement reached at the Constitutional Convention maintaining that slaves would be counted as three-fifths of a person for ascertaining the population to determine representation in the U.S. House of Representatives. This aspect of the Constitution, now rendered void by the Thirteenth and Fourteenth Amendments, demonstrates the fact that slaves were not considered citizens by the framers of the Constitution. At the time of its adoption, the compromise was viewed as a means of cooperation between the North and the South; yet, as the history of the nineteenth century reveals, this harmony between the two regions was short-lived.

Valence issues are the issues on which political candidates compete by claiming to stand for the same universally desired values without specifically explaining how they will achieve those values. For example, many candidates campaign as being antipoverty. Valence issues can have a critical impact on elections by influencing voter support for the candidate who most effectively articulates those values.

Vote dilution impedes the ability of minority voters to translate votes into the election of candidates of their choice. Devices such as at-large elections and racial gerrymandering have been used for this purpose.

Voting behavior is the way people vote in elections and the forces that influence those votes. Contrary to some perceptions, voting behavior varies both among and within minority groups.

White primary was a device used by southern states by which the Democratic Party would claim that as a private organization it could prohibit African Americans and other minorities from participating in primary elections to select its nominees. The South was a one-party region; thus, the primary election almost always determined the eventual winner. As a result of the white primary, blacks and other minorities were effectively disenfranchised. In 1944 the Supreme Court, in *Smith v. Allwright*, ruled that the Democratic Party was a public institution and that, therefore, the white primary violated the Fifteenth Amendment.

With all deliberate speed was a concept formed by the Supreme Court in the 1955 case *Brown v. Board of Education* (Brown II). The Court ruled that desegregation must be implemented as quickly as possible, although not immediately. The vagueness of this doctrine allowed southern communities to resist desegregation for almost two decades.

Timelines

Timeline of African American Political History

1619   The first twenty indentured servants arrive in Jamestown, Virginia, from Africa.
1641   Slavery is first officially recognized by American colonial law when Massachusetts incorporates slavery into its body of laws.
1776   The Declaration of Independence is issued; southern states force Thomas Jefferson to eliminate antislavery rhetoric from the document.
1777   Vermont becomes the first American territory to abolish slavery.
1781   The Articles of Confederation are ratified, extending citizenship to *all* free inhabitants. An effort by southern states to limit citizenship to all free whites is defeated; however, the states soon find ways to circumvent this edict.
1787   The U.S. Constitution is drafted. It considers slaves to be three-fifths of a person for apportionment purposes; it leaves citizenship requirements to the states; Article I, Section 9, forbids Congress to outlaw international slave trade prior to 1808 (after ratification, Delaware was the only state to forbid the importation of slaves).
1787   The Northwest Ordinances ban slavery in the Northwest Territory, which later includes Illinois, Indiana, Michigan, Ohio, and Wisconsin.
1793   The *Fugitive Slave Law* is passed (and is later upheld by the Supreme Court in 1842). It requires that the federal government assist in returning runaway slaves.
1804   Ohio passes a series of laws restricting the rights of freed blacks.
1807   Congress bans the importation of slaves. This action results in an increase in the number of domestic slave laws and in a stepped-up black-market international slave trade.
1820   The Missouri Compromise is passed, representing a settlement between slave owners and abolitionists. The act strikes a balance between the admission of slave states and free states to the union; it later turns out to be a failure.
1829   David Walker, a free black, begins publishing *Walker's Appeal,* calling for slaves and free blacks to rise up against slavery, using violence if necessary.
1831   The first National Negro Convention convenes in Philadelphia. It marks the first time African Americans from all over the country meet to advance the plight of all blacks (free and slaves) living in the United States.
1848   The Massachusetts Supreme Court, in *Sarah C. Roberts v. City of Boston,* upholds the practice of segregation. The language "separate but equal" appears in common law for the first time.
1850   The compromise of 1850 allows California to be admitted as a free state and halts slavery in the District of Columbia but requires stricter enforcement of

the *Fugitive Slave Law*. Alabama, Georgia, Mississippi, and South Carolina are disgruntled with the compromise and begin talk of secession.

1854   The Kansas-Nebraska Act rescinds the Missouri Compromise, allowing each state to decide for itself whether to be a free state or a slave state. For many states this decision ultimately leads to violence between the two factions.

1857   The Supreme Court decides *Dred Scott v. Sanford*. The decision, written by Chief Justice Taney, declares that the Constitution recognizes the slave owners' "property" rights regarding slaves above the citizenship rights of blacks; it also declares that any attempt by Congress to regulate slavery in the territories is unconstitutional.

1861   The Confederate States of America commence the Civil War with an attack on Fort Sumter in South Carolina.

1861   The Federal Confiscation Acts call for freeing the slaves; however, they make exceptions in the border states, where the Fugitive Slave Law continues to be enforced.

1863   The Emancipation Proclamation frees all but the eight hundred thousand slaves in the loyal border states.

1865   The Civil War ends, and the Thirteenth Amendment abolishing slavery is ratified.

1868   The Fourteenth Amendment is ratified, requiring states to grant full citizenship to all citizens regardless of race; this includes forbidding states to deny "equal protection of the law" and "due process of law." Section 5 grants Congress broad discretion in enforcing the amendment.

1870   The Fifteenth Amendment, barring states from denying anyone the right to vote because of race, is ratified; the southern states easily circumvent the spirit of this amendment with poll taxes, literacy tests, and even violence.

1875   The Civil Rights Act outlaws racial segregation in public accommodations and in the military; however, in the 1883 *Civil Rights Cases,* the U.S. Supreme Court declares the act to be unconstitutional.

1876   When the presidential race is thrown into the House of Representatives, Republican Rutherford B. Hayes bargains with southern Democrats, exchanging their support for ending Reconstruction. Upon assuming office in 1877, Hayes removes the military from the southern states, leaving blacks unprotected in the process.

1880   In *Strauder v. West Virginia,* the U.S. Supreme Court finds West Virginia's statute mandating all-white juries to be in violation of the Equal Protection Clause of the Fourteenth Amendment.

1881   Tennessee passes a railroad segregation law. Similar laws are passed in other states: Florida (1887); Mississippi (1888); Texas (1889); Louisiana (1890); Alabama, Arkansas, Georgia, Kentucky (1891); South Carolina (1898); North Carolina (1899); Virginia (1900); Maryland (1904); Oklahoma (1907).

1883   In the *Civil Rights Cases* the Supreme Court declares the Civil Rights Act of 1875 to be unconstitutional.

1884   In *Ex Parte Yarborough* the U.S. Supreme Court affirms the power of the federal government to enforce the Fifteenth Amendment. This case and several others, such as *Strauder,* demonstrate that the Court was willing to enforce the

Fourteenth and Fifteenth Amendments; however, this willingness was short-lived.

1895 Booker T. Washington delivers his Atlanta Exposition address, expounding the philosophy of his Tuskegee Institute, which purported that blacks should master labor skills and achieve economic independence before attempting to obtain political equality.

1896 In *Plessy v. Ferguson,* the U.S. Supreme Court upholds Louisiana's practice of racial discrimination, declaring that separation of the races is allowable as long as the facilities are equal. This is known as the separate but equal doctrine.

1900 In reaction to the Supreme Court's sanctioning of segregation, southern states begin to officially sanction segregated facilities. Some African Americans combat this unequal treatment with organized boycotts.

1905 W.E.B. DuBois and other black leaders organize the Niagara Movement, a crucial national political convention for the development of the civil rights movement.

1909 Developing out of the Niagara Movement, the NAACP is founded as the lobby organization for black rights. W.E.B. DuBois is the editor of *The Crisis,* the NAACP's official publication.

1915 The Grandfather Clause, a device used by southern states to deny the franchise to those whose grandparents were slaves—thereby effectively circumventing the Fifteenth Amendment—is declared unconstitutional by the U.S. Supreme Court in *Guinn v. United States;* the NAACP is instrumental in sponsoring this litigation.

1919 The Nineteenth Amendment is ratified, giving women the right to vote.

1924 Mary Montgomery Booze is the first woman elected to the Republican National Committee.

1925 The Brotherhood of Sleeping Car Porters and Maids is founded by A. Philip Randolph; this is the first major black labor union, made necessary by the discriminatory practices of the white unions.

1927 Minnie Buckingham-Harper assumes her husband's unexpired term in the West Virginia legislature, thus becoming the first African American female to serve in any legislative body in the country.

1932 In *Nixon v. Condon,* the Supreme Court rules that the Democratic Party in Texas is part of the state government; therefore, its white primary violates the Equal Protection Clause of the Fourteenth Amendment.

1941 A. Philip Randolph threatens a large-scale march on Washington as a means to protest racial discrimination. He calls off the march after the government creates the Fair Employment Practices Commission, which can only investigate instances of discrimination in the government's war industries.

1944 In *Smith v. Allwright,* the U.S. Supreme Court completely invalidates Texas's white primary as violating the Fifteenth Amendment.

1945 The Supreme Court, in *Screws v. U.S.,* rules that a Georgia sheriff did not violate a black man's Fourteenth Amendment rights by beating him to death "without the due process of law" for stealing a tire.

1946 The Supreme Court rules in *Morgan v. Virginia* that states cannot compel segregation on interstate buses.

1948   The Democratic Party and Harry Truman begin to extend themselves to
        African Americans by desegregating the military, creating a Commission on
        Civil Rights, and adopting a pro–civil rights platform at the party's nominating
        convention. The latter move causes many southern state delegations to aban-
        don the Democratic Party and form the States Rights Party, headed by South
        Carolina governor Strom Thurmond.

1948   Racially restrictive covenants in housing contracts are declared unenforceable
        by the Supreme Court in *Shelly v. Kraemer*.

1952   Charlotta Bass is the first African American female to be nominated for the U.S.
        vice presidency by a major political party (the Progressive Party).

1954   The Supreme Court issues its unanimous landmark ruling, *Brown v. Board of
        Education*, declaring that in education, separate facilities are inherently un-
        equal, thereby overturning the precedent set in *Plessy v. Ferguson*. This ruling
        renders segregated schools unconstitutional.

1955   The Supreme Court issues *Brown II*, which outlines the way the ruling in
        Brown I should be implemented. The Court's standard of "all deliberate speed"
        is sufficiently vague to allow the southern states to stall in desegregating their
        schools.

1955   Rev. Martin Luther King Jr., Rosa Parks, and other civil rights leaders organize
        the Montgomery bus boycott, which ultimately results in ending discrimina-
        tion on Montgomery, Alabama, buses.

1957   The first Civil Rights Bill since 1875 passes.

1957   President Dwight Eisenhower, who initially opposes the Supreme Court's
        Brown v. Board of Education ruling, dispatches federal troops to Little Rock,
        Arkansas, to enforce a court order to desegregate its schools.

1960   The Civil Rights Act of 1960 is passed.

1963   Dr. Martin Luther King Jr. organizes the historic march on Washington, which
        over two hundred thousand people of all races attend to protest racial discrimi-
        nation; it is here where Dr. King gives his immortal "I Have a Dream" speech.
        The march on Washington is arguably one of the largest nonviolent protests in
        American history.

1964   The Twenty-Fourth Amendment to the Constitution bans poll taxes in all fed-
        eral elections.

1964   As a result of intensive lobbying by civil rights leaders and the keen political
        skill of President Lyndon Johnson, Congress passes a comprehensive Civil
        Rights Act; this legislation gives the federal government enormous power in
        compelling states to end their practices of racial discrimination.

1964   Constance Baker Motley is the first African American female elected to the New
        York state senate.

1965   Again as the result of intensive lobbying by civil rights activists and the political
        know-how of Lyndon Johnson, Congress passes the Voting Rights Act; to ensure
        fair voting practices, this act places the voting practices of states that lag in ending
        voting-booth discrimination under the jurisdiction of the federal government.

1966   The U.S. Supreme Court invalidates poll taxes in state elections in *Harper v.
        Virginia Board of Elections;* this case opens broad access to the polls to many
        previously disenfranchised African Americans.

1967   Lyndon Johnson appoints Appeals Court judge and former U.S. solicitor general and director counsel of the NAACP LDF Thurgood Marshall to the Supreme Court; he is the first nonwhite to sit on the Court. The first big-city black mayors are elected—Carl Stokes in Cleveland, Ohio, and Richard Hatcher in Gary, Indiana.

1968   Dr. Martin Luther King Jr., arguably the most important civil rights leader in African American history, is assassinated in Memphis, Tennessee.

1968   Shirley Chisholm, from New York's Twelfth District, becomes the first African American female elected to the U.S. House of Representatives.

1972   Congresswoman Shirley Chisholm runs for president, becoming the first African American to launch a serious campaign for the U.S. presidency.

1973   Thomas Bradley is elected mayor of Los Angeles. Lelia K. Smith Foley is elected mayor of Taft, Oklahoma; she is the first African American woman mayor in the continental United States.

1976   Barbara Jordan becomes the first African American to deliver a keynote speech at a major political party convention when she does so at the Democratic National Convention. Yvonne Braithwaite Burke, a representative from California, is the first woman to chair the Congressional Black Caucus. Unita Blackwell is elected the mayor of Mayersville, Mississippi, becoming the first African American mayor in that state.

1978   The Supreme Court issues its complicated affirmative action decision in *Bakke v. California*. The Court rules that states may not use quotas as a means to ensure racial diversity; however, the Court does allow states to use race as a "plus" for admissions qualifications to universities and professional schools.

1981   Ronald Reagan takes office as president of the United States; he instantly scales back the federal government's role in protecting the rights of minorities in the name of the "New Federalism."

1981   Liz Byrd is elected to the Wyoming house of representatives; she is the first African American to be elected to Wyoming's state house.

1984   Rev. Jesse Jackson becomes the first African American candidate to run for president within one of the two major political parties when he enters the Democratic primary. Although his campaign suffers from logistical problems, he still finishes third behind Gary Hart and the eventual nominee, Walter Mondale. At the Democratic Convention Jackson contends that his level of influence does not match the proportion of votes he garnered.

1988   As a result of the liberalized primary process and a better organization Jesse Jackson runs a more successful campaign; he finishes second behind eventual nominee Michael Dukakis. At the Democratic Convention Jackson delivers his "Quilt Speech." In the general election Republican nominee George Bush employs the racially charged Willie Horton commercial.

1989   L. Douglas Wilder, the grandson of slaves, becomes the first African American to be *elected* governor of a state when he ekes out a victory over Marshall Coleman in Virginia. In the same month David Dinkins is the first African American elected mayor of New York City.

1989   *Wards Cove Packing, Inc. v. Atonio* and a series of other cases are decided. The Supreme Court rules that when employees file discrimination suits, the burden of proof is on the employee to show the existence of discrimination; statistics are no longer considered evidence of racial discrimination in the workplace.

1990   In response to the *Wards Cove* decision, Congress passes the Civil Rights Act of 1990, which allows for more statistical evidence to be used in employee discrimination suits. The act is vetoed by President Bush, and Congress is unable to override the veto.

1990   Sharon Pratt Dixon (Kelly) becomes the first woman and the first Washington, D.C., native to be elected mayor of the nation's capital.

1991   Thurgood Marshall retires from the Supreme Court, and President Bush appoints black conservative Clarence Thomas as his replacement. Thomas's nomination faces problems because of his judicial ideology and charges of sexually harassing his employees. His nomination becomes a public show trial, pitting him against his African American accuser, Anita Hill.

1991   Congress passes another Civil Rights Act, virtually identical to the one passed in 1991. President Bush, whose popularity is waning, signs the bill.

1992   Four white Los Angeles police officers are tried for use of excessive force against black motorist Rodney King. The beating was captured on videotape; however, the officers are acquitted by an all-white, all-suburban jury. As a result of the verdict, Los Angeles erupts with racial violence and rioting; the physical, economic, and psychological damage is enormous.

1992   Arkansas Governor Bill Clinton defeats incumbent George Bush as president of the United States; he promises to seek a new racial diversity.

1992   Carol Moseley-Braun from Illinois is elected to the U.S. Senate. She is the first African American female and the first African American Democrat elected to the Senate.

1993   The U.S. government pursues a federal civil rights case against the four Los Angeles police officers accused of beating Rodney King, resulting in convictions and prison terms for two of the officers. The city is peaceful following the verdicts.

Timeline of American Indian Peoples, All Tribes and All Regions

1000   This is the approximate date of the formation of the Iroquois League, the oldest political alliance in North America.

1638   The first reservation is established in Connecticut; remaining members of the Quinnipiac Tribe are placed on this reservation.

1775   American colonists declare war against England. The colonies' provisional government—the Continental Congress—establishes three Indian commissions (northern, middle, and southern); each commission is charged with preserving amiable relations with indigenous tribes and keeping them out of the violence. However, many Indians ally themselves with the British, and many join forces with the American colonists.

1777   The Articles of Confederation organize the new government of the United States. The articles assume authority over Indian affairs except when the "legislative right of any State within its own limits [is] infringed or violated."

1778   The United States signs its first Indian treaty with the Delaware Nation; in exchange for access to that nation's land by U.S. troops, the United States promises to defend and admit the Delaware Nation as a state.

1789   The U.S. Constitution is adopted. Article I, Section 8, grants Congress power to regulate commerce among foreign nations and *Indian tribes.*

1789   Congress places Indian affairs under the War Department.

1802   Congress appropriates over $10,000 for the "civilization" of Indians.

1803   As part of the Louisiana Purchase, the United States acquires lands on which numerous Indian tribes reside.

1815   The United States begins the process of removing Indians to western lands.

1816   Congress restricts licenses for trade with Indians to American citizens.

1824   The Bureau of Indian Affairs is created within the War Department.

1827   John Ross is elected president of the Cherokee Nation; he is the first president since the adoption of the nation's new constitution that year in New Echota, Georgia.

1830   President Andrew Jackson successfully pushes his Indian Removal Bill through Congress.

1831   The U.S. Supreme Court, in *Cherokee Nation v. Georgia,* holds that Indian tribes are domestic dependent nations, not foreign nations.

1832   In *Worcester v. Georgia,* the U.S. Supreme Court, in an opinion written by Chief Justice John Marshall, ensures the sovereignty of the Cherokees; however,

President Andrew Jackson refuses to follow the decision and initiates the westward removal of the Five Civilized Tribes (Cherokee, Chickasaw, Choctaw, Creek, and Seminole). The term *Five Civilized Tribes* originated because these five tribes modeled their governments after American and state institutions and had been assimilated into the white culture.

1835   The Treaty of New Echota is signed. Cherokees agree to westward removal.

1838   The Trail of Tears begins. Cherokee Indians are forced to travel almost thirteen hundred miles without sufficient food, water, and medicine; almost one-quarter of the Cherokees do not survive the journey. The Potawatomis in Indiana experience similar hardships on their Trail of Death.

1847   Pueblos in Taos, New Mexico, ally with Latinos to overthrow the newly established U.S. rule.

1848   The Treaty of Guadalupe Hidalgo (see Mexican American political chronology) is signed, bringing the Mexican War to an end. As a result of the vast amount of land ceded to the United States, many new Indian tribes fall under U.S. jurisdiction.

1849   The Department of the Interior is created, and the Bureau of Indian Affairs is shuffled from the War Department to the Interior Department.

1853   The Gadsden Purchase (see Mexican American timeline) is completed. More tribes come under the jurisdiction of the United States.

1854   Several southeast U.S. tribes (Cherokee, Chickasaw, Choctaw, Muscogee, and Seminole) form an alliance.

1861   The Civil War begins. Various Indian tribes fight on both sides. Stand Watie, a Cherokee, becomes the only Indian brigadier general in the Confederate Army; he leads two Cherokee regiments in the Southwest.

1864   Approximately eight thousand Navajos are forcibly marched to Fort Sumner, New Mexico, on the Navajo Long Walk; after three years of harsh imprisonment the survivors are released.

1865   Confederate General Robert E. Lee surrenders to Union General Ulysses S. Grant at Appomattox; at General Grant's side is Colonel Ely S. Parker, a fullblooded Seneca.

1867   The Indian Peace Commission finalizes treaty making between the United States and Indian tribes.

1869   President Ulysses S. Grant appoints Brigadier General Ely S. Parker to head the Bureau of Indian Affairs; he is the first Indian to fill this position.

1871   Congress passes legislation that ends treaty making with Indian tribes.

1884   In *Elk v. Wilkins,* the U.S. Supreme Court holds that the Fourteenth Amendment's guarantee of citizenship to all persons born in the United States does not apply to Indians, even those born within the geographical confines of the United States.

1901   Congress passes the Citizenship Act of 1901, which formally grants U.S. citizenship to members of the Five Civilized Tribes.

1921   Congress passes the Snyder Act, which appropriates money for Indians regardless of the amount of Indian blood or their residence.

1924   Congress passes the Indian Citizenship Act, conferring citizenship on all American Indians.

1934 Congress passes the Indian Reorganization Act, which allows for tribal self-government, and begins the Indian Credit Program; concurrently, the Johnson-O'Malley Act provides for general assistance to Indians.

1944 In Denver, Colorado, the National Congress of American Indians is founded.

1948 Through judicial means, Indians in Arizona and New Mexico win the right to vote in state elections.

1949 The Hoover Commission recommends "termination," which would mandate that Congress no longer recognize Indian sovereignty, thus eliminating all special rights and benefits.

1953 Congress passes a law—introduced by Wyoming Representative William Henry Harrison—that gives California, Minnesota, Nebraska, Oregon, and Wisconsin legal jurisdiction over Indian reservations, thus initiating the termination process.

1958 Secretary of the Interior Seaton begins to retract the termination policy.

1961 More than 210 tribes meet at the American Indian Chicago Conference, where the Declaration of Indian Purpose is drafted for presentation to the U.S. Congress.

1968 Congress passes the American Indian Civil Rights Act, giving individual Indians constitutional protection against their tribal governments. This protection is the same as the protection the U.S. Constitution provides against state and local governments.

1968 The American Indian Movement (AIM) is founded; it is a protest movement based on the model of the black civil rights protest groups.

1969 Indian activists occupy Alcatraz Island near San Francisco in addition to staging sit-ins at the Bureau of Indian Affairs.

1971 The Alaska Native Claims Settlement Act is passed; it eliminates 90 percent of Alaskan natives' land claims in exchange for a guarantee of 44 million acres and almost $1 billion.

1972 In protest of a history of broken promises to Indian tribes, two hundred Indians participate in the Trail of Broken Treaties march, ultimately occupying the Washington, D.C., office of the Bureau of Indian Affairs.

1973 AIM organizes an occupation of Wounded Knee on the Pine Ridge Reservation in South Dakota, near the Nebraska border; the occupation ends with an armed confrontation with the FBI. AIM member Leonard Peltier is still (as of 1995) held in federal prison for the murder of two FBI agents, despite evidence that his trial was unconstitutional and unfair.

1975 The Indian Self-Determination and Education Act is passed, giving Indian tribal governments more control over their tribal affairs and appropriating more money for education assistance.

1979 The U.S. Supreme Court awards the Lakota Nation $122.5 million in compensation for the U.S. government's illegal appropriation of the Black Hills in South Dakota.

1980 The Penobscots and Passamaquoddies accept monetary compensation from the U.S. government for their lands (the Massachusetts colony—now the state of Maine), which the government took illegally in 1790.

1986   Congress amends the Indian Civil Rights Act and grants tribal courts the power to impose criminal penalties.

1988   The Alaska Native Claims Settlement Act is amended, giving corporations the option to sell their stock after 1991.

1988   Congress officially repeals the thirty-five-year-old termination policy.

1992   Representative Ben Nighthorse Campbell, a Cheyenne from Colorado, is elected to the U.S. Senate.

1994   Three hundred representatives from the 545 federally recognized Indian tribes meet with President Bill Clinton, the first time since 1822 that Indians have been invited to meet officially with a U.S. president to discuss issues of concern to Indian peoples.

Timeline of Mexican Americans

1540   Explorers from Mexico first enter the Southwest.

1821   The Republic of Mexico gains its independence from Spain.

1829   The Republic of Mexico outlaws slavery, thereby creating a conflict with many Anglo immigrants who were invited to settle in northern Mexico (now Texas) to fill a capital void and who want to retain the practice of slavery.

1836   Anglos and dissident Mexicans in Texas revolt and secede from Mexico, creating the Republic of Texas, where slavery is legal. The United States instantly recognizes Texas, whereas Mexico does not.

1845   The Republic of Texas officially becomes an American state.

1846   After almost a decade of hostility, the United States declares war on the Republic of Mexico. Many Americans believe Mexico is weak and can be easily conquered.

1848   The *Treaty of Guadalupe Hidalgo* officially ends the hostilities between the United States and Mexico. Mexico cedes a tremendous amount of territory to the United States. The United States increases its territories by 33 percent, acquiring most of the present states of Arizona, New Mexico, California, Colorado, Texas, Nevada, Utah, Kansas, Oklahoma, and Wyoming. Mexican citizens living in the ceded territories are given the option to go to Mexico or to remain and live under U.S. rule. The United States grants Mexican citizens who elect to stay all guarantees of citizenship and freedom of religion; these guarantees, however, are not fully enjoyed.

1850   The California Foreign Miners Tax Law is passed, barring Mexicans from mining occupations. The hardships of the law are exacerbated by anti-Mexican violence.

1851   All native Mexicans are excluded from the California state senate, and California passes the California Land Law, which strips most native Mexicans of their land. The Mexican American population in California is divided into the rich Chicanos, called *Californios,* and the poor masses, the *Cholos.*

1853   The United States dispatches James Gadsen to Mexico to purchase land. Mexico is financially strapped and, therefore, is willing to sell the territory of what is now the southern portions of New Mexico and Arizona. The United States wants the land for a rail line to California.

1855   California passes a statute prohibiting vagrancy that is referred to colloquially as "the Greaser Law." The Bureau of Public Instruction in California requires that all schools use English exclusively.

1859   In Texas, Mexican Americans revolt against Anglo leaders; this is known as the Juan Cortinas revolt.

1884   Juan Patrón is murdered in the territory of New Mexico. Educated at Notre
        Dame University, Patrón had been elected speaker of the New Mexico house at
        age twenty-four. He was best known, however, for his support of Alex McSween
        in his battle against Judge Warren Bristol and District Attorney William
        Rynerson in the Lincoln County (New Mexico) wars, which began as a prop-
        erty feud and ended with a violent shoot-out; other notable participants in-
        clude Billy the Kid.

1889   In New Mexico Chicano resistance efforts begin. The two predominant groups
        directing the revolt are the *Gorras Blancas* and the *Mano Negras.*

1890   The political party for the *Gorras Blancas,* the United People's Party, has several
        candidates in local elections in New Mexico.

1894   One of the first *mutualistas* is formed in Tucson, Arizona. The Alianza Hispano
        Americano provides insurance and funeral services for Mexican Americans; it
        soon expands its activities to include political action and publishing.

1902   The United States passes the Reclamation Act, which significantly increases
        agricultural efforts in the Southwest and thus expands the demand for agricul-
        tural labor, which is satisfied by Chicanos.

1903   Two thousand Mexican American laborers march through Clifton-Morenci,
        Arizona, while striking against the arduous conditions they face in the Clifton-
        Morenci copper mines.

1907   Ricardo and Enrique Magon found El Partido Liberal Mexicano (PLM); the
        PLM organizes workers in southern California and, at times, is regarded as mil-
        itant. The PLM and followers of the Magon brothers spread throughout the
        United States, organizing Chicano workers.

1912   New Mexico and Arizona are admitted as states in the United States of
        America. In Arizona Anglos control both politics and industry, whereas
        Chicanos control little of either. In New Mexico, Anglos control industry, but
        Chicanos are better represented in state government.

1915   The first Latino to serve in the U.S. House of Representatives, Benigno "B.C."
        Hernandez from New Mexico, takes office; he serves from 1915 to 1916 and
        from 1919 to 1920.

1917   The Immigration Act of 1917 places a tax on Mexican employees and requires
        literacy tests. Industrialists and agriculturalists in the Southwest, who rely on
        this cheap source of labor, eventually pressure the government into repealing
        the law. Ezequiel Cabeza de Baca is inaugurated as governor of New Mexico af-
        ter serving as lieutenant governor (1912–1916) but dies after six weeks in office.

1928   The League of United Latin American Citizens (LULAC) is founded in Texas,
        composed primarily of relatively wealthy Chicanos. LULAC's main function is
        to compel all Chicanos to learn English as a means of getting ahead in the
        United States. LULAC is considered assimilationist in focus.

1929   The first Latino U.S. senator, O. A. Larrazola, a Republican from New Mexico, is
        elected to fill the unexpired term of a New Mexico senator who died in office.
        Larrazola serves only one year.

1935   Democratic member of Congress Dennis Chavez is appointed to fill one of
        New Mexico's senate seats, which became vacant when the incumbent was
        killed in a plane crash; Chavez is reelected five times and dies in office in 1962.

1940 Unity Leagues begin to arise in California; their primary objective is to combat segregation and discrimination directed at Chicanos.

1942 The federal government establishes the Bracero Program (Public Law 45) in response to the labor shortages caused by World War II; the program calls for Mexico to send workers to the United States to fill the void, with wages determined by both countries. This program increases the number of Chicanos in the Southwest, and the workers are given legal immigrant status. Chicano labor leaders oppose the program.

1944 The Comite Mexicano Contra el Racismo is founded to provide Chicanos with the necessary legal aid to fight discrimination and racism; its chief publication is *Fraternidad*.

1946 In what is later dubbed "the Lemon Grove Incident," California Judge Paul J. McCormick holds that segregation of Chicano schoolchildren violates both California law and the U.S. Constitution *(Mendez v. Westminster School District)*.

1948 Chicano World War II veterans in Corpus Christi, Texas, establish the American G.I. Forum to advance political and social progress of Mexican Americans.

1949 Edward Roybal becomes the first Latino to be elected to the Los Angeles City Council since 1881; his victory is in part a result of the Community Service Organization's (CSO) work in registering Chicano voters.

1950 Operation Wetback commences. Since the end of World War II there has been less need for agricultural labor; thus, many Mexicans are indiscriminately apprehended and deported to Mexico.

1951 The Bracero Program is renewed; many Chicano labor leaders view the Braceros as major hindrances in their unionization efforts.

1960 Chicanos who support John F. Kennedy's candidacy for the presidency form Viva Kennedy Clubs. The activity of these clubs significantly aids the Kennedy-Johnson results in California and Texas.

1962 Edward Roybal becomes the first Latino from California to be elected to the U.S. House of Representatives when he defeats a white Republican incumbent in the Thirtieth District in Los Angeles. César Chávez leaves the CSO to form the National Farmworkers Association (NFWA) to unite all farmworkers.

1964 The Bracero Program is ended. Joseph Montoya from New Mexico is elected to the U.S. Senate to the seat previously held by Dennis Chavez, serving until 1976 when he is defeated in his run for reelection.

1965 The NFWA supports the Filipinos in the Agricultural Workers Organizing Committee in their labor dispute with grape growers in Delano, California. This incident helps launch César Chávez to a position of national prominence.

1966 César Chávez negotiates contracts between his NFWA and the Schenley Corporation, Gallo, Christian Brothers, Paul Masson, Almaden, Franzia Brothers, and Novitiate.

1967 Reis Lopez Tijerina enters a courthouse in Tierra Amarilla, New Mexico, and attempts to place the district attorney under citizen's arrest. A shoot-out erupts, and Tijerina escapes. After a long manhunt he is apprehended but is later acquitted of all charges.

1967 David Sanchez establishes the Brown Berets, a paramilitary group interested in defending Chicano communities.

1967 Elizar Rico, Joe Raza, and Raul Ruiz found *La Raza,* a magazine that serves as a primary chronicler of the Chicano movement.

1968 Chicano students walk out of five Los Angeles high schools, demanding more Chicano administrators and teachers, courses in Mexican American history, and a cessation of discrimination against Chicano students. The walkouts receive national attention. The leaders of the walkouts are indicted by a Los Angeles grand jury, but the indictments are soon dismissed as unconstitutional.

1969 Chicano university students form El Movimiento Estudiantil Chicano de Aztlan; the organization leads the Chicano movement throughout the Southwest.

1969 The Ford Foundation funds the Mexican American Legal Defense and Education Fund as a legal aid group to fight for the rights of Chicanos.

1970 La Raza Unida Party (LRUP) chapters are formed to place candidates in races for office. LRUP's presence is felt in Colorado, Texas, California, Arizona, and New Mexico.

1970 Mexican American Ricardo Romo runs for governor of California on the Peace and Freedom Party ticket.

1971 In Crystal City, Texas (over 80 percent Chicano), LRUP candidates dominate the elections for the board of education and city council.

1971 The First Chicana Conference is organized. The conference examines the role of women in the Chicano movement.

1972 The Dixon-Arnett Law is passed by the State of California; it provides that any employer who knowingly hires undocumented workers will be fined. The Supreme Court of California deems the law unconstitutional.

1972 Chicano lawyer Ramsey Muniz runs for governor of Texas on the LRUP ticket.

1973 In *San Antonio v. Rodriguez,* the U.S. Supreme Court upholds Texas's school financing system despite claims that its inequities unconstitutionally deprive Mexican American students of their fundamental right to education. The Court reasons that the Mexican American students are not *absolutely* deprived of education and that education is *not* a fundamental constitutional right.

1974 Raul Castro is elected the first Chicano governor of Arizona. LRUP does relatively well in California, Texas, and Colorado.

1977 The Congressional Hispanic Caucus is established to monitor legislation and "other governmental activity that affects Hispanics" and to "develop programs and other activities that would increase opportunities for Hispanics to participate in and contribute to the American political system."

1981 Henry Cisneros is elected mayor of San Antonio, Texas, which is 55 percent Chicano; he is reelected in 1983, 1985, 1987, and 1989 and steps down as mayor in 1991.

1983 Federico Peña is elected mayor of Denver, Colorado; he is reelected in 1987.

1986 The Immigration Reform and Control Act, which is a major effort to reduce illegal immigration, is passed. The act increases border patrol activities and provides for harsh sanctions against employers who knowingly hire undocumented workers; additionally, the law provides for legalization of all people who have resided illegally in the United States since January 1, 1982.

1989 President George Bush appoints conservative former New Mexico representative Manuel Lujan as secretary of the interior.

1993 President Clinton appoints Federico Peña secretary of transportation and Henry Cisneros secretary of housing and urban development.

Timeline of Puerto Ricans

1493   Christopher Columbus lands on present-day Puerto Rico; he claims it as the Spanish island of Boriquén. Columbus calls the island San Juan Bautista. Approximately thirty thousand Taíno Indians are living on the island.

1508   Ponce de León is appointed governor of the island and founds the first settlement, known as Puerto Rico; he conscripts the Indians to mine for gold. The first school in Puerto Rico is established in Caparra.

1775   The population of Puerto Rico is 70,250, 6,467 of which are black slaves. The Indian population has been completely wiped out.

1873   Slavery is abolished on Puerto Rico.

1897   Spain grants autonomy to Puerto Rico; as a result of immigration the population approaches 900,000.

1898   The Spanish-American War begins. By July, American forces land on the island.

1899   The Treaty of Paris is ratified, ending the Spanish-American War. The United States annexes the island of Puerto Rico.

1900   The Foraker Act is passed, making Puerto Rico an "unincorporated" U.S. territory. President McKinley appoints a governor to administer the territory. The first fifty-six Puerto Ricans arrive in Hawaii.

1901   Luis Muñoz publishes the first bilingual Spanish-English newspaper in New York City.

1917   The Jones Act grants U.S. citizenship to all Puerto Ricans.

1937   Oscar Garcia Rivera becomes the first Puerto Rican to be elected to the New York state legislature.

1942   Hiram C. Bithorn becomes the first Puerto Rican major league baseball player (with the Chicago Cubs).

1950   Public Law 600 gives Puerto Rico a chance to draft its own constitution.

1950   Nationalists attack the governor's mansion killing twenty-seven and wounding ninety. In Washington, D.C., they attempt to assassinate President Truman, killing a White House police officer. Pedro Albizu Campos and other Nationalist leaders are given lengthy prison sentences.

1952   The commonwealth of Puerto Rico ratifies its new Commonwealth Constitution. In the first election, the Popular Democratic Party wins the most votes, and the Independence Party finishes second.

1953   The United Nations directs the United States to discontinue classifying Puerto Rico as a nonself-governing territory.

1954   Four Puerto Rican Nationalists begin shooting in the U.S. House of Representatives; five members of Congress are wounded.

1958   Tony Mendez becomes the first Puerto Rican to be appointed Democratic Party district leader in El Barrio, New York.

1966   Herman Badillo becomes the first Puerto Rican to be elected Bronx borough president, New York City.

1970   The 1970 Census reveals that 2.8 million people live on the island of Puerto Rico and that 1.5 million Puerto Ricans live in the United States. Herman Badillo becomes the first Puerto Rican member of Congress from the mainland.

1973   Maurice Ferré, a Puerto Rican, is elected the first Latino mayor of Miami. He serves six terms before he is defeated in 1985.

1974   A consent decree is signed between the New York City school system and Puerto Rican plaintiffs represented by PRLDEF mandating bilingual programs in New York City schools.

1978   Olga Mendez becomes the first Puerto Rican woman elected to a major post in the United States, the New York state senate.

1979   Luis Roviera is appointed Colorado state Supreme Court justice.

1993   Nydia Velazquez (D-NY) becomes the first Puerto Rican woman to be elected to the U.S. Congress.

Timeline of Cuban Americans

1801   Spain allows Cuba to engage in open commerce; although the Spanish government withdraws this privilege in 1809, many Cubans still engage in free trade.

1823   The United States issues the Monroe Doctrine, thus indicating U.S. willingness to become involved in Spain's dealings with Cuba.

1885   Vicente Martínez Ybor, who migrated to Cuba from Spain to avoid compulsory military service, purchases a plot of land immediately northeast of Tampa, Florida. On his land he develops a cigar manufacturing operation, which grows at a phenomenal rate. Ybor's development eventually becomes Ybor City, and the Cuban American population in Tampa mainly resides there. Cubans migrate to Ybor City to work on the tobacco farms and in the cigar factories.

1886   Slavery is abolished in Cuba.

1894   José Martí, a Cuban exile living in Florida, and others unsuccessfully attempt to raid Cuba from Jacksonville; the expedition is funded by donations from Cuban tobacco-field workers in Key West and Tampa.

1895   With the support of the U.S. government, Cuba launches a war of independence against Spain.

1898   The U.S. battleship *Maine* is attacked by Spanish troops off the coast of Cuba, which begins the Spanish-American War. The United States ultimately wins the war, thus achieving Cuba's independence from Spain. Cuba, however, remains under U.S. military rule.

1901   Congress approves the Platt Amendment, granting Cuba conditional independence; the United States reserves the right to intervene on "Cuba's behalf."

1959   Fidel Castro successfully overthrows General Fulgencio Batista y Zaldívar as president of Cuba. Castro soon becomes prime minister of Cuba, declaring that free elections will be held in four years, after problems are solved. Upper-income and professional Cubans, with financial help from the United States, begin to arrive in Florida.

1961   In the infamous Bay of Pigs operation, 1,500 Cuban American exiles, supported by the U.S. government, attempt to invade Cuba. The invaders are handily defeated, as almost 1,200 (80 percent) of the exiles are captured and imprisoned in Cuba.

1962   U.S. intelligence services spot Soviet missiles in Cuba; President John F. Kennedy blockades the island with air and naval forces. The United States and the Soviet Union are pushed to the brink of nuclear war over the issue. Soviet Secretary Khrushchev admits that missiles are present and promises to withdraw them.

1973   The "freedom flight," which brought over 250,000 anti-Castro Cubans to the United States, ceases operations.

1980   President Jimmy Carter publicly announces that the United States will accept 3,500 Cuban refugees from the port of Mariel, thus beginning an immense wave of Cuban immigration to the United States. The United States is deluged with Cuban immigrants, many of whom are not political prisoners but ordinary criminals. The United States detains the new immigrants for an indefinite period.

1980   President Carter declares a state of emergency in Florida and authorizes $10 million for refugee assistance. He also calls up nine hundred Coast Guard reservists to help administer aid to Cuban refugees.

1980   Cuba halts the 159-day Mariel boat lift.

1980   A group of politically conservative, anti-Castro Cuban Americans in Miami, Florida, form the Cuban-American National Foundation, which functions as a trade association and political lobbying organization; Miami construction mogul and Cuban American community leader Jorge Mas Canosa is elected the foundation's first president.

1982   With the support of the Cuban-American National Foundation and the Reagan administration, Congress authorizes the Voice of America to initiate Radio Martí, an anti-Castro, anti-Communist radio broadcast transmitted to Cuba. Radio Martí angers Fidel Castro, who suspends agreements and dialogue with the United States.

1984   Miami, Florida's, African American city manager, Howard Gray, who is extremely unpopular with the Cuban community, is fired. This incident demonstrates the emerging political power of Miami's Cuban American community.

1985   Nonideological technocrat Xavier Suarez becomes the first Cuban-born mayor of Miami, Florida (although it is important to note that the first Latino mayor of Miami was Maurice Ferre, a Puerto Rican). Suarez defeats Democratic incumbent Ferre and Raul Masvidal, a Reagan supporter and a member of the Cuban-American Foundation.

1986   The former mayor of Tampa Bob Martinez (R) is elected governor of Florida; Martinez, a Cuban American, is the first Latino governor of the state.

1990   Martinez, who is extremely unpopular, is defeated by former U.S. Senator Lawton Chiles (D) in his bid for reelection.

Timeline of Asian Americans:
Chinese, Japanese, Koreans, Filipinos, East Indians, Southeast Asians

1785   Three Chinese sailors land in Baltimore, Maryland.

1790   The first known native of India is reported in the United States in Salem, Massachusetts.

1790   The Naturalization Act of 1790 grants the right of U.S. citizenship to all "free white persons."

1834   The first Chinese woman in the United States, Afong Moy, is put on display in a New York theater.

1843   The first known Japanese immigrants arrive in the United States.

1848   The *Eagle* docks in the San Francisco harbor, bringing the first reported Chinese immigrants.

1850   Following an influx of Chinese immigration to California as a result of the discovery of gold, the Foreign Miners Tax is imposed on the Chinese to impede further immigration.

1852   Sugar plantation owners in Hawaii bring in 180 Chinese indentured servants.

1868   The first Japanese contract workers are brought to sugar plantations in Hawaii.

1869   The first transcontinental railroad is built with the labor of Chinese immigrants; two thousand Chinese railroad workers go on strike for better working conditions.

1870   The anti-Chinese movement is initiated. Many communities single out Chinese immigrants through discriminatory laws and violence.

1875   The Page Law prohibits prostitution and "coolie" labor in the United States.

1880   The California Civil Code forbids marriage between a white person and a "Negro, Mulatto, or Mongolian."

1882   The Chinese Exclusion Act is passed and signed into law; it bars the immigration of Chinese laborers and prohibits Chinese from becoming naturalized citizens.

1885   The Japanese government allows its workers to go to Hawaii as contract laborers; in the ensuing decade over thirty thousand workers migrate.

1898   The United States officially annexes Hawaii.

1898   The Spanish-American War ends with the signing of the Treaty of Paris. The Philippine Islands are given to the United States. Filipinos are viewed as "wards" of the United States and thus do not need visas to travel there. Filipino women who marry American veterans are allowed to migrate to the United States as war brides.

1905   The Asiatic Exclusion League is formed; it lobbies to prevent the immigration of Asians.

1913   The California Land Act is passed; it bars aliens from owning land. Many Japanese farmers are adversely affected.

1917   The 1917 Immigration Act prohibits immigration of labor from all parts of Asia except Japan.

1918   The Act of May 9 allows all people who served in the U.S. armed forces in World War I, *regardless of race,* to become naturalized citizens.

1922   The Cable Act rescinds the citizenship of women who marry aliens who are ineligible for citizenship (which includes all Asians except Hawaiians and Filipinos).

1923   The Supreme Court rules in *United States v. Thind* that Indian immigrants are not eligible for U.S. citizenship.

1924   The Immigration Quota Act excludes all aliens who are ineligible for citizenship. It allows the entry of alien wives of Chinese merchants but not of alien wives of U.S. citizens.

1931   Filipinos who served in the U.S. armed forces are eligible for U.S. citizenship.

1934   The ruling in *Morrison v. California* mandates that Filipinos are not eligible for citizenship.

1935   A reparations bill is passed by Congress, encouraging Filipinos to return to the Philippines; only two thousand leave.

1942   President Franklin Roosevelt signs Executive Order 9066, which creates zones from which the military has the power to exclude people; consequently, over 112,000 Japanese residing in these zones are forcefully removed to ten "relocation" camps.

1943   Congress repeals the Chinese Exclusion Acts; however, Congress establishes an annual quota of 105 Chinese immigrants.

1952   The McCarran-Walter Act upholds the national origin quotas for Asian Americans based on the figures from the 1924 Immigration Quota Act. Aliens previously ineligible for citizenship are subsequently allowed naturalization rights.

1956   The first Asian American—Californian Dalip S. Saund—is elected to the U.S. House of Representatives.

1964   The Civil Rights Act is passed, outlawing all racial discrimination.

1965   The Voting Rights Act is passed, forbidding outright electoral discrimination on account of race.

1965   The Immigration and Naturalization Act eliminates national origin quotas; hemisphere-based quotas are used instead. The Eastern Hemisphere's quota is set at 170,000, limited to 20,000 immigrants per country.

1971   The provisions of the McCarran-Walter Act providing for detention camps are repealed.

1974   *Lau v. Nichols* rules that school districts must provide special education for students who speak little or no English.

1975   Congress establishes the Indochinese Refugee Assistance Program (Public Law 94-23); this act resettles approximately 130,000 Southeast Asians (mostly Vietnamese and Cambodians) to the United States.

1976   *Wong v. Hampton* allows resident aliens to be eligible for federal jobs.

1976 After thirty-four years in existence, Executive Order 9066 is repealed by Gerald Ford.

1982 Following a racially motivated argument in a Detroit, Michigan, bar, twenty-seven-year-old Vincent Chin is clubbed to death with a baseball bat; the two white assailants receive light sentences. In response, Chinese Americans (with the assistance of other Asian American groups) form the Citizens for Justice. A federal grand jury investigates, and one of the assailants is given a twenty-five-year prison sentence. His conviction is later overturned by the Sixth Circuit Court of Appeals.

1982 A Southeast Asian immigration quota of ten thousand is set by Ronald Reagan.

1983 With the assistance of the Japanese American Citizens League, the National Committee for Japanese American Redress initiates federal litigation, seeking monetary compensation for the more than one hundred thousand Japanese Americans who were interned during World War II. Meanwhile, the convictions of Fred Korematsu, Minoru Yasui, and Gordon Hirabayashi, who were convicted of curfew violations during World War II, are reversed.

1985 Michael Woo is elected to the Los Angeles City Council; he is the first Chinese American to serve in that position.

1986 California passes an initiative declaring English as the official state language.

1988 The U.S. Congress, with the reluctant agreement of President Reagan, publicly apologizes for interning Japanese Americans during World War II and authorizes payment of twenty thousand dollars to each former internee.

1993 Michael Woo loses his race for mayor of Los Angeles to Richard Riordan.

Notes

Chapter 1

1. This and subsequent epigraphs are drawn largely from issues of the *Intelligence Report*, a bimonthly publication of the Klanwatch project of the Southern Poverty Law Center in Montgomery, Alabama. Each issue includes pages of such incidents that are only a sample from the project's files. One incident is reported by the American Indian Relief Council in Rapid City, South Dakota.

2. The term *civilized* came about because historically, these tribes had associated with, and adopted the culture of, whites—especially their commercial culture. The fertile southeast land coupled with a commercial mindset enabled these tribes to amass great wealth, furthering their image as "civilized." It should be noted that the fertility of the land of the Southeast was not lost on whites, who coveted the territory. Beginning in the 1830s, the U.S. government, especially under the administration of President Andrew Jackson, removed the Five Civilized Tribes from their land to reservations in the relatively barren Oklahoma Territory.

Chapter 3

1. Ralph J. Bunche, the first African American to receive a Ph.D. in political science (Harvard, 1934), was the founder of the Department of Political Science at Howard University. Bunche later worked for the United Nations and in 1950 received the Nobel Peace Prize for his negotiations with Israelis and Arabs in the Middle East. Mary McLeod Bethune, founder and president of Bethune-Cookman College in Daytona Beach, Florida, was the director of the Division of Negro Affairs of the National Youth Administration. Robert C. Weaver served in the Department of the Interior under Franklin Roosevelt and later became secretary of labor under President Lyndon Johnson. Rayford W. Logan, a pioneer in the development of the study of what he preferred to call "Negro history," served as a consultant to the State Department, particularly on issues related to the Caribbean basin and to Africa.

2. Earl Warren was a former Republican governor of California, and Eisenhower, who was pursuing a southern white strategy, assumed—incorrectly—that Warren would hold the line on civil rights issues. After the 1954 *Brown* decision, when it became clear that the Warren Court was moving forward to dismantle segregation, Eisenhower is quoted as saying that his appointment of Earl Warren as chief justice "was the biggest damn fool mistake I ever made" (Rodell 1968:12).

Chapter 4

1. Shirley Chisholm, the first African American woman ever elected to Congress, ran for the presidency in 1972 as a Democrat. She garnered only 3 percent of the primary votes and 5 percent of the delegate votes.

2. These regulations clearly noted that segregation was still mandated for "members of the Negro race or persons of Negro ancestry" but not for "members of any other race" (quoted in San Miguel 1987:126).

3. In Arizona, a similar case banned the segregation of Mexican American students in 1951 (see *Gonzales v. Sheely*).

4. The plaintiffs in this case challenged the local school board's practice of segregating Mexican American students for the first two grades and requiring these students to spend four years in these grades regardless of their academic achievement. Thus, Mexican American youngsters could not enter the third grade until their fifth year of school. The school board countersued, asking that the parents of the children involved in the suit be enjoined from speaking any language other than English in the presence of school-age children and that they keep their children from associating with anyone who did not speak English. The federal judge dismissed the defendants' counterclaim in a terse footnote.

Chapter 5

1. This section draws heavily on the excellent work of Sonenshein (1993).

Chapter 6

1. This statement is necessarily tentative because implementation of Proposition 187 has been blocked by court order.

References

Alexander v. Holmes. 1969. 396 U.S. 19.

Alston v. School Board of Norfolk. 1940. 112 F.2d 992.

Ambrecht, Beliana C., and Harry P. Pachon. 1974. "Ethnic Political Mobilization in a Mexican American Community: An Exploratory Study of East Los Angeles, 1965–1972." *Western Political Quarterly* 27:500–519.

American Friends Service Committee et al. 1970. *The Status of School Desegregation in the South, 1970.* American Friends Service Committee, Delta Ministry of the National Council of Churches, Lawyers Committee for Civil Rights Under Law, Lawyers Constitutional Defense Committee, NAACP Legal Defense and Educational Fund, and Washington Research Project.

Bean, Frank, and Marta Tienda. 1987. *The Hispanic Population of the United States.* New York: Russell Sage Foundation.

Bennett, Claudette E. 1992. *The Asian and Pacific Islander Population in the United States: March 1991 and 1990.* U.S. Bureau of the Census, Current Population Reports, P20-459. Washington, DC: Government Printing Office.

———. 1993. *The Black Population in the United States.* U.S. Bureau of the Census, Current Population Reports, P20-471. Washington, DC: Government Printing Office.

Blalock, Herbert M. 1967. *Toward a Theory of Minority-Group Relations.* New York: John Wiley & Sons.

Bobo, Lawrence D., James H. Johnson Jr., Melvin Oliver, James Sidanius, and Camille Zubrinsky. 1992. *Public Opinion Before and After a Spring of Discontent: A Preliminary Report on the 1992 Los Angeles County Social Survey.* Los Angeles: UCLA Center for the Study of Urban Poverty, Occasional Working Paper.

Boswell, Thomas D., and James R. Curtis. 1983. *The Cuban-American Experience: Culture, Images and Perspectives.* Totowa, NJ: Rowen and Allanheld.

Bradley v. Milliken. 1975. 402 F. Supp. 1096.

Brown v. Board of Education. 1954. 347 U.S. 483.

Brown v. Board of Education. 1955. 349 U.S. 294.

Browning, Rufus P., Dale Rogers Marshall, and David H. Tabb. 1984. *Protest Is Not Enough.* Berkeley: University of California Press.

———, eds. 1990. *Racial Politics in American Cities.* New York: Longman.

Cain, Bruce E. 1988. "Asian-American Electoral Power: Imminent or Illusory?" *Election Politics* 9:27–30.

Cain, Bruce E., and D. Roderick Kiewiet. 1984. "Ethnicity and Electoral Choice: Mexican-American Voting Behavior in the California 30th Congressional District." *Social Science Quarterly* 65:315–317.

———. 1986. "California's Coming Minority Majority." *Public Opinion* 9:50–52.

Cain, Bruce E., D. Roderick Kiewiet, and Carole J. Uhlaner. 1991. "The Acquisition of Partisanship by Latinos and Asian Americans." *American Journal of Political Science* 35:390–442.

Calvo, M., and Steven Rosenstone. 1989. *Hispanic Political Participation*. San Antonio: Southwest Voter Education Project.

Carmichael, Stokely, and Charles V. Hamilton. 1967. *Black Power: The Politics of Liberation in America*. New York: Random House.

Catawba Indian Tribe of South Carolina v. U.S. 1993. 982 F.2d 1564.

Chafe, William H. 1993. *Never Stop Running: Allard Lowenstein and the Struggle to Save American Liberalism*. New York: Basic Books.

Chaudhuri, Joytopaul. 1982. "American Indian Policy: An Overview of the Legal Complexities, Controversies, and Dilemmas." *Social Science Journal* 19:9–21.

Cherokee Nation v. State of Georgia. 1831. 5 Peters 1.

Cheyenne-Arapaho Tribes of Oklahoma v. U.S. 1992. 966 F.2d 583.

Children's Defense Fund. 1974. *Children Out of School in America*. Washington, DC: Children's Defense Fund of the Washington Research Project.

———. 1975. *School Suspensions: Are They Helping Children?* Washington, DC: Children's Defense Fund of the Washington Research Project.

Cisneros v. Corpus Christi Independent School District. 1970. 324 F. Supp. 599, *appeal docketed* No. 71-2397 (5th Cir. July 16, 1971).

Civil Rights Cases. 1883. 109 U.S. 3.

Clifford, Harlan C. 1992. "Big Ben." *Boston Globe Magazine* (August 2, 1992):16, 32–34.

Cobb, Roger W., and Charles D. Elder. 1983. *Participation in American Politics: The Dynamics of Agenda-Building*, 2d ed. Baltimore: Johns Hopkins University Press.

Cobb, Roger W., Jennie-Keith Ross, and Marc Howard Ross. 1976. "Agenda Building as a Comparative Political Process." *American Political Science Review* 70:126–138.

Cohen, Gaynor. 1982. "Alliance and Conflict Among Mexican Americans." *Ethnic and Racial Studies* 5:175–195.

Cooke, W. Henry. 1971. "Segregation of Mexican-American School Children." In *A Documentary History of Mexican Americans*, edited by Wayne Moquin, with Charles Van Doren. New York: Praeger, 325–328.

Cruse, Harold W. 1987. *Plural But Equal: A Critical Study of Blacks and Minorities and America's Plural Society*. New York: William Morrow.

Cumming v. County Board of Education. 1899. 175 U.S. 545.

Davidson, Chandler. 1992. "The Voting Rights Act: A Brief History." In *Controversies in Minority Voting*, edited by Bernard Grofman and Chandler Davidson. Washington, DC: Brookings Institution, 7–51.

Day, Jennifer Cheeseman. 1993. *Population Projections of the United States, by Age, Sex, Race, and Hispanic Origin: 1993 to 2050*. U.S. Bureau of the Census, Current Population Reports, P25-1104. Washington, DC: Government Printing Office.

de la Garza, Rodolfo O., Louis DeSipio, F. Chris Garcia, John A. Garcia, and Angelo Falcon. 1992. *Latino Voices: Mexican, Puerto Rican, and Cuban Perspectives on American Politics*. Boulder: Westview Press.

Delgado et al. v. Bastrop Independent School District of Bastrop County et al. 1948. Docket No. 388, W.D. Tex. June 15.

Doherty, Steven J. 1994. "Native American Voting Behavior." Paper presented at the Midwest Political Science Association Annual Meeting, Chicago.

Dred Scott v. Sanford. 1857. 19 Howard 393.

Eisinger, Peter K. 1976. *Patterns of Interracial Politics: Conflict and Cooperation in the City.* New York: Academic Press.

Elk v. Wilkins. 1884. 112 U.S. 94.

Espiritu, Yen Le. 1992. *Asian American Panethnicity: Bridging Institutions and Identities.* Philadelphia: Temple University Press.

Estrada, Leobardo, F. Chris Garcia, Reynaldo F. Marcias, and Lionel Maldonado. 1981. "Chicanos in the United States: A History of Exploitation and Resistance." *Daedalus* 110:103–132.

Eyler, Janet, Valerie J. Cook, and Leslie Ward. 1983. "Resegregation: Segregation Within Desegregated Schools." In *The Consequences of School Desegregation,* edited by Christine H. Rossell and Willis D. Hawley. Philadelphia: Temple University Press, 126–162.

Falcón, Angelo. 1988. "Black and Latino Politics in New York City." In *Latinos in the Political System,* edited by F. Chris Garcia. Notre Dame, IN: Notre Dame University Press, 171–194.

Fernández, Ricardo R., and Judith T. Guskin. 1981. "Hispanic Students and School Desegregation." In *Effective School Desegregation,* edited by Willis D. Hawley. Beverly Hills: Sage, 107–140.

Foner, Eric. 1992. "From Slavery to Citizenship: Blacks and the Right to Vote." In *Voting and the Spirit of American Democracy,* edited by Donald W. Rogers. Urbana: University of Illinois Press, 55–65.

Franklin, Frank George. 1906. *The Legislative History of Naturalization in the United States.* Chicago: University of Chicago Press.

Franklin, John Hope. 1969. *From Slavery to Freedom,* 3rd ed. New York: Vintage Books.

Goldman, Sheldon, and Matthew D. Saranson. 1994. "Clinton's Nontraditional Judges: Creating a More Representative Bench." *Judicature* 78 (September-October):68–73.

Gomes, Ralph, and Linda Faye Williams, eds. 1992. From *Exclusion to Inclusion: The Long Struggle for African American Political Power.* Westport, CT: Greenwood Press.

Gong Lum v. Rice. 1927. 275 U.S. 78.

Gonzalez v. Sheely. 1951. 96 F. Supp. 1004.

Grebler, Leo, Joan Moore, and Ralph Guzman. 1970. *The Mexican American People.* New York: Free Press.

Green v. New Kent County School Board. 1968. 391 U.S. 390.

Guadalupe Organization, Inc. v. Tempe Elementary School District. 1978. 587 F.2d 1022.

Guinier, Lani. 1994. *The Tyranny of the Majority: Fundamental Fairness in Representative Democracy.* New York: Free Press.

Guinn v. U.S. 1915. 238 U.S. 347.

Gulick, Sidney L. 1918. *American Democracy and Asiatic Citizenship.* New York: Charles Scribner's Sons.

Gurin, Patricia, Shirley Hatchett, and James S. Jackson. 1989. *Hope and Independence: Blacks' Response to Electoral and Party Politics.* New York: Russell Sage Foundation.

Hart v. Community School Board of Brooklyn District #2. 1974. 383 F. Supp. 699, *aff'd* 512 F.2d 37, 1975.

Henry, Charles P. 1980. "Black and Chicano Coalitions: Possibilities and Problems." *Western Journal of Black Studies* 4:222–232.

Henry, Charles P., and Carlos Muñoz Jr. 1991. "Ideological and Interest Linkages in California Rainbow Politics." In *Racial and Ethnic Politics in California*, edited by Byran O. Jackson and Michael B. Preston. Berkeley: Institute of Governmental Studies, 323–338.

Hernandez v. Driscoll Consolidated Independent School District. 1957. 2 *Race Relations Law Reporter* 329.

Hero, Rodney E. 1992. *Latinos and the U.S. Political System.* Philadelphia: Temple University Press.

Higham, John. 1963 [1955]. *Strangers in the Land: Patterns of American Nativism 1860–1925.* Westport, CT: Greenwood Press.

Hochschild, Jennifer L. 1984. *The New American Dilemma: Liberal Democracy and School Desegregation.* New Haven: Yale University Press.

Holt, Len. 1966. *The Summer That Didn't End.* London: Heinemann.

Ichioka, Yuji. 1988. *The Issei: The World of the First Generation Japanese Americans, 1885–1924.* New York: Free Press.

In re Wallace. 1959. 4 Race Relations Law Reporter 97.

Independent School District v. Salvatierra. 1930. 33 S.W.2d 790., *cert. denied,* 284 U.S. 580, 1931.

James, Marlise. 1973. *The People's Lawyers.* New York: Holt, Rinehart and Winston.

Jarvis, Sonia R. 1992. "Historical Overview: African Americans and the Evolution of Voting Rights." In *From Exclusion to Inclusion: The Long Struggle for African American Political Power,* edited by Ralph Gomes and Linda Faye Williams. Westport, CT: Greenwood Press, 17–33.

Jennings, Jerry T. 1993. *Voting and Registration in the Election of November 1992.* U.S. Bureau of the Census, Current Population Reports, P20-466. Washington, DC: Government Printing Office.

Johnson, James H. Jr., and Melvin L. Oliver. 1989. "Interethnic Minority Conflict in Urban America: The Effects of Economic and Social Dislocations." *Urban Geography* 10:449–463.

Joint Center for Political and Economic Studies (JCPES). 1993. "Political Trend-letter." *Focus* 21:n.p.

———. 1994. *Black Elected Officials: A National Roster, 1993.* Washington, DC: JCPES Press.

Keyes v. School District No. 1, Denver, Colorado. 1973. 380 F. Supp. 673.

Kitano, Harry H.L. 1981. "Asian-Americans: The Chinese, Japanese, Koreans, Filipinos, and Southeast Asians." *Annals of the Academy of Political and Social Sciences* 454:125–138.

Kleppner, Paul. 1990. "Defining Citizenship: Immigration and the Struggle for Voting Rights in Antebellum America." In *Voting and the Spirit of American Democracy,* edited by Donald W. Rogers. Urbana: University of Illinois Press, 43–53.

Kousser, J. Morgan. 1992. "The Voting Rights Act and the Two Reconstructions." In *Controversies in Minority Voting,* edited by Bernard Grofman and Chandler Davidson. Washington, DC: Brookings Institution, 135–176.

Lau v. Nichols. 1974. 414 U.S. 563.

Lewis, Anthony. 1965. *Portrait of a Decade.* New York: Bantam.

Lindblom, Charles E. 1980. *The Policy-Making Process,* 2d ed. Englewood Cliffs, NJ: Prentice-Hall.

Logan, Rayford Wittingham. 1954. *The Negro in American Life and Thought: The Nadir, 1877–1901.* New York: Dial Press.

Loving v. Virginia. 1967. 388 U.S. 1.

Low, Victor. 1982. *The Unimpressible Race: A Century of Educational Struggle by the Chinese in San Francisco.* San Francisco: East/West Publishing Company.

Márquez, Benjamin. 1989. "The Politics of Race and Assimilation: The League of United Latin American Citizens." *Western Political Quarterly* 42:355–377.

McClain, Paula D. 1993a. "The Changing Dynamics of Urban Politics: Black and Hispanic Municipal Employment—Is There Competition?" *Journal of Politics* 55:399–414.

McClain, Paula D., ed. 1993b. *Minority Group Influence: Agenda Setting, Formulation, and Public Policy.* Westport, CT: Greenwood Press.

McClain, Paula D., and John A. Garcia. 1993. "Expanding Disciplinary Boundaries: Black, Latino, and Racial Minority Group Politics in Political Science." In *Political Science: The State of the Discipline, II,* edited by Ada W. Finifter. Washington, DC: American Political Science Association, 247–279.

McClain, Paula D., and Albert K. Karnig. 1990. "Black and Hispanic Socioeconomic and Political Competition." *American Political Science Review* 84:535–545.

McCool, Daniel. 1982. "Voting Patterns of American Indians in Arizona." *Social Science Journal* 19:101–113.

———. 1985. "Indian Voting." In *American Indian Policy in the Twentieth Century,* edited by Vine Deloria Jr. Norman: University of Oklahoma Press, 105–133.

McDonald, Laughlin, and john a. powell. 1993. *The Rights of Racial Minorities: The Basic ACLU Guide to Racial Minority Rights,* 2d ed. Carbondale: Southern Illinois University Press.

Meier, Kenneth J., and Joseph Stewart Jr. 1991. *The Politics of Hispanic Education.* Albany: State University of New York Press.

Meier, Kenneth J., Joseph Stewart Jr., and Robert E. England. 1989. *Race, Class, and Education: The Politics of Second-Generation Discrimination.* Madison: University of Wisconsin Press.

Mendez v. Westminster School District. 1946. 64 F. Supp. 544, *aff'd* 161 F.2d 774, 1947.

Missouri ex rel. Gaines v. Canada. 1938. 305 U.S. 337.

Mollenkopf, John H. 1990. "New York: The Great Anomaly." In *Racial Politics in American Cities,* edited by Rufus P. Browning, Dale Rogers Marshall, and David H. Tabb. New York: Longman, 75–87.

Montgomery, Patricia A. 1994. *The Hispanic Population in the United States: March 1993.* U.S. Bureau of the Census, Current Population Reports, P20-475. Washington, DC: Government Printing Office.

Moore, Joan, and Harry Pachon. 1985. *Hispanics in the United States.* Englewood Cliffs, NJ: Prentice-Hall.

Morgan v. Hennigan. 1974. 379 F. Supp. 410.

Morris, Aldon D. 1984. *The Origins of the Civil Rights Movement: Black Communities Organizing for Change.* New York: Free Press.

Morrison, Peter A., and Ira S. Lowry. 1994. "A Riot of Color: The Demographic Setting." In *The Los Angeles Riots: Lessons for the Urban Future*, edited by Mark Baldassare. Boulder: Westview Press, 19–46.

Muñoz, Carlos Jr. 1989. *Youth, Identity, Power: The Chicano Movement*. New York: Verso.

Myrdal, Gunnar. 1944. *An American Dilemma*. New York: Harper and Brothers.

Nagel, Joanne. 1982. "The Political Mobilization of Native Americans." *Social Science Journal* 19:37–45.

Nakanishi, Donald. 1991. "The Next Swing Vote: Asian Pacific Americans and California Politics." In *Racial and Ethnic Politics in California*, edited by Byran O. Jackson and Michael B. Preston. Berkeley: Institute of Governmental Studies, 25–54.

National Center for Education Statistics. 1978. *The Children's English and Services Study*. Washington, DC: Government Printing Office.

National Conference of Christians and Jews. 1993. *Taking America's Pulse: The Full Report of the National Conference Survey on Inter-Group Relations*. New York: National Conference of Christians and Jews.

National Council of La Raza. 1990. "Background Paper for Black-Latino Dialogue." Unpublished paper.

National Institute of Education. 1977. *Conference Report: Desegregation and Education Concerns of the Hispanic Community*. Washington, DC: Government Printing Office.

Native American Rights Fund (NARF). 1993. *Annual Report*. Boulder: NARF.

Nolan, Martin F. 1992. "Candidates Offer Vivid Contrast in Biographies." *Boston Globe*, October 18, 1992, A19.

O'Connor, Karen, and Lee Epstein. 1984. "A Legal Voice for the Chicano Community: The Activities of the Mexican American Legal Defense and Educational Fund, 1968–82." *Social Science Quarterly* 65:245–256.

Oliver, Melvin L., and James H. Johnson Jr. 1984. "Inter-Ethnic Conflict in an Urban Ghetto: The Case of Blacks and Latinos in Los Angeles." *Social Movements, Conflicts, and Change* 6:57–94.

Olsen, Marvin C. 1970. "Social and Political Participation of Blacks." *American Sociological Review* 35:682–697.

Orfield, Gary W. 1969. *The Reconstruction of Southern Education: The Schools and the 1964 Civil Rights Act*. New York: Wiley-Interscience.

———. 1978. *Must We Bus?* Washington, DC: Brookings Institution.

Orfield, Gary W., with Sara Schley, Diane Glass, and Sean Reardon. 1993. *The Growth of Segregation in American Schools: Changing Patterns of Separation and Poverty Since 1968*. National School Board Association, Council of Urban Boards of Education.

Panetta, Leon E., and Peter Gall. 1971. *Bring Us Together: The Nixon Team and the Civil Rights Retreat*. Philadelphia: Lippincott.

Peltason, Jack W. 1971. *Fifty-Eight Lonely Men: Southern Federal Judges and School Desegregation*. Urbana: University of Illinois Press.

Pinderhughes, Dianne M. 1987. *Race and Ethnicity in Chicago Politics: A Reexamination of Pluralist Theory*. Urbana: University of Illinois Press.

Plessy v. Ferguson. 1896. 163 U.S. 537.

Pohlman, Marcus. 1991. *Black Politics in Conservative America*. New York: Longman.

Rangel, Jorge C., and Carlos M. Alcala. 1972. "Project Report: *De Jure* Segregation of Chicanos in Texas Schools." *Harvard Civil Rights–Civil Liberties Law Review* 7:307–392.

Ritt, Leonard. 1979. "Some Social and Political Views of American Indians." *Ethnicity* 6:45–72.

Robertson, David B., and Dennis R. Judd. 1989. *The Development of American Public Policy: The Structure of Policy Restraint.* Glenview, IL: Scott, Foresman–Little, Brown.

Robinson, Donald L. 1971. *Slavery in the Structure of American Politics 1765–1820.* New York: Harcourt Brace Jovanovich.

Rodell, Fred. 1968. "The Complexities of Mr. Justice Fortas." *New York Times Magazine*, July 28, p. 12.

Rodgers, Harrell R. Jr., and Charles S. Bullock III. 1976. *Coercion to Compliance.* Lexington, MA: D. C. Heath.

Romero v. Weakley. 1955. 131 F. Supp. 818.

Ross v. Eckels. 1970. 434 F.2d 1140.

Saito, Leland Tadaji. 1992. *Politics in a New Demographic Era: Asian Americans in Monterey Park, California.* Unpublished Ph.D. dissertation, Department of Sociology, UCLA.

San Miguel, Guadalupe Jr. 1987. *"Let All of Them Take Heed": Mexican Americans and the Campaign for Educational Equality in Texas, 1910–1981.* Austin: University of Texas Press.

Schattschneider, E. E. 1960. *The Semi-Sovereign People.* Hinsdale, IL: Dryden.

Seelye, Katherine Q. 1995. "Democrats Lose 1 in Senate with Switch by Coloradan." *New York Times* (national edition), March 4, p. 8.

Serna v. Portales Municipal Schools. 1974. 499 F.2d 1147.

Sigelman, Lee, and Susan Welch. 1991. *Black Americans' Views of Racial Inequality: The Dream Deferred.* Cambridge: Cambridge University Press.

Sigler, Jay A. 1975. *American Rights Policies.* Homewood, IL: Dorsey Press.

Simmons, Cassandra A., and Nelvia M. Brady. 1981. "The Impact of Ability Group Placement Decisions on the Equality of Educational Opportunity in Desegregated Elementary Schools." *Urban Review* 13:129–133.

Slaughterhouse Cases. 1873. 16 Wallace 36.

Smith v. Allwright. 1944. 321 U.S. 649.

Smith, Robert C. 1990. "From Insurgency to Ward Inclusion: The Jackson Campaigns of 1984 and 1988." In *The Social and Political Implications of the 1984 Jesse Jackson Campaign*, edited by Lorenzo Morris. New York: Praeger, 215–230.

Smith, Robert C., and Richard Seltzer. 1992. *Race, Class, and Culture.* Albany: State University of New York Press.

Sonenshein, Raphael J. 1990. "Biracial Coalition Politics in Los Angeles." In *Racial Politics in American Cities*, edited by Rufus P. Browning, Dale Rogers Marshall, and David H. Tabb. New York: Longman, 33–48.

———. 1993. *Politics in Black and White: Race and Power in Los Angeles.* Princeton: Princeton University Press.

Spickard, Paul R. 1989. *Mixed Blood: Intermarriage and Ethnic Identity in Twentieth Century America.* Madison: University of Wisconsin Press.

Spring, Joel. 1989. *The Sorting Machine Revisited: National Educational Policy Since 1945*, updated edition. New York: Longman.

Stokes, Bruce. 1988. "Learning the Game." *National Journal* 20:2649–2654.

Sundquist, James L. 1968. *Politics and Policy: The Eisenhower, Kennedy, and Johnson Years*. Washington, DC: Brookings Institution.

Takaki, Ronald. 1993. *A Different Mirror: A History of Multicultural America*. Boston: Little, Brown.

Tate, Katherine. 1993. *From Protest to Politics: The New Black Voters in American Elections*. Cambridge, MA: Harvard University Press and Russell Sage Foundation.

Teitelbaum, Herbert, and Richard J. Hiller. 1977. "Bilingual Education: The Legal Mandate." *Harvard Educational Review* 47:138–170.

Thielemann, Gregory S., and Joseph Stewart Jr. 1995. "A Demand-Side Perspective on the Importance of Representative Bureaucracy: AIDS, Ethnicity, Sexual Orientation, and Gender." *Public Administration Review* (n.v. or pp.).

Tocqueville, Alexis de. 1966 [1835]. *Democracy in America*. Edited by J. P. Mayer and Max Lerner. New York: Harper and Row.

Tuck, R. 1946. *Not with the Fist*. New York: Harcourt Brace and World.

Tushnet, Mark V. 1987. *The NAACP's Legal Strategy Against Segregated Education, 1925–1950*. Chapel Hill: University of North Carolina Press.

UCLA Asian American Studies Center. 1993. "CrossCurrents" (Fall/Winter):1, 5.

Uhlaner, Carole J. 1991. "Perceived Prejudice and the Coalition Prospects of Blacks, Latinos and Asian Americans." In *Ethnic and Racial Politics in California*, edited by Byran O. Jackson and Michael B. Preston. Berkeley: Institute of Governmental Studies, 339–371.

Uhlaner, Carole J., Bruce Cain, and D. Roderick Kiewiet. 1989. "Political Participation of Ethnic Minorities in the 1980s." *Political Behavior* 11 (September):195–231.

United States Bureau of the Census. 1993. *Asians and Pacific Islanders in the United States*. Series 1990 CP-3-5, August.

United States Commission on Civil Rights. 1968. *Political Participation*. Washington, DC: Government Printing Office.

United States Office of Personnel Management. 1994. *Annual Report to Congress on the Federal Equal Opportunity Recruitment Program* (Fiscal Year 1993). CE-104, January. Washington, DC: Career Entry Group, Office of Affirmative Recruiting and Employment.

United States Senate. 1969. *Indian Education: A National Tragedy—A National Challenge*. Report of Special Subcommittee on Indian Education, Committee on Labor and Public Welfare, 91st Cong., 1st sess., S. Rep. No. 501.

U.S. v. Cruikshank. 1876. 92 U.S. 542.

U.S. v. Georgia. 1969. Civil No. 12972, N.D. Ga.

U.S. v. Harris. 1883. 106 U.S. 629.

U.S. v. Reese. 1876. 92 U.S. 214.

U.S. v. Texas Education Agency. 1972. 467 F.2d 848.

Verba, Sidney, and Norman Nie. 1972. *Participation in America*. New York: Harper and Row.

Vigil, Maurilio E. 1987. *Hispanics in American Politics: The Search for Political Power*. Lanham, MD: University Press of America.

Vose, Clement E. 1958. "Litigation as a Form of Pressure Group Activity." *Annals* 319:20–31.

———. 1959. *Caucasians Only: The Supreme Court, the NAACP, and the Restrictive Covenant Cases.* Berkeley: University of California Press.

Warren, Christopher L., John G. Corbett, and John F. Stack Jr. 1990. "Hispanic Ascendancy and Tripartite Politics in Miami." In *Racial Politics in American Cities,* edited by Rufus P. Browning, Dale Rogers Marshall, and David H. Tabb. New York: Longman, 155–178.

Wei, William. 1993. *The Asian American Movement.* Philadelphia: Temple University Press.

Weinberg, Meyer. 1977. *Minority Students: A Research Appraisal.* Washington, DC: National Institute of Education, Government Printing Office.

Welch, Susan, and Lee Sigelman. 1992. "A Gender Gap Among Hispanics? A Comparison with Blacks and Anglos." *Western Political Quarterly* 45:181–199.

Welch, Susan, Albert K. Karnig, and Richard A. Eribes. 1983. "Changes in Hispanic Local Employment in the Southwest." *Western Political Quarterly* 36:660–673.

Weyler, Rex. 1982. *Blood on the Land: The Government and Corporate War Against the American Indian Movement.* New York: Everest House.

Williams, Linda F. 1987. "Black Political Progress in the 1980s: The Electoral Arena." In *The New Black Politics: The Search for Political Power,* 2d ed., edited by Michael B. Preston, Lenneal Henderson, and Paul Puryear. New York: Longman, 97–135.

Wollenberg, Charles M. 1978. *All Deliberate Speed: Segregation and Exclusion in California Schools, 1855–1975.* Berkeley: University of California Press.

About the Book and Authors

RODNEY KING framed what might be called the enduring question of American politics from the Founding forward: "Can we all get along?" In a nation built by immigrants and bedeviled by the history and legacy of slavery, issues of liberty, equality, and community continue to challenge Americans. Whether we look at the Los Angeles riots, the patterns of ethnic representation in Congress, or examples of discrimination in schools, we see that "getting along" is intimately connected with "who gets what, when, and how"—the traditional definition of politics.

Here, Paula McClain and Joseph Stewart combine traditional elements of political science analysis—history, Constitutional theory, institutions, political behavior, and policy actors—with a thoroughgoing survey of the political status of four major groups: African Americans, Latinos, Asian Americans, and American Indians. They show similarities and differences in these groups' political action and experience, and point the way toward coalition, competition, and consensus-building in the face of ongoing conflict. Two dilemmas shape the book: How do we as a nation reconcile a commitment to equality with persistent inequality and discrimination? And what can we do about it—from the perspective of ethnic and racial minorities as well as within the dominant culture?

Paula D. McClain is professor of government and chair of the Woodrow Wilson Department of Government and Foreign Affairs at the University of Virginia. **Joseph Stewart Jr.** is professor of government, politics, and political economy at the University of Texas at Dallas.

Index

Abernathy, Ralph, 43
Adams, John, 12
Adoption, policy, 87. *See also* Policymaking
Affirmative action, 128
African Americans. *See* Blacks
Age distribution, 31–32
Agenda setting, 87, 88–89, 121
  and Jesse Jackson campaigns, 94–95
  See also Policymaking
AIM. *See* American Indian Movement
Akaka, Daniel, 95–97
Alabama, 50, 52, 74, 107
Alaska, 50, 108, 109(table)
Alaska Federation of Natives, 82
Alston v. School Board of Norfolk, 110
American Dilemma, An (Myrdal), 3
American G.I. Forum, 114
American Indian Movement (AIM), 48, 175
American Indians
  citizenship in U.S. history, 10, 12–13, 15–16
  civil rights movements, 48
  demographics, 30(table), 37, 38(map), 152
  education issues, 118
  in government bureaucracy, 104
  identification of, 6–7, 9
  as identifying term, 6
  interest groups, 80–81, 82
  political ideology, partisanship, 65, 72–74, 151–152
  political representation, 89, 98–100, 99(table), 107–108 109(table)
  and presidential actions, 90–91, 92
  registration and voting behavior, 78
  and suffrage, 22–23, 51
  timeline of political history, 173–176
  See also specific tribes
Americanization, 112, 117
American Samoa, 97
Anaya, Tony, 107
Anderson, Jesse, 153
Antimiscegenation laws, 8
Apodaca, Jerry, 107
Arizona
  antimiscegenation laws, 8
  and Indian suffrage, 22–23
  and Mexican Americans, 178, 190(n3)
  minority representation in, 107, 108
  and Voting Rights Act, 50
Arkansas, 107
Articles of Confederation, 12–13, 167, 173
Asian American Legal Defense and Education Fund, 80
Asian Americans
  citizenship in U.S. history, 17–19
  civil rights movements, 47–48
  current discrimination against, 148

demographics, 30(table), 32, 32(table), 33, 37, 39(map), 152
education issues, 117–118
ethnic identification, 7, 9
in government bureaucracy, 104
interest groups, 80, 82
in Los Angeles, 128, 131, 133, 137, 139–143
political attitudes, 61–62
political ideology, partisanship, 64–65, 70–72, 73(table), 151–152
political representation, 89, 95–98, 98(table), 107
presidential appointments of, 92
registration and voting behavior, 74, 77, 77(table), 78, 79(table)
and suffrage, 51
timeline of political history, 185–187
See also Chinese Americans; Filipinos; Japanese Americans; Korean Americans
Asian Indians, 7
Asian Law Caucus, 80
Asian Pacific American Legal Center, 80
Asian Pacifics, 72. *See also* Asian Americans
Attitudes, political
  group cohesiveness, 59–62
  identifying, 58–59
  ideological orientations, 62–65. *See also* Ideology, political
  partisan identification, 65–74. *See also* Partisan identification

Banks, Dennis, 48
Baton Rouge bus boycott, 41–44
Bellecourt, Clyde, 48
Bethune, Mary McLeod, 67, 189(n1)
BIA. *See* Bureau of Indian Affairs
Black and Tan Republicans, 66
Black Power (Carmichael and Hamilton), 126–127
Blacks
  citizenship in U.S. history, 11, 13–14
  civil rights movement, 41–46
  demographics, 30, 30(table), 33, 34, 35(map), 152
  education issues, 108–112, 120, 190(n2)
  in government bureaucracy, 103
  group competition with Latinos, 129–130
  as identifying term, 5
  interest groups, 80, 81
  interminority coalitions with, 127–129, 135–141
  and Jesse Jackson campaigns, 93–94
  in Los Angeles, 131–143
  political attitudes, 60–62, 60(table)
  political ideology, partisanship, 63, 63(table), 65–69, 68(table), 151

political representation, 89, 95, 96
(table), 107
presidential appointments of, 91, 92
registration and voting behavior, 74–77,
75–76(table), 77(table), 78–79, 79(table)
slavery and importation, 7–8, 10–11
suffrage in U.S. history, 20–22, 49, 50
on the Supreme Court, 102
"Born in East LA" (Marín), 148
Bradley, Thomas, 94, 135, 136, 137, 138–141
Brooke, Edward, 95, 107
Brown, George, 107
Brown, Jesse, 91
Brown, Lee, 91
Brown, Ronald, 91
Brown v. Board of Education of Topeka, 68, 80,
110, 170
Bunche, Ralph J., 67, 189(n1)
Bureaucracy, government
minority representation in, 102–105,
104(table), 105(table)
and policy implementation, 112
Bureau of Indian Affairs (BIA), 48, 81, 82, 173
Burrage, Billy Michael, 92
Burris, Roland, 107
Bush, George, 68, 102, 106, 147

Cabeza de Baca, Ezequiel, 107
Cain and Kiewiet survey (1984), 64
California
anti-Asian sentiment, 19, 131
gold rush and development of, 17–18
interracial marriage laws, 8
minority group population, 152
minority representation in, 107
Proposition 187, 148, 190(n1)
segregated Mexican schools, 113, 114
and suffrage issues, 50
See also Los Angeles
California Indian Legal Services (CILS), 80
California Rural Legal Assistance (CRLA), 80
Campbell, Ben Nighthorse, 98–100, 152
Candidacy, minority, 92–95, 190(n1)
Carmichael, Stokely, 126–127
Carter, Jimmy, 74, 184
Castro, Raul, 107
Castro, Sal, 47
Catawba Indian Land Claim Settlement Act,
81
Catawba Tribe of South Carolina, 81
Chaney, James, 45–46
Chávez, César, 46, 179
Cherokee Nation v. State of Georgia, 15, 173
Cherokees, 15, 90, 174
Cheyenne-Arapaho Tribes of Oklahoma, 81
Chicano power movement, 46–47
Chickasaw, 15, 90
Chinese Americans
citizenship in U.S. history, 17–19
ethnic grouping, 7
and interest groups, 82
in Los Angeles, 131
political ideology, partisanship, 64, 70–71,
72, 128
population, 32
and school segregation, 117–118
socioeconomic status, 33
See also Asian Americans
Chinese Exclusion Act (1882), 18, 131, 185
Chisholm, Shirley, 190(n1)
Choctaw, 15, 90
CILS. *See* California Indian Legal Services

Cisneros, Henry, 91, 180
*Cisneros v. Corpus Christi Independent School
District*, 116
Citizenship
current concerns over, 148
and minorities in U.S. history, 12–19
racial/ethnic identification and, 9
Civil rights
and presidential elections, 66–68
versus states' rights, 106
See also Citizenship; Civil rights move-
ments; Education; Suffrage
Civil Rights Act (1866), 20
Civil Rights Act (1875), 106, 168
Civil Rights Act (1960), 170
Civil Rights Act (1964), 90, 106, 112, 186
Civil Rights Act (1991), 172
Civil Rights Cases, 106, 168
Civil rights movements
American Indian, 48
Asian American, 47–48
black, 41–46
and interest group activity, 81
Latino, 46–47
role in policymaking of, 89
and suffrage issues, 50, 53
Class
bias and pluralism, 58
and interminority relations, 130, 140
and racism, 7
Classical liberalism, 10
Clinton, Bill, 81, 90–92, 151, 176
Coalitions
definition of political, 125
group relations and forming, 126–130,
143,150
in Los Angeles politics, 135–141
political ideology and, 65, 127, 128, 140
COFO. *See* Council of Federated Organizations
Colorado, 107
Competition, intergroup, 126, 129–130
and Los Angeles politics, 136–137, 141–143
Congress, U.S.
citizenship acts, 13, 15–16, 18, 19. *See also*
Citizenship
minority representation in, 95–100,
96(table), 97(table), 98(table), 99(table)
and school desegregation issues, 111–112.
See also Education
suffrage acts, 20–21. *See also* Voting Rights
Act
Congressional Asian Pacific American Caucus,
97–98
Congressional Black Caucus, 93, 95
Congressional Hispanic Caucus, 95, 180
Congress of Racial Equality, 81
Conservative. *See* Ideology, political
Continental Congress, 12
Council of Federated Organizations
(COFO), 45
Courts. *See* Judicial system; Supreme
Court, U.S.
Creek, 15, 90
CRLA. *See* California Rural Legal Assistance
Crystal City, Texas, 47, 180
Cuba, 17, 183
Cuban Americans
citizenship in U.S. history, 17
in Congress, 95
as identifying term, 6
political attitudes, 60–61, 63, 69–70
political ideology and partisanship, 128, 151

population and geographic distribution,
32, 37
socioeconomic status, 33
timeline of political history, 183–184
See also Latinos
Cumming v. County Board of Education, 108
Cumulative voting, 52–53

Dade County, Florida, 60
Davidson, T. Whitfield, 111
Davis, Reverend A. L., 43
Dawes Act (1887), 15
Declaration of Independence, 9–10
Delaware, 107
*Delgado et al. v. Bastrop Independent School
District of Bastrop County et al.,* 114–115
Democracy, principles of, 3–4, 9, 148
Democracy in America (de Tocqueville), 3
Democratic Party
and Jesse Jackson, 93–95
and Latinos, 69
and minority groups, 151–152
relationship with blacks, 50, 66–69
See also Partisan identification
Demographics, 29–37, 53
urban changes in, 125
See also Geographic distribution;
Population
Department of Health, Education, and Welfare
(HEW), 112
Desegregation. *See* Education
de Tocqueville, Alexis, 3, 148
Dewey, Thomas, 67
Discrimination
Asians and educational system, 117
and conservatism in Los Angeles, 132–135
democratic principles versus, 3–4, 9, 147
against Latinos and Asians, 148
perceptions by black women, 79
perceptions of, 59–62, 61(table)
presidential action on, 90
role of group competition in, 126
second-generation, 120–121, 152
in U.S. history, 24–25
See also Citizenship; Education; Suffrage
Dixiecrats, 67
Dominated groups, 37–40
Dred Scott v. Sanford, 13–14, 168
DuBois, W.E.B., 66, 169
Duke, David, 153
Dymally, Merv, 107

EchoHawk, Larry, 107
Education
Asians and equal opportunities in, 117–118
bilingual, 117–118, 118–120
blacks and equal opportunities in, 108–112,
190(n2)
current segregation in, 152
and equal opportunity policy, 108, 121–122
federalism and school desegregation, 106
Hispanics and equal opportunities in,
112–117, 190(nn 3, 4)
Indians and equal opportunities in, 118
minority group attainments in, 33
resegregation, 120
second-generation discrimination, 120–121
Education Amendments Act (1978), 118
Eisenhower, Dwight, 67–68, 111, 189(n2)
Elementary and Secondary Education Act (1965), 112
Elk v. Wilkins, 15, 22, 174

Employment
and group competition, 130
Los Angeles and, 133, 141
Enforcement Acts, 21
Espy, Michael, 91
Ethnicity, defined, 8–9
Evaluation, policy, 87
Evers, Medger, 44

FBI. *See* Federal Bureau of Investigation
Federal Bureau of Investigation (FBI), 48
Federalism, 88, 105–106
Federalist Papers, 10, 57
Fifteenth Amendment, 20–21, 22, 49–50, 168
Filipinos, 185, 186
ethnic grouping, 7
political ideology, 65
socioeconomic status, 33
and United Farm Workers, 46
Five Civilized Tribes, 15, 90, 174, 189(n2)
Florida, 8, 50, 107
Ford Foundation, 80
Formulation, policy, 87. *See also* Policymaking
Fort Laramie Treaty, 48
Fourteenth Amendment, 14, 49, 50, 168
Franklin, Benjamin, 12
Freedom Riders, 44
Freedom Vote, 44–45
Funding
and black civil rights movement, 42, 43, 46
importance to social movements, 40
for Indian education, 118
school desegregation and federal, 106
truant children and school, 113

Gender
differences in political attitudes and partici-
pation, 58, 68, 70, 78–79, 79(table)
and racism, 7
See also Women
Generational differences
in ideology/partisanship, 65, 68–69
in perceptions of discrimination, 61, 62
Geographic distribution, 33–37, 35(map),
36(map), 38(map), 39(map), 152
effect on political attitudes, 60
Georgia, 8, 50, 74, 107
Ginsberg, Ruth Bader, 102
Gong Lum v. Rice, 117
González, Rodolfo "Corky," 47
Goodman, Andrew, 45–46
Grandfather clause, 49
Guam, 97
Guinier, Lani, 52
Guinn v. United States, 49
Gutiérrez, José Angel, 47

Hamilton, Charles V., 126–127
Hatcher, Richard, 138
Hawaii, 19, 107, 185
Hawaiians, 6, 72, 95–97
Hayes, Rutherford B., 18, 21, 66, 168
*Hernandez v. Driscoll Consolidated Independent
School District,* 115, 190(n4)
HEW. *See* Department of Health, Education
and Welfare
Hispanics. *See* Latinos
Hollingsworth, Joe, 136, 137
Hoover, Herbert, 67
Housing, 133, 143

Idaho, 107
Identity
  as American Indian, 6–7
  and Asian Americans, 7
  group, 58, 59–62, 60(table)
  and suffrage/citizenship issues, 9
Ideology, political, 58, 62–65, 63(table),
    64(table)
  effect on policymaking, 87
  role in coalitions, 65, 127, 128, 140
Illinois, 52, 107
Immigration
  Chinese, 17–18
  Cuban, 17
Immigration Quota Act (1924), 19
Implementation, policy, 87, 110–112, 122. *See
    also* Policymaking
Income. *See* Socioeconomic status
Independent School District v. Salvatierra, 114
Indiana, 8
Indian Citizenship Act (1924), 16
Indian Education Act (1972), 118
Indian Removal Bill, 90
Indians. *See* American Indians
Indian Self-Determination and Education
    Assistance Act (1975), 118, 175
Ink Fund. *See* National Association for the
    Advancement of Colored People, Legal
    Defense and Educational Fund
Inouye, Daniel, 95
Inside access model, 88–89
Institute for the Development of Indian
    Law, 82
Intelligence Report, 189(n1)
Interest groups, 58, 79–82
Intergroup relations, 126–130, 149–150,
    150(table). *See also* Coalitions; Competi-
    tion, intergroup
Iroquois Confederacy, 12, 173

Jackson, Andrew, 90, 189(n2)
Jackson, Jesse, 69, 77, 93–95, 171
JACL. *See* Japanese American Citizens League
Japanese American Citizens League (JACL), 82
Japanese Americans
  citizenship in U.S. history, 19
  ethnic grouping, 7
  in Los Angeles, 131, 133
  political ideology, partisanship, 64, 72, 128
  population, 32
  socioeconomic status, 33
  World War II internment, 82, 90
  See also Asian Americans
Jefferson, Thomas, 9, 10, 12
Jemison, Reverend T. J., 42–43
Jews, coalitions with, 127, 134, 137, 138
Johnson, Frank, 111
Johnson, Lyndon, 82, 90, 102, 111–112
Jones Act (1917), 16, 181
Judicial system
  minorities in, 92
  and school desegregation issues, 111, 112,
    114–117, 119, 121–122

Kennedy, John F., 68, 111
*Keyes v. School District No. 1, Denver,
    Colorado*, 116–117
Kim, Jay, 97
King, Martin Luther, Jr., 43
King, Rodney, 125, 172
Kitchen Cabinet, 67

Korean Americans
  ethnic grouping, 7
  and Los Angeles 1992 riots, 3, 141–142
  political ideology, 64, 65, 128
  See also Asian Americans
Ku Klux Klan, 6
Ku Klux Klan Act, 106

Language
  and pan-Asian identification, 7
  See also Education, bilingual
LAPD. *See* Los Angeles Police Department
Larrazolo, Octavian Ambrosio, 107
Latino National Political Survey, 1990
    (LNPS), 6, 59, 69–70
Latinos
  bilingual education for, 118–120
  citizenship in U.S. history, 16–17
  civil rights movements, 46–47
  current discrimination against, 148
  demographics, 31(table), 32, 33, 34–37,
    36(map), 152
  education issues, 112–117, 120, 190(nn 3, 4)
  ethnicity issues, 9
  in government bureaucracy, 104
  group competition with blacks, 129–130
  as identifying term, 5–6
  interest groups, 80, 81–82
  interminority coalitions with, 127–129,
    135–141
  in Los Angeles, 131, 133, 134, 135–143
  and Los Angeles 1992 riots, 3
  political attitudes, 60–61, 61(table), 62
  political ideology, partisanship, 63, 64
    (table), 69–70, 69(table), 151
  political representation, 89, 95, 97
    (table), 107
  presidential appointments of, 91–92
  registration and voting behavior, 74, 75–76
    (table), 77, 77(table), 78, 79(table)
  and suffrage, 51
  timelines of political history, 177–184
  See also Cuban Americans; Mexican
    Americans; Puerto Ricans
Lau v. Nichols, 117–118, 186
LDF. *See* National Association for the
    Advancement of Colored People, Legal
    Defense and Educational Fund
Leadership
  and American Indian Movement, 48
  and Asian American civil rights move-
    ments, 48
  and black civil rights movement, 42–43, 44
  Chicano movement, 47
  importance to social movements, 40
League of United Latin American Citizens
    (LULAC), 81, 113–115, 178
Lewis, James, 107
Liberal. *See* Ideology, political
Lily White Republicans, 66
Lindsay, Gilbert, 136, 137
Little Bighorn National Monument, 100
LNPS. *See* Latino National Political Survey,
    1990
Locke, John, 10
Logan, Rayford W., 67, 189(n1)
Los Angeles
  Hispanic education, 119
  history of politics in, 130–135
  intergroup competition in, 141–143
  minority coalitions in, 127–129, 135–141

race riots of 1960s, 137–138
riots of 1992, 3, 135, 142–143, 172
student strike, 47, 180
Los Angeles County Social Survey (1992), 64, 70
Los Angeles Police Department (LAPD), 134–135, 136, 137, 138, 139
reform of, 140–141
Los Angeles Times, 128, 134
Louisiana, 153
legal restrictions on blacks, 8
minority representation in, 107
and suffrage, 49, 50, 74
Loving v. Virginia, 8
Lowenstein, Allard, 45
LULAC. *See* League of United Latin American Citizens
Lynch, John R., 66

Madison, James, 57
MALDEF. *See* Mexican American Legal Defense and Education Fund
Marin, Cheech, 148
Marriages, interracial, 8
Marshall, Thurgood, 102, 110–111, 171
Martinez, Elizabeth Sutherland, 46
Martinez, Robert, 107
Maryland, 8, 53
Massachusetts, 107
McCarran-Walter Act (1952), 19
Means, Russell, 48
Media, mass, 122
Mendez v. Westminster School District, 114
Mexican American Legal Defense and Education Fund (MALDEF), 80, 115–117, 119, 180
Mexican Americans
Chicano power movement, 46–47
citizenship in U.S. history, 16
coalitions with blacks, 127, 129, 138
in Congress, 95
education issues, 112–117, 190(nn 3, 4)
geographic distribution of, 37
as identifying term, 6
interest groups, 80, 81–82
in Los Angeles, 131, 133
political attitudes, 60, 63, 69
political ideology, partisanship, 128, 151
timeline of political history, 177–180
See also Latinos
Mexican-American War, 16, 174, 177
Miami, 130
Michigan, 50, 107
Mink, Patsy T., 97–98
Minnesota, 107–108
Minority groups
current citizenship and suffrage issues for, 148–149. *See also* Citizenship; Suffrage
demographics, 29–37
differential status of, 29
intergroup relations, 126–130, 149–150, 150(table)
policymaking and, 89, 121. *See also* Policymaking
political attitudes, 58–59, 83. *See also* Attitudes, political
political power of, 53, 126, 129–130. *See also* Political power
political representation, 89–105. *See also* Representation, minority
strategies for action, 4. *See also* Tactics/strategy

studying politics of, 4–5
See also American Indians; Asian Americans; Blacks; Latinos
Mississippi
civil rights movement in, 44–46
minority representation in, 107
racism in, 8, 117
and suffrage, 49, 50
voter registration in, 74
Mississippi Freedom Democratic Party, 46
Missouri, 8
Missouri ex rel. Gaines v. Canada, 110
Mobilization model, 88
Mondale, Walter, 94
Monroe Doctrine, 17
Montana, 108
Monterey Park, California, 70–72, 73 (table), 82
Montgomery bus boycott, 42
Montoya, Joseph, 95
Morales, Dan, 107
Moseley-Braun, Carol, 95
Moses, Robert, 44, 45
Myrdal, Gunnar, 3

NAACP. *See* National Association for the Advancement of Colored People
NARF. *See* Native American Rights Fund
National Asian Pacific American Legal Consortium, 80
National Association for the Advancement of Colored People (NAACP), 44, 81, 169
and Jesse Jackson campaigns, 93
Legal Defense and Educational Fund (LDF), 80, 108–110
National Association of Latino Elected and Appointed Officials, 89
National Black Election Study, 1984–1988 (NBES), 58, 59, 68
National Center for Education Statistics, 119
National Conference of Christians and Jews (NCCJ), 59, 64, 70
National Congress of American Indians, 82
National Council of La Raza (NCLR), 81–82
National Council on Indian Opportunity, 82
National Farm Workers Association, 46, 179
National Indian Youth Council, 82
National Tribal Chairman's Association, 82
National Urban League, 81, 93
Native American Rights Fund (NARF), 80–81, 82
Native Americans. *See* American Indians
Naturalization Acts (1790, 1870), 13
Navajos, 73, 74, 108, 174
NBES. *See* National Black Election Study, 1984–1988
NCCJ. *See* National Conference of Christians and Jews
NCLR. *See* National Council of La Raza
Nebraska, 8
New Hampshire, 50
New Jersey, 107
New Mexico, 178
and Indian suffrage, 22–23
minority representation in, 107, 108
New York, 50, 107
New York City, 119
Nixon, Richard, 74, 106, 112
North Carolina, 8, 50, 74
minority representation in, 107, 108
North Dakota, 8

O'Connor, Sandra Day, 102
OCR. *See* Office for Civil Rights
Office for Civil Rights (OCR), 112, 115–116, 119–120
Officeholders
congressional, 95–100, 96(table), 97(table), 98(table), 99(table)
effect of Voting Rights Act on minority, 51, 89
presidential appointments, 91–92
states and minority, 107–108, 109(table)
See also Representation, minority
Oklahoma, 107
O'Leary, Hazel, 91
Oregon, 8
Outside initiative model, 88, 89

Pagagos, 73
Parker, William, 135, 136, 137
Participation, political
connection to socioeconomic status, 32
group cohesion in, 62
interest group activities, 58, 79–82
and Jesse Jackson campaigns, 94
Los Angeles and minority, 130–141, 143
and pluralist theory, 57–58
and social movements, 37–40
voter registration and behavior, 58, 74–79, 75–76(table), 77(table), 79(table)
and voting rights law, 49–53. *See also* Suffrage
See also Coalitions
Partisan identification, 58, 65–66, 151–152
American Indians, 72–74, 108
Asian Americans, 70–72, 73(table)
and Ben Nighthorse Campbell, 100
blacks, 66–69, 68(table)
Latinos, 69–70, 69(table)
PASSO. *See* Political Association of Spanish Speaking Peoples
Peña, Federico, 91–92, 180
Pine Ridge Reservation, 48
Plessy v. Ferguson, 21, 80, 108, 169
Pluralism, 57–58, 79
Policymaking
agenda setting in, 88–89, 121
education issues, 108–122
minority participation in, 24, 150–151
stages of, 87
states and, 105–106
Supreme Court and, 100–102
Political Association of Spanish Speaking Peoples (PASSO), 47
Political parties
and black civil rights movement, 46
and urban politics, 132, 143
See also Partisan identification
Political power
and coalition politics in Los Angeles, 134–141. *See also* Coalitions
and Cuban Americans, 60
effects of group competition on, 126, 129–130
Los Angeles history of, 131–135
and minority groups, 53
representation methods and, 52–53
and social movements, 40, 49
See also Policymaking; Representation, minority
Population, 29–31, 30(table), 31(table)
increase in Asian American, 131

increases and group competition, 129–130
increases in minority group, 152
Los Angeles black, 135
voting, 74
Pottinger, Stanley, 115–116
Poulson, Norris, 135
Presidency
Jesse Jackson campaigns, 93–95
minority appointments, 91–92
and minority issues, 90
PRLDEF. *See* Puerto Rican Legal Defense and Education Fund
Proposition 187 (California), 148, 190(n1)
Puerto Rican Legal Defense and Education Fund (PRLDEF), 80, 119, 182
Puerto Ricans
citizenship in U.S. history, 16–17
in Congress, 95
education issues, 117, 119
geographical distribution of, 37
as identifying term, 6
interest groups, 80
nationalist movement, 46
political attitudes, 60, 63, 69
political ideology, partisanship, 128, 151
timeline of political history, 181–182
See also Latinos
Puerto Rico, 16, 95, 181, 182

Race
as dividing American society, 57, 147
history of concept in America, 7–8
See also Minority groups
Racism, 7, 8, 147. *See also* Discrimination
Rainbow Coalition, 93
Reagan, Ronald, 68, 82, 93, 106, 147, 171
Reapportionment
debates, 4, 148–149
in Los Angeles, 135, 141
and vote dilution, 51–52
Registration, voter, 74–79, 75–76(table), 77(table), 79(table)
and Jesse Jackson campaigns, 94
Representation, minority
and agenda setting, 121, 150–151
in Congress, 95–100, 96(table), 97(table), 98(table), 99(table)
and cumulative voting arguments, 52–53
and executive branch, 90–95, 102–105, 104(table), 105(table)
and Los Angeles politics, 134–141
and reapportionment issues, 4, 148–149
and state government, 107–108
in Supreme Court, 100–102
Republican Party
and Cuban Americans, 69–70
and minority groups, 151–152
relationship with blacks, 65–66
See also Partisan identification
Resegregation, 120
Riordan, Richard, 141
Roosevelt, Eleanor, 67
Roosevelt, Franklin D., 67, 90
Ross v. Eckels, 116
Roybal, Edward, 134, 135, 136, 137

San Francisco, 117–118
Schattschneider, E. E., 58, 122
Schwerner, Michael, 45–46
SCLC. *See* Southern Christian Leadership Conference

Segregation. *See* Education
Seminole, 16, 90
Separate but equal doctrine, 21, 108–110, 167
Slaughterhouse Cases, 106
Slavery
  history in America, 7–8, 9
  as issue in framing U.S. Constitution, 10–11
Smith, Susan, 153
Smith v. AllWright, 49–50
SNCC. *See* Student Nonviolent Coordinating
  Committee
Social change
  and black civil rights movement, 41
  policymaking in, 121–122
  and social movements, 40
Social movements
  defined, 37–40
  elements for successful, 40
  See also Civil rights movements
Social organizations, 40, 43
Socioeconomic status
  defined, 29
  effect on group competition, 129–130,
    141–143
  of minorities, 32–33
  minorities in Los Angeles, 131–134
  political ideology and, 63
South Africa, 149
South Carolina, 8, 50, 74, 107
South Dakota, 50, 52, 107
Southeast Asians, 7
Southern Christian Leadership Conference
  (SCLC), 81
Southern Manifesto, 111
Spanish-American War, 16, 17, 181, 183
States
  federalism and power of, 105–106
  minority officeholders in, 107–108,
    109(table)
  policymaking in, 88
  suffrage and citizenship issues, 11–12, 13
  suffrage and southern, 20–22, 49
Steele, Reverend C. K., 43
Stokes, Carl, 138
Stuart, Charles, 153
Student Nonviolent Coordinating Committee
  (SNCC), 44, 81
Students, and civil rights movements, 45–47,
  47–48
Suffrage
  minorities and issues of, 49–53, 148–149
  and minorities in U.S. history, 11–12, 13,
    19–23
  racial/ethnic identification and, 9
Summer Project, 1964, 45–46
Supreme Court, U.S.
  and antimiscegenation laws, 8
  citizenship cases, 13–14, 15, 19, 106, 168
  civil rights decisions, 67–68, 106
  Indian decisions, 90
  policymaking and minority representation
    in, 100–102
  school segregation decisions, 108, 110,
    117–118
  suffrage decisions, 21, 22, 49–50, 106
  Warren Court, 189(n2)
  See also Judicial system

Tactics/strategy
  and Asian American civil rights move-
    ments, 48
  and black civil rights movement, 43, 44–46
  and Chicano movement, 47
  litigation and interest group, 79–81
  litigation and school desegregation, 110,
    113–117
  and social movements, 40
  See also Coalitions
Tafoya, Richard, 136, 137
Takao Ozawa, 19
Takei, George, 139
Taney, Chief Justice, 13–14
Tennessee, 8
Texas
  Mexican-only schools, 112–113, 114–115,
    190(n2)
  minority representation in, 107
  and suffrage issues, 50
  white primary, 49–50
Thomas, Clarence, 102
Three-fifths compromise, 11
Thurmond, Strom, 67, 102
Tijerina, Reies López, 47
Timelines, political history
  African American, 167–172
  American Indian, 173–176
  Asian American, 185–187
  Cuban American, 183–184
  Mexican American, 177–180
  Puerto Rican, 181–182
Trail of Tears, 90, 174
Truman, Harry, 67, 170

UCLA Asian Pacific American Voter
  Registration Project, 70
UDL. *See* United Defense League
Unemployment levels, 33. *See also*
  Employment
United Defense League (UDL), 42
Unruh, Jesse, 139
U.S. Census Bureau, 9, 78, 152
U.S. Constitution
  classical liberalism in, 9–10
  and Indians, 173
  post–Civil War amendments, 49. *See also*
    Fifteenth Amendment; Fourteenth
    Amendment
  slavery and suffrage issues, 11, 13, 14,
    19–20, 167
U.S. v. Cruikshank, 21
U.S. v. Harris, 106
U.S. v. Reese, 21, 106
U.S. v. Texas Education Agency, 116
Utah, 22–23

Valence issues, 94
Varela, Maria, 46
Vietnamese, 128
Vietnam War, 48
Virginia, 50, 107
Vote dilution, 51–52
Voting behavior, 75–76(table), 77(table),
  78–79, 79(table)
  and group cohesion, 62
  See also Registration, voter
Voting rights. *See* Suffrage
Voting Rights Act (1965) (VRA), 50–51, 53,
  74, 90, 186
  continuing debates over, 148–149
  effect on minority representation, 89
  Latinos and, 128
VRA. *See* Voting Rights Act

Warren, Earl, 67, 189(n2)
Washington (state), 107
Watts, 133
Weaver, Robert C., 67, 189(n1)
West San Gabriel Valley Asian Pacific
    American Democratic Club
    (WSGVAPADC), 82
Wheat, Alan, 94
Wilder, L. Douglas, 107
Wilson, Woodrow, 66–67
Women
    officeholders, 89, 95
    political attitudes and participation, 58
    in state government, 107

Supreme Court justices, 102
voting behavior and black, 78–79
Woo, Michael, 141, 187
Worcester v. Georgia, 90, 174
World War II, 18
Wounded Knee (village), 48
WSGVAPADC. *See* West San Gabriel Valley
    Asian Pacific American Democratic Club
Wyman, Rosalind, 136

Yorty, Samuel, 135–136, 137, 138–139
Young, Andrew, 94
Young, Coleman, 94